PRAISE FOR *UNDERDOGMA*

"Michael Prell's book, *Underdogma*, explains in detail how the Left masks anti-Americanism and anti-Western sentiment behind the American tradition of rooting for the underdog and how we can fight back against their rhetoric by reviving the American spirit of our founding fathers that transformed us from the 'underdog' to the greatest country on earth."

—Newt Gingrich, former Speaker of the House,
New York Times best-selling author

"*Underdogma* is the first great Tea Party book. All Tea Party Patriots should read *Underdogma*."

—Jenny Beth Martin, one of *TIME* Magazine's 100 most influential people in the world, 2010 Tea Party Patriots co-founder and national coordinator

"Michael Prell skillfully exposes how our misplaced emphasis to cheer on the underdogs, especially in the international community, will erode America's status not only as a superpower, but also as the greatest nation in the world. A must-read for anyone who believes in maintaining America's presence as a global leader."

—Congresswoman Michele Bachmann, (R, MN-6),
leader of the Tea Party Caucus

"Analyzing and refuting the common assumptions of anti-Americanism is a critical contribution to the global political debate. Thank goodness for this effort."

—UN Ambassador John Bolton,
author of *Surrender Is Not an Option*

"We don't need 'social justice.' We need to become umpires who call it fair and square. Three cheers for Michael Prell's timely reminder that the best society is a merit society, not the grievance society that feeds on *Underdogma*."

—Andrew C. McCarthy, prosecutor of the "Blind Sheikh" (1993 World Trade Center bombing), senior fellow at the National Review Institute, author of *The Grand Jihad* and *Willful Blindness*

"Americans have sympathy for the underdog. But that sympathy, Michael Prell argues, can be used by America's enemies to undermine faith in our culture and our country. In *Underdogma*, Prell shows how that works—and what we can do to combat it."

—Michael Barone, FOX News contributor, resident fellow, American Enterprise Institute, senior political analyst, *The Washington Examiner*, co-author, *The Almanac of American Politics*

"*Underdogma* is the *Liberty and Tyranny* of 2011"

—Ezra Levant, author of *Shakedown*

"Clever, accurate, droll and timely: The meek shall inherit contrariness."

—John Batchelor, nationally-syndicated radio host

"I love, love, love it. The title is fantastic."

—Rabbi Shmuley Boteach, best-selling author, television, and radio host

"Compelling; well done."

—Daniel Pipes, author, founder of the Middle East Forum

"*Underdogma* is the Rosetta Stone for our time's most portentous puzzle: Why do so many in this country—including some in leadership positions—abhor our national greatness and seek to diminish it at every turn? Michael Prell has 'broken the code,' and in so doing made an invaluable contribution to preserving and strengthening American exceptionalism."

—Frank Gaffney, Founder and President of the Center for Security Policy, Ronald Reagan's Assistant Secretary of Defense for International Security Policy

Underdogma

Underdogma

How America's Enemies Use Our Love for the Underdog to Trash American Power

Michael Prell

BenBella Books, Inc.
Dallas, Texas

BenBella Books, Inc.
10300 N. Central Expressway, Suite 400
Dallas, TX 75231
www.benbellabooks.com
Send feedback to feedback@benbellabooks.com

Printed in the United States of America
10 9 8 7 6 5 4 3 2 1

Library of Congress Cataloging-in-Publication Data is available for this title.
ISBN 978-1-935618-13-3

Editing by Erin Kelley
Copyediting by Erica Lovett
Proofreading by Michael Fedison
Printed by Bang Printing

Distributed by Perseus Distribution
perseusdistribution.com

To place orders through Perseus Distribution:
Tel: 800-343-4499
Fax: 800-351-5073
E-mail: orderentry@perseusbooks.com

ACKNOWLEDGMENTS

Scott Hoffman, the world's best agent. Scott is the reason why *Underdogma* is in your hands. May you all have someone who believes in you the way Scott Hoffman believed in me.

Mark Spiro, the world's best friend and business partner. Mark is the reason I had time to write *Underdogma* (and he is the reason I wound up on Benjamin Netanyahu's sofa). May you all have a friend like Mark Spiro.

A SPECIAL THANKS TO THOSE WHO CONTRIBUTED TO *UNDERDOGMA*

Ambassador John Bolton, Charles Krauthammer, Rabbi Shmuley Boteach, Jenny Beth Martin and Mark Meckler of the Tea Party Patriots, Newt Gingrich, Professor Walter E. Williams, Hugh Hewitt, Hillsdale College president Larry P. Arnn, Bjørn Lomborg, Peter Hessler, John Batchelor, Ezra Levant, Joseph Vandello, Frank Gaffney, Andrew C. McCarthy, Michael Barone, Lee Phillip McGinnis, Richard Rhodes, Andrew Breitbart, Larry Kudlow, John Tamny, Burton Folsom, and Tony Robbins. Special thanks to my exceptional publicist, Stephen Manfredi.

TO THE BENBELLA TEAM

Gratitude and respect for your professionalism, savvy, and support. Thank you to Glenn Yeffeth, Erin Kelley, Adrienne Lang, Debbie Harmsen, Laura Alberter, Aida Herrera, the sales team, and everyone in the BenBella family who dedicated their time, passion, and expertise to *Underdogma*.

"How I first came to conceive the notion of the *great liberal death wish* was not at all in consequence of what was happening in the USSR, which, as I came to reflect afterward, was simply the famous lines in the Magnificat working out, 'He hath put down the mighty from their seat and hath exalted the humble and meek,' whereupon, of course, the humble and meek become mighty in their turn and have to be put down.

"It was from that moment that I began to get the feeling that a liberal view of life was not what I'd supposed it to be—a creative movement which would shape the future—but rather a sort of death wish. How otherwise could you explain how people, in their own country ardent for equality, bitter opponents of capital punishment and all for more humane treatment of people in prison, supporters, in fact, of every good cause, should ... prostrate themselves before a regime ruled over brutally and oppressively and arbitrarily by a privileged party oligarchy? I still ponder over the mystery of how men displaying critical intelligence in other fields could be so astonishingly deluded. I tell you, if ever you are looking for a good subject for a thesis, you could get a very fine one out of a study of [this phenomenon]."

—Malcolm Muggeridge (1903–1990), Moscow correspondent for the Manchester Guardian, British Intelligence Agent (WWII), deputy editor of the *Daily Telegraph*, *Esquire* book reviewer, author, playwright.
Excerpt from speech to Hillsdale College, May 1979 issue of Imprimis.

TABLE OF CONTENTS

FOREWORD

ON SEPTEMBER 9, 2002, a mob of young, multicultural North American university students clashed with police, spat on Jews, smashed glass, and hurled anti-Semitic slurs to stop a free man from engaging in free speech.

Gordon Beck, The Gazette (Montreal)

September 9, 2002. Protest at Concordia University against the visit of [then] former Israeli Prime Minister Benjamin Netanyahu.

That free man was Benjamin Netanyahu.

Six years later, I found myself in Benjamin Netanyahu's Jerusalem home, working shoulder-to-shoulder with him as a writer on what would become his victorious 2009 campaign to become Israel's ninth Prime Minister.

What happened in between is what you will find between the covers of this book.

When I saw those young, multicultural students—on the campus of a university that prides itself on its "diversity"—spitting on Jews and rioting against free speech, it ripped apart the fabric of the world I thought I understood. I had to know: what changed? And so I conducted years of primary research into what happened that day, and into similar events and case studies around the world, and discovered to my surprise that *nothing* had changed. Those students, and the scores of people and institutions exposed in this book, were doing what they and others like them have always done. Their actions were fully consistent with a belief system that we can now trace to our first, formative moments as human beings—a belief system that drives today's most pressing issues. This book is a biography of that belief system, which I have named "Underdogma."

I dedicate *Underdogma* to those who have the courage to speak truth—to power, while in power, and while under attack.

—Michael Prell

PART ONE

The Roots of Underdogma

1
Underdogma

DURING THE HEIGHT OF THE IRAQ WAR, a group called the Christian Peacemaker Teams went to Baghdad to oppose the "illegal occupation of Iraq by Multinational Forces" and to shine a light on the "abuse of Iraqi detainees by U.S. soldiers"[1]. On November 26, 2005, four members of this pro-Iraqi / anti-Coalition group were kidnapped by the very Iraqis they had come to champion.

One of the Peacemakers was shot in the head by his Iraqi captors, and his bound and gagged corpse was later found in a dumpster. After months in captivity, the remaining Peacemakers were rescued and set free by the same powerful Coalition forces they had come to oppose. Once released, the Peacemakers did not thank their rescuers; instead they heaped scorn on their rescuers and blamed their "illegal occupation of Iraq" as "the root cause of the insecurity which led to this kidnapping and so much pain and suffering in Iraq."[2] And they continued to defend the terrorists who had kidnapped them, held them for months, and murdered one of their colleagues by declaring their "love" for their captors

[1] Christian Peacemaker Teams, Talking Points
[2] Christian Peacemakers Official Statement, March 23, 2006

and asking that they "be granted all possible leniency"[3] because the kidnappers' violent actions were "inextricably linked to the US-led invasion and occupation."[4]

Contrary to the Stockholm Syndrome, the Christian Peacemakers maintained the same worldview throughout their ordeal. Before, during, and after their kidnapping, their views remained unchanged: the more powerful Coalition forces were bad, and the less powerful Iraqis were good.

What gave their belief system the power to withstand kidnapping and murder at the hands of the "good," and rescue and salvation at the hands of the "bad," without their views changing at all?

On September 13, 2006, Kimveer Gill donned a black trench coat, packed an assault rifle and several other guns, drove to Montreal's Dawson College, and opened fire on students in the courtyard. He then entered the school and shot up the cafeteria. Police officers arrived and exchanged fire with Gill, hitting the twenty-five-year-old gunman once in the arm. Gill then turned a weapon on himself and committed suicide. Nineteen people were injured that day, inside and outside of the school, and one eighteen-year-old female student was killed.

---

[3] Statement by Norman Kember, James Loney, and Harmeet Singh Sooden regarding the prosecution of their kidnappers, December 8, 2006

[4] Ibid

A local talk radio station interviewed a witness to the carnage. Moments earlier, when the gunman trained his weapon on him, the witness ducked out of the way and then personally dragged a shot and bleeding student to safety. When asked what the gunman looked like, the witness replied:

> "I'm a bit shook up, I'm okay, but I just want to say what happened, and I don't want to enforce any stereotypes, I don't want to scare anybody...Like I said, I don't want to enforce stereotypes, and I really don't mean to be saying anything wrong, but this guy seemed to me as the kind of person we would classify as a Goth...but, like I said, I *really* don't want to enforce stereotypes about Goths or anything like that."
>
> —CFRB Radio, September 13, 2006

Less than one hour removed from a rampaging murderer pointing an assault rifle at his head, and with the blood of one of his classmates still fresh on his clothes, why did this young man feel compelled—three times in a two-minute interview—to stand up for the underdog Goth community, a member of which had just shot up his school?

On July 11, 2009, a UK study found that "one in four Britons would like to see the [human] population reduced by up to a third."[5] On December 10, 2009, seventy-three

[5] "Cut Population by a Third, Say Crowded Britons," *UK Daily Mail Online*, July 14, 2009

members of the U.S. Congress signed a letter that urged the White House to spend $1 billion on "slowing the [human] population's rapid growth."[6]

These people are not alone in their belief that the world would be a better place with fewer people. Prince Philip, past president of the World Wildlife Fund, said, "if I were to be reincarnated, I would wish to be returned to the earth as a killer virus, to lower human population levels."[7] The Sierra Club's first executive director, the late David Brower, said childbearing should be "a punishable crime against society."[8] And President Obama's so-called "Science Czar" John Holdren cowrote a book that discussed "a Planetary Regime" to reduce the number of human beings, including "compulsory population-control laws, even including laws requiring compulsory abortion," "involuntary fertility control," "a program of sterilizing women after their second or third child," and "adding a sterilant to drinking water or staple foods [as long as it does not harm pets or livestock]."[9]

Antihuman humans make an important distinction: they do not think that all life should be reduced on Planet Earth, just the lives of Earth's most powerful creatures—human beings. Why? So that less powerful life forms, like plants, animals, and even viruses might thrive.

---

[6] Letter to the Director of the Office of Management and Budget, December 10, 2009

[7] Prince Philip, quoted in the *Standard Handbook of Environmental Science, Health, and Technology*, by Jay H. Lehr & Janet K. Lehr, 2000

[8] William Norman Grigg, *The New American*, Vol. 18, August 12, 2002

[9] *Ecoscience: Population, Resources, Environment*, by Paul Ehrlich, Anne Ehrlich, & John Holdren, 1978

From an evolutionary perspective, how could humans develop a belief system that overrides our will to survive, thrive, and reproduce?

In *Dreams From My Father*, Barack Obama recalled a lesson his stepfather taught him about power: "men take advantage of weakness in other men. They're just like countries in that way. The strong man takes the weak man's land. He makes the weak man work in his fields. If the weak man's woman is pretty, the strong man will take her." In his second book, *The Audacity of Hope*, Barack Obama again shared his views on power: "I am angry about policies that constantly favor the wealthy and powerful."

In Chicago in the 1980s, "a group of [Saul Alinsky] disciples hired Barack Obama, a 23-year-old Columbia University graduate, to organize black residents on the South Side while learning and applying Alinsky's philosophy of street-level democracy."[10] Saul Alinsky literally wrote the book on community organizing; a book called *Rules for Radicals*. On page one, this is what it says about power:

> "The Prince was written by Machiavelli for the Haves on how to hold power. Rules for Radicals is written for the Have-Nots on how to take it away."
>
> —*Rules for Radicals*, Saul Alinsky, 1971

[10] "For Clinton and Obama, a Common Ideological Touchstone," the *Washington Post*, March 25, 2007

As a U.S. Senator, Barack Obama continued to focus on power dynamics. When John Roberts was nominated as Chief Justice of the Supreme Court, "Sen. Barack Obama argued that the role of a justice is to favor the 'weak' over the 'strong.'"[11] In justifying his vote against Justice Samuel Alito, Barack Obama said, "I found that in almost every case he consistently sides on behalf of the powerful against the powerless."[12]

As President of the world's lone superpower, Barack Obama traveled the world, bowing down to less powerful world leaders and speaking out against power: specifically American power. On April 3, 2009, in Strasbourg, France, he decried American power and "arrogance," saying, "In America, there's a failure to appreciate Europe's leading role in the world."[13] Later that month, in Trinidad and Tobago, Barack Obama told the assembled leaders of Venezuela, Haiti, Grenada, Ecuador, Columbia, Chile, Suriname, and others: "I pledge to you that we seek an equal partnership. There is no senior partner and junior partner in our relations."[14] During his first address to the United Nations, President Obama said, "No world order that elevates one nation or group of people over another will succeed. No balance of power among nations will hold."[15] And during his visit to China in November 2009, Barack

[11] "Obama's Class War Court," *Washington Times*, March 1, 2008

[12] Ibid

[13] The White House, "Remarks by President Obama at Strasbourg Town Hall," April 3, 2009

[14] The White House, "Remarks by the President at the Summit of the Americas Opening Ceremony," April 17, 2009

[15] U.S. President Barack Obama, Address to the United Nations, September 23, 2009

Obama spoke of the need for America to show "modesty" and "humility"[16] on the world stage.

At home, President Obama has, in the words of the *New York Times*, "return[ed] to a more traditional Democratic approach of positioning the party as fighting against the rich and powerful. In Mr. Obama's telling, he is taking on entrenched interests in the form of banks, insurance companies, large agribusinesses, oil and gas companies, and others."[17]

Big banks, big insurance companies, big agribusiness, big oil and big gas companies. What do they all have in common?

Why would kidnap victims champion their captors and vilify their rescuers? Why would a student stand up for a shooter who almost shot him? Why would humans call for a reduction of human beings so that less powerful life forms might thrive? And why does the world's most powerful man have so many issues with power?

Underdogma answers these questions and others by showing how an "Axis of Power"—between the power haves and power have-nots, the underdogs and overdogs—has superseded traditional notions of Left and Right to become the central pivot point for the defining issues of our time, including the Global Financial Crisis, the presidency of Barack Obama, the conflicts in the Middle East, the

[16] President Obama's China town hall, November 16, 2009

[17] *New York Times*, Peter Baker, March 1, 2009

environmental movement, anti-Americanism, the "new anti-Semitism," global terrorism, and the rise of China, to name a few.

This book also reveals the effect of Underdogma in our personal lives, from the delight we take in the misfortune of celebrities to small-town protests over "big box" stores to the runaway success of *American Idol* to the underdog advertising methods used by Madison Avenue to sell us everything from cola to new cars.

As you turn the pages of this book, you will pull back the curtain on Underdogma and see for yourself how Underdogmatists are using our love/hate relationship with power to manipulate us, to shift world affairs, and, oddly, to acquire your power. And you will find, at the end of this book, a way to take your power back.

But first some definitions. What is Underdogma?

> "Americans have a severe disease—worse than AIDS. It's called the winner's complex."
>
> —"Gorbachev: Americans Have a Severe Disease," ABC, Mikhail Gorbachev, July 12, 2006

An old Russian fable tells the story of a farmer who stumbles across a lamp. He rubs it and a genie appears, offering him one wish. The farmer says: "my neighbor just got a cow. It gives enough milk for his entire family and he is finally prospering."

"Would you like a cow such as his?" the genie replies. "Or perhaps two?"

"No," says the farmer. "I want you to kill his cow."

The story of the Russian farmer depicts jealousy, not envy, and not Underdogma. To understand the differences, let us revisit the Russian farmer:

- Jealousy is wishing for the neighbor's cow to be killed.
- Envy is wishing for the neighbor himself to be killed, or to be stripped of his ability to ever possess such a cow.
- Underdogma is to automatically assign virtue to the cowless farmer, *simply because he has less*, and to heap scorn on the farmer who has one cow, *simply because he has more*.

Underdogma

noun ˈʌn•dər•ˈdɔg•mə

Underdogma is the belief that those who have less power are virtuous and noble—*because they have less power*—and the belief that those who have more power are to be scorned—*because they have more power*.

Underdogma is not simply standing up for "the little guy," but *reflexively* standing up for the little guy and assigning him nobility and virtue—*because he has less power*. My friend Rabbi Shmuley Boteach calls this first part of Underdogma the "Always Root for the Underdog school of morality [which] sides with the weaker party, however wicked or immoral."[18] The second part of Underdogma

---

[18] "Why Jimmy Carter is Not an Anti-Semite," *Jerusalem Post*, December 26, 2006

states that those who have more power (overdogs) are to be reflexively scorned—*because they have more power.* Ayn Rand called this second part of Underdogma "hatred of the good for being good."[19]

Together, the two sides of Underdogma act like a "gag-reflex" to power—against those who have it, and for those who do not. And evidence of this reflex is all around us.

By the end of his second term, nearly half of Americans blamed President Bush for the attacks of 9/11,[20] while the self-confessed architect of those attacks (Khalid Sheikh Mohammed) was characterized by the American media as "thoughtful about his cause and craft" and "folksy."[21] Gay and lesbian activists protest those who defend gay rights (America, Israel), while championing those who outlaw and execute homosexuals (radical Islamists).[22] Environmentalists focus their rage on America, even though China has eclipsed the United States as the world's No. 1 emitter of greenhouse gases.[23] And Amnesty International, Jimmy Carter, and scores of activist groups around the world have somehow found themselves on the same side of an issue (Israelis vs. Palestinians) as Osama bin Laden and Mahmoud Ahmadinejad.

---

[19] "The Age of Envy," Ayn Rand, *The Objectivist*, July–August 1971
[20] "Poll: More Americans Blame Bush for 9/11," *USA Today*, September 11, 2006
[21] Josh Meyer, *LA Times*, March 16, 2007
[22] Queers Undermining Israeli Terrorism (QUIT)'s official website declares its members to be "part of the growing international movement seeking active ways to express our solidarity with the people of Palestine"
[23] "China now no. 1 in CO2 emissions; USA in second position," Netherlands Environmental Assessment Agency, June 19, 2007

What is the common thread? Reflexive opposition to the more powerful overdog, and automatic support for the less powerful underdog—even when those underdogs fly planes into buildings (9/11 attackers), bury homosexuals up to their necks and stone them to death (radical Islamists), open an average of one new coal-fired plant each week (China), and use child suicide bombers to kill innocent civilians (Palestinians).

Underdogma is not scorn for the powerful for exploiting the less powerful. Nor is it sympathy for the less powerful for being exploited. Underdogma reflexively assigns virtue and scorn based on whichever side has less or more power—regardless of either side's actions.

WHY?

Kidnap victims praising their captors and demonizing their rescuers. A shooting survivor defending the shooter. Humans spouting anti-human rhetoric. Gays and lesbians championing those who kill gays and lesbians, and railing against those who protect gay rights. If these behaviors do not seem logical or rational to you, it is because they are not logical or rational. They are also not based on facts.

In 2007, Joseph Vandello of the University of South Florida conducted a study on underdogs.[24] His experiment

[24] "The Appeal of the Underdog," Joseph A. Vandello, Nadav P. Goldschmied, & David A. R. Richards, Personality and Social Psychology Bulletin, December 2007

was simple. First, he asked test subjects to read an identical, one-page essay that described the Israeli-Palestinian conflict from each side's perspective. Then, he gave half of his subjects (Group A) a map that showed Israel as big, and the other half (Group B) a map that showed Israel as small.

Same information. Same country. The only difference: Group A's map had a big Israel, and Group B's map had a small Israel.

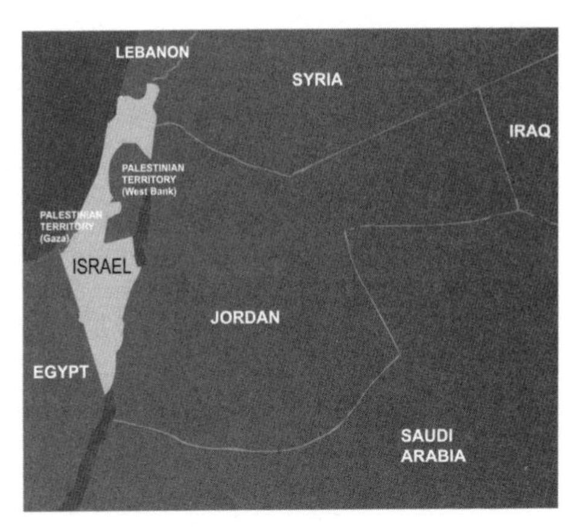

GROUP A's MAP GROUP B's MAP

Participants were then asked which side they viewed as the underdog in the conflict. The results were astounding. Group A (big Israel map) chose Palestinians as the underdog (70%). Group B (small Israel map) chose Israelis as the underdog (62.1%).

The groups were then asked which side they supported—Israelis or Palestinians. Same information. All that differed was the size of Israel on their maps. The results? The majority of Group A (big Israel) sided with Palestinians (53.3%) while Group B (small Israel) sided with Israel (76.7%).

What does this tell us?

It tells us these test subjects based their decisions on something other than facts. The facts were identical (each group read the same one-page essay). The results, however, were far from identical. The lone variable was the map. When Israel was small on the map, test subjects saw an "underdog" and threw their support behind Israel. When Israel was big on the map, test subjects saw an "overdog" and threw their support to the Palestinians. Which leads us to the first of four keys to understanding Underdogma:

KEY 1: Bypasses rational thought and is immune from facts.

The second key trait of Underdogma is that it is remarkably widespread. In Japan, a horse named Haru-urara became a national hero in 2004 after losing 113 consecutive races. Underdog surveys in Singapore and South Korea show that "love for the underdog" is alive and well in the Far East. Germans coined the term "Schadenfreude" and gave us the beloved underdog fairy tale *Cinderella*. Underdog researcher Nadav Goldschmied found that "data showed an [underdog] effect that was largely consistent across cultures. 'The underdog,' he says, 'is a global phenomenon.'"[25] And the *Freakonomics* blog in the *New York Times* observed: "our preference for the underdog is

[25] "The Underdog Effect," *Slate*, April 30, 2010. The underdog effect doesn't span all cultures, however—there are a few notable exceptions, detailed later in this book.

global."[26] From David and Goliath to the American Revolutionaries to the "Little Engine That Could," Team USA's "Miracle on Ice," the Star Wars Rebel Alliance, Rocky Balboa, the Jamaican bobsled team, and Christ's blessed meek—nearly everyone, it seems, loves an underdog. This conflict between the power haves and the power have-nots, overdogs and underdogs, is so widespread that virtually the entire world has come together, under the flag of the United Nations (see Chapter 6—THE UNITED NATIONS: INSTITUTIONALIZED UNDERDOGMA), to try to equalize "the global power imbalance that Kofi Annan identifies as one of the main challenges of our age."[27] Which gives us the second key to understanding Underdogma:

KEY 2: Underdogma is remarkably widespread.

How, exactly, did Underdogma become so widespread? Collusion? Secret meetings? Talking points? Vast right-wing or left-wing conspiracies? As someone who has spent years helping politicians stay "on message," I can tell you that maintaining message discipline is difficult at best when everyone involved belongs to the same political party—even when they are all in the same room. So it is not just technically unfeasible, it is frankly impossible for kidnapped Christian Peacemakers, the target of a Goth gunman, antihumanists from every part of the globe, representatives from the 192 member states of the United

[26] "Why Do We Love the Underdog?" *Freakonomics*, *New York Times*, May 4, 2010

[27] Greeting at the 9th COSATU National Congress

Nations, and U.S. President Barack Obama to get together each day—along with Hollywood storytellers and anyone who ever wrote a tale that featured an underdog hero—to make sure they are all on the same page when it comes to choosing sides along Underdogma's Axis of Power. And yet, somehow, they wind up on the same side.

If not through collusion, then how did these millions of people around the world come to the same conclusion? Is Underdogma something we learn? If so, who teaches it to us? Again, the worldwide reach of Underdogma makes this impossible. It is difficult enough to implement standardized testing and curricula in schools within the same district, let alone in schools around the world, in different countries, with different languages and cultures. Which leads us to the third key:

KEY 3: Underdogma is not taught or spread through collusion or communication.

If Underdogma is not taught, if it is not spread through collusion or communication, and if we do not arrive at Underdogma through our own logic or reasoning, how exactly did Underdogma come to be? Are we biologically predisposed to stand up for the little guy and to rail against those who have more power?

Actually, our biological instincts are the direct opposite of Underdogma.

Think back to the antihuman humans. They believe that reducing the number of Earth's most powerful creatures—human beings—would be good for Mother Nature. The problem with such a "pro-nature" belief is that holding it *goes against nature itself.*

As Richard Dawkins wrote in his best-selling book, *The Selfish Gene*: "we are survival machines—robot vehicles blindly programmed to preserve the selfish molecules known as genes." Underdogma, therefore, should not exist. If evolution is the survival of the fittest, then Underdogma is the polar opposite: scorning of the fittest and championing of the weakest. Underdogma goes against our biological instinct to survive. It makes human beings the first and only species that actively seeks to limit its own strength and numbers so that other, less powerful life forms might thrive. Natural selection should have bred this belief system out of our collective psyche long ago.

And yet here it is, with millions of humans around the world believing that the world would be a better place without humans. Which leads us to:

KEY 4: We are not biologically predisposed to Underdogma.

What is the door that fits all these keys? Perhaps the better question is: since all these people around the world have Underdogma in common, what else do they have in common?

One thing all human beings have in common is: we were all born.

Regardless of where we grew up or how we were raised, each of us has a tangible, personal understanding of what it feels like to be a small and powerless underdog surrounded by those who have more power. We begin life tiny and helpless, at the mercy of those who are bigger and more powerful than us; parents and guardians who tell us what to eat, what to wear, how to behave—even when to sleep and wake up. Then we encounter schoolteachers and professors who work us, test us, and assign grades to us that could shape the future directions of our lives. After school, we emerge into the workforce, where we face new Goliaths: bosses and supervisors who interview us, hire us, set our incomes, and hold the power to promote or fire us.

The reason we love underdogs is because each of us knows what it feels like to be a powerless underdog, to be a David in a world full of Goliaths. The reason we heap scorn on powerful overdogs is because each of us knows what it feels like to live under the thumb, or under the boot, or under the roof, of those who have more power than us. As world-renowned expert on human behavior Tony Robbins observed in his exclusive interview for *Underdogma*, "the basis of this [phenomenon], I believe, is in the structure of growing up for a child: this long dependency period that doesn't just go six months, a year, two years, three years, five years—how long are children dependent?—seven years, ten years, fifteen years, these days thirty-five years? That long dependency period makes us feel like someone else has power over us, because they *do* at some stage. And almost everyone has been at the brunt of that power."

But just because we are all susceptible to Underdogma does not make us all Underdogmatists. In fact there is one nation, an exceptional nation, which for most of its history has forged a philosophical path far different than Underdogma. In doing so, this nation has become the greatest superpower the world has ever known. Unfortunately, at the time of this writing, this same great nation—the United States of America—finds its reins of power in the hands of a President and a political movement with a far different view of American power. In the final chapter of *Underdogma*, I propose a way to take back those reins of power and to reverse the damage being done to America by Underdogma and Underdogmatists.

Underdogma is all around us. It is at work in virtually every corner of our lives. Underdogma is a driving force in our history (Chapter 4—THE HISTORY OF UNDERDOGMA), in our personal lives (Chapter 7—PERSONAL UNDERDOGMA), in the way we distinguish between right and wrong (Chapter 3—THE POWER OF UNDERDOGMA: RIGHT, WRONG...IT DEPENDS), in the way we choose between life and death (Chapter 2—DOES UNDERDOGMA EXIST? FIELD-TESTING THE THEORY), in the way we choose our leaders (Chapter 10—POLITICAL UNDERDOGMA), in the Global Financial Crisis (Chapter 12—UNDERDOGMA AND THE GLOBAL FINANCIAL CRISIS), in the rise of China and militant Islam (Chapter 13—OUR ENEMIES DO NOT PRACTICE UNDERDOGMA), and in the Tea Party Movement that has swept across the nation (Chapter 15 —THE ANTIDOTE TO UNDERDOGMA).

Although Underdogma plays a pivotal role in our lives and in the most pressing issues of our time, the mechanics of Underdogma and its strength and reach have yet to be explored. In the next chapter, Underdogma will be put to the test.

2

Does Underdogma Exist? Field-Testing the Theory

WHAT HAPPENS WHEN A SELF-PROCLAIMED neo-Marxist professor and champion of the underdog is born and raised a New York Yankees fan? What could lead prominent members of America's media to call the 9/11 terrorists "thoughtful," "folksy," and "brave"? And why do some people support murderous underdogs who would kill them if given the chance?

In this chapter, Underdogma is put through a series of field-tests that show Underdogma's true nature, its effect on our lives, its prevalence in our world, and its awesome power—even causing some to put adherence to Underdogma ahead of their own lives.

Field-Test 1: "The Day Underdogma Stood Still"

AP Photo/Richard Drew

This is an image that forces people to choose sides. Clearly, this falling office worker was an innocent victim and, clearly, the people who hijacked those planes and smashed them into those buildings were evil and wrong.

On September 11, 2001, the civilized world declared its solidarity with America. A *Time* magazine editorial called the attacks of 9/11 a "moment of clarity" that "separate[d] the civilized world from the uncivilized."[1] French newspaper *Le Monde* famously announced "We are all Americans!"[2] on its front page. In a flash of exploding jet fuel, Underdogma was turned on its head. America, the most powerful country on Earth, had become the underdog.

> "It is the American way. We love an underdog story, and we have become one now."
> —"We Rise Because We Must," Steve Serby, *New York Post*, September 17, 2001

But the biggest, richest, most powerful buildings in the biggest, richest, most powerful city in the biggest, richest, most powerful country in the world could not hold on to the mantle of underdog forever. In the years that followed the 9/11 attacks, the phrase "We are all Americans" gave way to "America is the real terrorist" and other such slogans. Did the world realign itself naturally along the traditional Underdogmatist lines of power and virtue, or

[1] "The Case for Rage and Retribution," Lance Morrow, *Time* magazine, September 12, 2001

[2] "We Are All Americans," Jean-Marie Colombani, *Le Monde*, Paris, France, September 12, 2001

did Underdogma—and Underdogmatists—have a hand in bringing about that change?

There was no "Vast Underdogma Conspiracy" formed in the years since September 11, 2001. No secret meetings were held. No messengers were dispatched between millions of media outlets, politicians, opinion leaders, protesters, and casual observers around the world. Collusion on such a scale would have been impossible. The "collusion of common purpose" theory also falls short, as it would have required vast numbers of people from every corner of the world to share an identical, clearly drawn goal (to knock America down and lift its attackers up) and the will to systematically act on that shared goal over time.

Could it be that Underdogma—the belief that those who have less power are virtuous and noble *because they have less power*, and that those who have more power are to be scorned *because they have more power*—was the gut-level instinct that brought millions of disconnected people from every part of the globe together around the shared notion that "America-as-underdog" simply could not stand?[3]

If Underdogma did play a role in America's transformation from underdog hero to "the most hated country in the world,"[4] how did that transformation happen? And what were the steps along the way?

---

[3] NOTE: This field-test focuses on the change in worldwide opinion regarding the 9/11 attacks and those who carried them out—not America's response to those attacks.

[4] *Reader's Digest*, October 2006

STEP ONE: KNOCK AMERICA FROM ITS UNDERDOG PERCH

Make 9/11 images disappear

The shocking images of helpless office workers plummeting to their deaths forced civilized people to immediately take the side of the 9/11 victims and, by extension, the United States of America. If Underdogma played a role in knocking America down from its underdog perch, a logical first step would be for Underdogmatists to remove those sympathy-inducing images from the airwaves.

That is exactly what happened.

Shortly after the 9/11 terrorist attacks, the "photographs of people falling to their deaths [which] shocked the nation" and cast America as an underdog under attack began to vanish from the media. "Most newspapers and magazines ran only one or two photos, [and] then published no more."[5] And "across the network and cable news spectrum, there is a virtual blackout of the video of the actual terrorist attacks of 9/11...Put it all together, and that means the moving pictures of the September 11 attacks—surely the most powerful of the television age—have virtually disappeared from American life."[6]

Change the language

The word "terrorist" immediately conjures negative feelings and draws a clear distinction between good and evil (America good, terrorists evil). Such black-and-white dis-

---

[5] "Desperation Forced a Horrific Decision," Dennis Cauchon & Martha Moore, *USA Today*, September 2, 2002

[6] "Taboo: Abu Ghraib Images Are One Thing. But 9/11? Off limits," Byron York, *National Review*, July 26, 2004

tinctions made it difficult for Underdogmatists to create any movement along Underdogma's Axis of Power. So, shortly after 9/11, the language began to change, with the BBC, Canada's CBC, and most notably Reuters refusing to call terrorism by its name.

> "We all know that one man's terrorist is another man's freedom fighter and that Reuters upholds the principle that we do not use the word terrorist...To be frank, it adds little to call the attack on the World Trade Center a terrorist attack."
> —Steven Jukes, global news head for Reuters News Service, internal memo cited by *Washington Post* reporter Howard Kurtz, September 24, 2001

Shortly after President Obama was elected, his administration ramped up efforts to change the language around terrorism. His Homeland Security Secretary insisted that acts of terrorism be called "man-caused disasters."[7] The Pentagon was instructed that "this administration prefers to avoid using the term 'Long War' or 'Global War on Terror' [GWOT]. Please use 'Overseas Contingency Operation.'"[8] And, in his weekly radio address of January 2, 2010, President Obama himself said "the United States is at war with a 'far-reaching network of violence and hatred,'"[9] not terrorists. President Obama also refused to call the radical jihadist Fort Hood shooter a terrorist, even though Major Nidal Malik Hasan "allegedly wore ritual

[7] Janet Napolitano, interview with *Spiegel*, March 16, 2009

[8] "'Global War On Terror' Is Given New Name," *Washington Post*, March 25, 2009

[9] Haaretz, January 2, 2010

Muslim garb [and] shouted 'God is great' in Arabic when opening fire on a group of soldiers on the base."[10]

Establish moral equivalence

One of the ways for Underdogmatists to close the gap between America and its attackers would be to draw moral equivalence between them, which has happened repeatedly since 9/11. Britain's "Archbishop of Canterbury himself has expressed just such moral equivalence"[11] in his book *Writing in the Dust*, which reads in part, "we are at once vulnerable to the charge that there is no moral difference in kind between our military action and the terror which it attacks."[12] The *Daily Telegraph* (London) and the *Sydney Morning Herald* observed, "a moral equivalence is set up, in which Osama bin Laden and Bush are presented as two sides of a fundamentalist coin."[13] And NBC's Brian Williams even drew moral equivalence between the 9/11 terrorists and America's Founding Fathers, saying, "someone brought up today the first several U.S. presidents were certainly revolutionaries and might have been called 'terrorists' by the British crown."[14]

Blame American foreign policy

The terrorist attacks were then recast as natural and understandable reactions to American foreign policy. This Underdogmatist line of argument had the dual effect of knocking America down from its underdog

[10] "GOP Rep.: Ft. Hood Report 'Sanitized,'" *Politico*, January 18, 2010
[11] *UK Daily Mail*, March 24, 2003
[12] "Writing in the Dust: After September 11," Rowan Williams, 2002
[13] *Sydney Morning Herald*, October 30, 2004
[14] NBC's Brian Williams, June 30, 2005

perch (for causing the problem in the first place) while lifting some blame for the attacks off of the terrorists' shoulders. George Stephanopoulos of ABC News called for "a real open debate about the effect of our policies in the world, about why some people in the world do hate us and the effect of our policies on them."[15] Canada's "Prime Minister Jean Chretien's remarks—that the Western world should assume some responsibility for the Sept. 11 attacks"[16]—linked the 9/11 attacks to America "being arrogant, self-satisfying, greedy and with no limits."[17] And Walter Cronkite, the "most trusted man in America," said, "I think very definitely that foreign policy could have caused what has happened [on 9/11]. This is a revolution in effect around the world. A revolution is in place today. We are suffering from a revolution of the poor and have-nots against the rich and haves and that's us."[18]

Blame America itself

Other Underdogmatists went further and blamed America itself for the 9/11 attacks; for instance, the "NEA [National Education Association] lesson plans—compiled together under the title 'Remember September 11' and appearing on the teachers union health information network Web site—[took] a decidedly blame-America approach."[19]

---

[15] George Stephanopoulos, ABC New Year's Eve broadcast, December 31, 2001

[16] Catholic News, October 6, 2002

[17] Ibid

[18] Former CBS Evening News anchor Walter Cronkite on CNN's *Larry King Live*, September 9, 2002

[19] "NEA Delivers History Lesson," *Washington Times*, August 19, 2002

ABC News reported that President Barack Obama's pastor said, "God Damn America, U.S. to Blame for 9/11."[20] And a columnist quoted in the *New York Times* asserted that Osama bin Laden "has been sculpted from the spare rib of a world laid waste by [America]."[21]

America: More evil than terrorists?

Meeting with little resistance, Underdogmatists knocked America down even further by suggesting that the United States was somehow worse than the 9/11 terrorists. The *Boston Globe* printed a story that called America "the world's leading exporter of the tools of death and destruction."[22] Others called the 9/11 attacks "not as bad as the things the American government has itself carried out."[23] And, of course, there is the phrase we have all heard too many times and seen on too many bumper stickers: "America is the real terrorist."

America had it coming

After establishing that America had caused the terrorist attacks, and that America's actions were worse than those of the terrorists, the next step for Underdogmatists would be to advance the notion that America somehow deserved what happened to it on 9/11, that "America had it coming"[24]—a phrase that first appeared in the media just eight days after

[20] ABC News, March 13, 2008
[21] *New York Times*, November 3, 2001
[22] Derrick Z. Jackson, *Boston Globe*, September 12, 2001
[23] "Young, Educated and Anti-American," Interview with three young Jordanians, Cameron W. Barr, *Christian Science Monitor*, September 27, 2001
[24] Haroon Siddiqui, "It's the U.S. Foreign Policy, Stupid," *Toronto Star*, September 19, 2001

the 9/11 attacks, and, by October 1, 2001, had become the "dominant"[25] notion on American campuses. CNN reported that "in the American mind [where] arrogance coexists with a surprising, even squirming self-effacement [there is] a perverse impulse, for example, to think that somehow Americans may have deserved 9/11."[26] President Obama's preacher and others piled on, saying, "America's chickens are coming home to roost" and "God damn America for as long as she acts like she is God and she is supreme."[27]

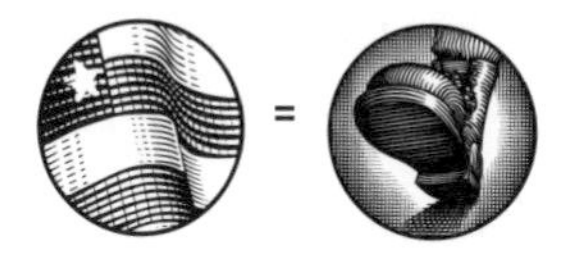

The evidence suggests that one part of Underdogma (vilifying the powerful) played a role in the United States' dramatic fall from its underdog perch in the months and years since the terrorist attacks of 9/11. But, before it can be said that Underdogma was truly at work in the seachange of world opinion that followed the 9/11 attacks, the other part of Underdogma—the belief that those who have less power are automatically deemed virtuous and noble—must also be present.

STEP TWO: CHAMPION THE UNDERDOG

A *Time* magazine editorial captured the nation's mood on September 12, 2001. It flatly stated that "anyone who

[25] "Learning to Love Terrorists," John Leo, October 1, 2001
[26] "Who's More Arrogant?" CNN, December 3, 2001
[27] ABC News, March 13, 2008

does not loathe the [terrorists] who did these things, and the people who cheer them on, is too philosophical for decent company."[28] In that atmosphere, surely no Underdogmatist would dare make the philosophical argument that the 9/11 attackers were virtuous and noble underdogs. At least not right away. Transforming terrorists into noble and virtuous underdogs would take time and effort. And the first step would be to:

Downplay the actions of the terrorists

When Khalid Sheikh Mohammed proudly confessed to planning the 9/11 attacks as Osama bin Laden's right-hand man, Underdogmatists in the media quickly responded by downplaying his claims and casting doubt on the validity of his confession, saying, "Khalid Sheikh Mohammed's claims that he was responsible for dozens of successful, foiled, and imagined attacks in the last 15 years relies on a loose definition of the word 'responsible.'"[29]

Later in that same story, Ms. Schrader of the Associated Press wrote a point-by-point refutation of the crimes to which Mr. Mohammed had confessed, under headings entitled "THE CLAIM" and "THE TRUTH." It is difficult to find another example of a journalist ever investing that much effort to disprove the proud confession of any known killer, let alone within the first news cycle.

Humanize the terrorists

The confession of Khalid Sheikh Mohammed unleashed another wave of stories that seemed geared to humanizing

[28] "The Case for Rage and Retribution," Lance Morrow, *Time* magazine, September 12, 2001

[29] Katherine Schrader, Associated Press, March 16, 2007

the man who took credit for planning the 9/11 attacks ("from A to Z," as he put it). One such story contended that Khalid Sheikh Mohammed "showed himself to be ambitious, boastful and, when given the chance, talkative. He was even ***thoughtful about his cause and craft***. At other times, he appeared contrite about such killings, and at moments seemed downright ***folksy***."[30]

Evoke sympathy for the terrorists

How does one evoke sympathy for terrorists? By painting them as powerless underdog victims. "To understand terrorism," an article in the *Washington Post* read, we "must learn of the suffering it thrives on...don't lose sight of the suffering, which is systemic and deeply rooted—in colonialism, racism, religious bigotry, and greed." And, "when one U.S. congressman said on the House floor that he wanted to make those responsible for the acts of terrorism 'rue the day they were born,' he seemed unaware that for many people in the targeted areas, death would be a relief."[31] "Perhaps it is too much to hope," asked a *Guardian UK* special report, "that, as rescue workers struggle to pull firefighters from the rubble, any but a small minority might make the connection between what has been visited upon them and what their government has visited upon large parts of the world."[32]

---

[30] Josh Meyer, *LA Times*, March 16, 2007 [emphasis added]

[31] Courtland Milloy, *Washington Post*, September 19, 2001

[32] "They Can't See Why They're Hated," Seumas Milne, *The Guardian UK*, September 13, 2001

The "brave" and noble terrorists

In the case of the 9/11 attacks, the final stage of Underdogma would be to ascribe nobility and virtue to the underdog terrorists for having the courage to stand up to their overdog oppressors (the United States) by crashing planeloads of innocent people into buildings filled with thousands of other innocent people. As outlandish as this may sound, it is exactly what happened. Colorado professor Ward Churchill wrote, "whatever else can be said of them, the men who struck on September 11 manifested the courage of their convictions, willingly expending their own lives in attaining their objectives."[33] Susan Sontag added, "whatever may be said of the perpetrators of Tuesday's slaughter, they were not cowards."[34] Bill Maher piled on, saying, "we have been the cowards, lobbing cruise missiles from 2,000 miles away. That's cowardly. Staying in the airplane when it hits the building, say what you want about it, it's not cowardly."[35] And CNN founder Ted Turner said of the 9/11 hijackers, "I think they were brave at the very least."[36]

"Brave at the very least." Brave terrorists who killed innocent secretaries, janitors, office workers, firefighters, flight attendants, pilots, airline commuters, mothers, fathers, brothers, and sisters—innocent human beings who got up on September 11, 2001, and went about their

[33] Ward Churchill, University of Colorado at Boulder professor, September 11, 2001

[34] Susan Sontag, *The New Yorker*, September 24, 2001

[35] Bill Maher, *Politically Incorrect*, September 17, 2001

[36] "Ted Turner: Sept. 11 An Act of Desperation," *Rock Hill Herald*, Associated Press, February 13, 2002

lives in peace until murdering terrorists ended their lives with multiple, brutal, and carefully-planned acts of war against innocent civilians. Acts of war, which American Underdogmatists have called "brave." Do these American Underdogmatists also call American soldiers "brave" for hunting down terrorists and bringing them to justice? Of course not. That would go against the other part of Underdogma: heap scorn on those who have more power.

Underdogma's post-9/11 transformation is now complete: the terrorists are "brave" underdogs, and America is "the real terrorist."

There are those who claim that America squandered its goodwill after the attacks of 9/11, citing the oft-quoted "We are all Americans" story that appeared in France's *Le Monde* newspaper on September 12, 2001. To argue that America squandered its goodwill, rather than Underdogmatists proactively chipping it away, is to admit to not having read beyond the headline of that very same *Le Monde* story. This so-called solidarity and goodwill failed to survive the *Le Monde* story's halfway mark, at which point the Underdogmatist manifesto reared its head and blamed America for bringing the 9/11 attack upon itself.

> "And America, in the solitude of its power, in its status as the sole superpower, now in the absence of a Soviet counter-model, has ceased to draw other nations to itself; or more precisely, in certain parts of the globe, it seems to draw nothing but hate.

> "Beyond their obvious murderous madness, these latest attacks nonetheless follow a certain logic."
>
> —"We are all Americans," Jean-Marie Colombani, *Le Monde*, Paris, France, September 12, 2001

The burst of empathy and solidarity for America that followed the 9/11 attacks was real. America was the underdog for a brief moment in time. How long would that moment have lasted if Underdogmatists had not eroded America's support around the world? We will never know.

But we can look at the broad and sustained assault on America's post-9/11 underdog status, and at the equally broad campaign to systematically ascribe nobility and virtue to the 9/11 hijackers, and ask: what force could have brought these millions of disconnected people together in an undirected campaign to realign the world along Underdogma's lines of power and virtue? That force was Underdogma.

And now, the event that led me to discover Underdogma: the 2002 riot against Benjamin Netanyahu.

Field-Test 2: "The Riot against Benjamin Netanyahu"

On September 9, 2002, Concordia University students raised their fists and rioted against then-former Israeli Prime Minister Benjamin Netanyahu. But their fists were not raised against just one man or even his nation—they were raised in solidarity with Palestinians.

Gordon Beck, *The Gazette* (Montreal)

The Concordia riot, organized by "Solidarity for Palestinian Human Rights" (SPHR)

When Palestinians take the side of Palestinians, it is called self-interest. When non-Palestinian university students halfway around the world take the side of Palestinians, it is called something else. Many books explore which side is right or wrong in the Israeli-Palestinian conflict. *Underdogma* explores why people—even those who have no personal involvement in an issue—choose sides the way they do and what role, if any, that power imbalances play in their choices. In the case of the Concordia rioters, North American University students—even those who had no personal stake in the Israeli-Palestinian conflict—chose the side of Palestinians. Why? Was there something about the culture, beliefs, or actions of Palestinians that resonated deep within the hearts of Western university students?

WESTERN UNIVERSITY STUDENTS	PALESTINIANS
Taught to be tolerant of other cultures.	Incite hatred of, and violence toward, other cultures, calling them "descendents of monkeys and pigs,"[1] and 91% of university-aged Palestinians deny Israel's right to exist.[2]

continued on following page . . .

continued from previous page . . .

WESTERN UNIVERSITY STUDENTS	PALESTINIANS
Taught to be peace-loving. Many students protest the use of force.	Teach students (through television shows, cartoons, and school curricula) to kill innocent people,[3] and 72% of school-aged Palestinians said they aspire to be martyrs.[4]
Taught that women are equal.	When raped, Palestinian women are sometimes stoned to death under the "honor killing" provision of sharia law, in which "maintaining honor is deemed a woman's responsibility, whether or not she has been educated about sex or consented to the act."[5]
Tolerate homosexuals.	Outlaw and execute homosexuals.[6]
Many students believe in separation of church and state.	In Islam, "religion is the state and the state is the religion."[7]
A 2001 study entitled "Hooking Up" confirmed what most Western university students already know; that "sex without commitment, is widespread on campuses and profoundly influences campus culture."[8]	In Gaza, women are "punished, even murdered, on the suspicion of having been involved in a sexual relationship" with "20 honor killings in Gaza and the West Bank in 1996"[9] in order to maintain the "patriarchal control and repression of female sexuality."[10]

TABLE FOOTNOTES

[1] "O Allah, destroy America as it is controlled by Zionist Jews ... Allah will avenge, in the name of His Prophet, the colonialist settlers who are the descendents of monkeys and pigs ..." Ikrime Sabri, Mufti of the Palestinian Authority, Voice of Palestine, July 11, 1997

[2] Near East Consulting poll, May 2007

[3] "Every Palestinian child, say someone aged twelve, says: 'O Lord, I would like to become a Shahid [Martyr]'"— from a videotaped interview with "Yussra," an eleven year-old Palestinian girl, Palestinian Authority TV, June 9, 2002

[4] Palestinian poll, reported in the Palestinian *Al-Ayyam* newspaper, January 24, 2002

[5] "Commodifying Honor in Female Sexuality: Honor Killings in Palestine," Suzanne Ruggi, Middle East Report No. 206, Spring 1998

[6] "'Death Threat' to Palestinian Gays," BBC News, March 6, 2003

[7] Brigitte Gabriel, President, American Congress For Truth, "Exposed: The Extremist Agenda," CNN Headline News, November 15, 2006

[8] Institute for American Values, July 26, 2001

[9] "Commodifying Honor in Female Sexuality: Honor Killings in Palestine," Suzanne Ruggi, Middle East Report No. 206, Spring 1998

[10] Palestinian women: "Patriarchy and Resistance in the West Bank," by Cheryl Rubenberg

What was it about intolerant, violent, misogynist, homosexual-killing, fundamentalist, sexually repressive Palestinians that inspires such feelings of solidarity among tolerant, peaceful, egalitarian, open-minded, largely secular, and free-spirited Western university students? For that matter, what is it about the Palestinian cause that has attracted such diverse supporters as President Jimmy Carter, the U.S. Democratic Party, the Green Party, the late Saddam Hussein, Mahmoud Ahmadinejad, the worldwide labor movement, gay and lesbian activists, women's groups, Noam Chomsky, the United Nations, Amnesty International, former U.S. Attorney General Ramsey Clark, numerous Christian churches, numerous Jewish groups, Osama bin Laden, solidarity groups from America, England, Germany, Canada, Spain, India, Norway, Scotland, Ireland, France, Sweden, Australia, Italy—even Israel—and campus groups from America's most respected institutes of higher learning including Harvard, Georgetown, Duke, Princeton, Rutgers, Yale, Columbia, Brandeis, Berkeley, and the Universities of Chicago, Minnesota, Texas, North Carolina, Maryland, New York, Oklahoma, Michigan, Oregon, and others?[37] Are these millions of supporters attracted by the fact that Palestinians torture and kill homosexuals and women, or are they united in the Underdogmatist belief that those who have less power are virtuous and noble and worthy of support *because they have less power*?

To answer that question, let us go back to the university campus riot against Benjamin Netanyahu.

University campuses are historical breeding grounds for underdog activism, from the civil rights movement in the 1960s to women's rights in the '70s to Nelson Mandela in the '80s to the "Free Tibet" movement in the '90s to today's protests against globalization, frankenfoods, American imperialism, multinational corporations, the WTO, the G8, NATO, the IMF, and others. Wherever power is

[37] Sources: official university websites and Campus Watch

held or exerted, these young, politically active students can be counted on to raise their fists and take the side of the underdog.

Jews have traditionally been the underdogs of history—chased, rounded up, and killed by some of the world's most vicious and powerful tyrants. Underdog-championing university students (at least those who have studied history) should, therefore, naturally side with the Jews. But that is not what happened at Concordia. At Concordia, students rioted against a Jew and spat on Jewish families and students who came to hear Mr. Netanyahu speak.

What at first seemed like an explosion of "new anti-Semitism," or some fundamental and dangerous shift in our society, was in fact nothing new. The Concordia rioters were being consistent, doing what university students and countless others have always done. They were taking the side of the underdog.

And Jews are no longer the underdog.

Today's Jews have a homeland (Israel), advanced weapons, and a fearsome, well-equipped army. As Steve Crowder wrote, "much like when Michael Jordan set foot on the court, or Gretzky touched blades on the ice; it really isn't even fair to the other players. It's because of Israel's efficient and battle-hardened techniques that it's become quite popular to pre-maturely condemn them."[38] Plus, Israel's strongest ally is the world's most powerful country; the United States. To Underdogmatists, Jews committed an unforgivable sin. They became powerful. And, according

[38] "Did Israel Act Stupidly?" FOXNews.com, June 1, 2010

to Underdogma, those who have more power are to be scorned *because they have more power*.

> "When I was first here, we had the advantages of the underdog. Now we have the disadvantages of the overdog."
>
> —Former Israeli Foreign Minister Abba Eban, 1915–2002, quoted in the *World Book* dictionary, 2003

The new underdogs in this equation are the Palestinians. And although Palestinians occasionally use women and children as human bombs that kill university students, university students around the world stand up for them. And these students have company.

- Iranian President Mahmoud Ahmadinejad said, "Palestine is the point of convergence and differentiation of right and wrong."[39]
- Lesbian activist group Queers Undermining Israeli Terrorism (QUIT) proudly declares itself as "part of the growing international movement seeking active ways to express our solidarity with the people of Palestine."[40]
- "Former President Jimmy Carter has turned to 'malicious advocacy' for the Palestinians and against Israel,"[41] causing fourteen

[39] Iranian President Mahmoud Ahmadinejad, April 14, 2006

[40] Queers Undermining Israeli Terrorism (QUIT) official website

[41] CAMERA, January 11, 2007. The final paragraph of the resignation letter reads: "As a result it seems that you have turned to a world of advocacy, including even malicious advocacy. We can no longer endorse your strident and uncompromising position. This is not the Carter Center or the Jimmy Carter we came to respect and support. Therefore it is with sadness and regret that we hereby

members of his own Carter Center advisory board to resign.

- Osama bin Laden said, "the Palestinian cause is the major issue for my [Islamic] nation," and cited solidarity for Palestinians as "an important element in fueling me from the beginning and the 19 others [9/11 hijackers]."[42]
- "Amnesty International uses uncorroborated personal anecdotes, emotional language, undefined legal terminology, as well as factual errors and the omission of the context of terror, to portray the Palestinians solely as victims."[43]
- The United Nations hosted "International Day of Solidarity with the Palestinian People,"[44] during which a map at the head of the room—flanked by Palestinian and UN flags—showed Israel literally wiped from it.

Underdogma is about power imbalances. And there are few places on Earth where the balance of power is drawn in starker contrast than at "Ground Zero" for Underdogma:

---

tender our resignation from the Board of Councilors of the Carter Center effective immediately." For the full text of the resignation letter, visit www.under-dogma.com

[42] Osama bin Laden audio tape, May 16, 2008

[43] Israeli Justice Ministry, response to a June 2007 Amnesty International report

[44] "[Kofi Annan and] Eliminating Israel Politely," Daniel Pipes, *New York Sun*, December 13, 2005

the Israeli-Palestinian conflict. Perhaps that is why Palestinians have become the world's leading recipients of Underdogmatist support.

> "Palestinians [are] the largest per capita recipients of international development assistance in the world."
>
> —"Dollars and Diplomacy: Foreign Aid and the Palestinian Question," Scott Lasensky, August 2006

For Underdogma to be truly present in the relationship between Israelis and Palestinians, it is not enough to show evidence of people around the world standing up for underdog Palestinians. There must also be evidence of the second part of Underdogma: reflexive scorn for the more powerful overdog. Does that mean Israel should be blamed for, say, the fact that Palestinians stone to death their own women for the "dishonor" of being raped? According to Amnesty International, the answer is: yes.

> "Israel is implicated in this violence by Palestinian men against Palestinian women."
>
> —"Amnesty Int'l Redefines 'War Crimes,'" *Jerusalem Post*, August 30, 2006

What does Amnesty International mean when it says that "Israel is implicated" in the fact that Palestinians stone to death their own raped women? According to "Women of Palestine" founding member Hanadi Loubani, "without the establishment of an independent state [for Palestinians], it is impossible to develop an indigenous legal framework that can defend Palestinian women's rights—and this is a direct result of the Israeli occupation."[45]

To recap: when Palestinian men rape Palestinian women—and when Palestinian men then kill those same Palestinian women for the "dishonor" of being raped—Underdogmatists blame Israel.

When it comes to overdog Israel, Underdogmatist scorn knows no bounds. Although enlightened Westerners generally bristle at any hint of intolerance or bigotry toward any identifiable group, hatred toward Israel is openly practiced in American cities.

Photos courtesy of zombietime.com

Photos, taken at various protests in California, 2003–2006

The United Nations' founding charter states that its purpose is "to practice tolerance and live together in peace with one another as good neighbors." So where does the UN stand on all of this anti-Israel scorn? Steadfastly against the overdog. After Israel withdrew from the Gaza Strip in 2005, "the United Nations bankrolled the production of

[45] "Occupation, Patriarchy, and the Palestinian Women's Movement," Association for Women's Rights in Development, November 10, 2003

thousands of banners, bumper stickers, mugs, and T-shirts bearing the slogan 'Today Gaza and Tomorrow the West Bank and Jerusalem,' which have been widely distributed to Palestinian Arabs in the Gaza Strip, according to a U.N. official … many of the materials displayed the logo of the United Nations Development Program."[46] The United Nations has also singled out Israel for condemnation more than any other country and passed "an outrageous number of resolutions against Israel, the largest number of resolutions against any nation and equal to all the resolutions against all other states combined."[47] The UN has voted against Israel 87.5% of the time.[48] And the UN once passed a resolution (which UN Ambassador John Bolton, a contributor to this book, later helped overturn) that equated Zionism with racism.

With lesbians, Osama bin Laden, Amnesty International, Mahmoud Ahmadinejad, the United Nations, and activist groups from around the world joining together to fight the overdog oppressor Israel—while championing homosexual and rape-victim-killing Palestinians—it appears that Underdogma is alive and well when it comes to choosing sides between Israelis and Palestinians. Those who have more power (Israelis) are scorned, and those who have less power (Palestinians) are championed as the worldwide kings of the underdogs.

---

[46] "United Nations Bankrolled Latest Anti-Israel Propaganda," Jacob Gershman, *New York Sun*, August 17, 2005

[47] Israel's UN Ambassador Professor Gabriela Shalev, November 4, 2009

[48] 1991 statistical analysis of UN voting records, commissioned by the office of Prime Minister Yitzhak Shamir

Field-Test 3: "The New York Yankees"

> "Rooting for the Yankees is like rooting for U.S. Steel."
> —Joe E. Lewis

> "You've got to root for the underdog, and the idea of rooting for the Yankees seems to me so bizarre."
> —"Damn Yankees" interview with David Shields

> "The New York Yankees have become the 'evil empire' of the baseball world."
> —*Why I Hate the Yankees*, Kevin O'Connell & Josh Pahigian, 2005

The New York Yankees are the richest, most powerful baseball team in the richest, most powerful city, in the richest, most powerful country in the world.

No wonder people hate them.

But it wasn't always this way. In the book *Why I Hate the Yankees*, Kevin O'Connell and Josh Pahigian observe that many people around the world view the New York Yankees and the United States of America through the same lens. When America was loved, the Yankees were loved. And no Yankee was more loved than Babe Ruth, who personified the Yankees, and the America, of his day.

> "Babe Ruth's big appetites for home runs, food, drink, women, and even life itself helped deliver the message that America was an up-and-coming power. We were young, strong, uninhibited, and had that can-do attitude that war-ravaged Europe sorely lacked."
> —*Why I Hate the Yankees*, Kevin O'Connell & Josh Pahigian, 2005

Fast-forward to today and the New York Yankees are viewed by many as too rich, too powerful, too arrogant, and "the epitome of the capitalist enemy within the world of baseball,"[49] much the same way America is viewed within the world of nations. If it is true that, as America goes, so go the Yankees, then what has changed about America and the Yankees since the days of Babe Ruth?

In the 1920s, America was an "up-and-coming power."[50] So were the New York Yankees. Then the Yankees and America both went on a winning streak. When Babe Ruth first joined the Yankees, the team had never won the World Series. As of 2009, the Yankees had won the World Series twenty-seven times—more than any other team and almost triple that of their nearest competitor. The Yankees and America went from underdogs to superpowers. *That* is what changed since the days of Babe Ruth.

> "In other words, the Yankees *are* the United States. Those Americans puzzled by the ambivalence, to put it gently, with which U.S. leadership in the world is met might consider their own love-hate relationship with New York's finest. The parallels run deep and true."
> —Alex Massie, *The Spectator*, November 5, 2009

The first part of Underdogma—championing of the underdog—is on full display when it comes to the New York Yankees. People hate the more powerful Yankees *because they have more power*, and often lend their Un-

---

[49] "Rooting for the 'Devil,'" George Ritzer, *South Atlantic Quarterly*, Spring 2006

[50] *Why I Hate the Yankees*, Kevin O'Connell & Josh Pahigian, 2005

derdogmatist support to *any* team that is not as powerful as the Yankees, *because they have less power*. As the earlier University of South Florida study on underdogs noted, we have a reflexive urge to side with the underdog—any underdog—in the face of a more powerful overdog.

> "My favorite team is whoever is playing the Yankees."
>
> —"The Appeal of the Underdog," Joseph A. Vandello, et al., 2007

Underdogma's scorn for those who have more power (because they have more power) is clearly present in the way people react to the New York Yankees; sometimes referred to as "Yankee Derangement Syndrome." Some sportswriters felt that Yankee-hatred had less to do with scorn for the Yankees' power and success, and more to do with that "top dog…that stinking, flea-bitten, mangy mutt, [the late George] Steinbrenner."[51] Those sportswriters should have checked in with their brethren from the past. In 1950, almost a quarter century before the late George Steinbrenner era began, James Murray penned an article in *Life* magazine called "I Hate the Yankees." In it, he wrote that the blackest day in baseball history was not the "Black Sox" scandal, but instead, "Oct. 2, 1936, when the Yankees won the second game of the World Series…18–4. That was the day the great illusion was dispelled. Formerly, it had been thought that the Yankee domination was due in large measure to that large, lovable outfielder-of-all-time, Babe Ruth. But in 1936 came the first post-Ruthian World

[51] *Why I Hate the Yankees*, Kevin O'Connell & Josh Pahigian

Series. For some reason I thought they might now be cut down to a level with their competition…But the second game ruined that hope by the score of 18–4."[52]

One thing about the Yankees that sets off Underdogmatists even more than the team's greatness is the fact that the Yankees *know* they are great. They are confident in their greatness and comfortable with their power. They have that same swagger about them that George W. Bush had—the kind that rubs Underdogmatists the wrong way. The Yankees know that people hate them and they view being hated as par for the course. The cost of greatness. A badge of honor. As Yankees senior VP Hank Steinbrenner said, "we'd rather be Darth Vader. Let them [Boston] be the underdog."[53] Which is the kind of self-confident quip that sets off Underdogmatists even more. Especially Underdogmatists from Boston.

> "We hate the Yankees because they epitomize greatness and remind us of our own historical mediocrity, both as a team and as a town when compared to the great metropolis. New York loves a winner. We mistrust anyone who speaks so openly about trying to achieve greatness…We are deeply suspicious of ambition."
>
> —*Boston Globe* columnist Kevin Cullen "Loving to Hate the Yankees," Daniel Rubin, Philly.com, October 28, 2009

Hatred of the powerful overdog Yankees is not limited to Bostonians. Or even to non-New Yorkers. Or even to

[52] "I Hate The Yankees," James Murray, *Life* magazine, April 17, 1950
[53] New York Yankees senior vice president Hank Steinbrenner, Associated Press, February 20, 2008

non-Yankees fans. Devout Underdogmatist and self-proclaimed neo-Marxist professor George Ritzer, who admits he has "a distaste for the rich and successful and a corresponding appreciation of the underdog,"[54] was born and raised a New York Yankees fan. In a battle between his love for the underdog and love for his home team, which side did Mr. Ritzer choose: his ideology or his team?

He chose neither. And both.

> "How…could I possibly root for the Yankees, given that they symbolized, among other things, the fundamental unfairness and inequality of the capitalist system?…I increasingly focused on the team's marginal players; the most proletarian of players on an otherwise highly capitalistic team."
>
> —"Rooting for the 'Devil,'" George Ritzer, *South Atlantic Quarterly*, Spring 2006

If Underdogma is the driving force behind anti-Yankee scorn, then some of that scorn should dissipate when the New York Yankees stop behaving like overdogs and/or face more powerful opponents. Which is exactly what happened in 2009, when former special counsel to President Clinton and lifelong Yankee hater Lanny Davis went against his "family history," against his "DNA," and did what he said would make "grand-pa cry in Heaven."[55] He rooted for the Yankees.

---

[54] "Rooting for the 'Devil,'" George Ritzer, *South Atlantic Quarterly*, Spring 2006

[55] "Ok, I Surrender—Yeah for the Yankees!" Lanny Davis, *Huffington Post*, November 9, 2009

> "So it happened. A miracle. In the 2009 World Series, I became a Yankee Fan. May Dad forgive me."
> —"Ok, I Surrender—Yeah for the Yankees!"
> Lanny Davis, *Huffington Post*, November 9, 2009

What caused Lanny Davis to break the generational cycle of Underdogma? The first crack in his belief system came in the '80s and early '90s. As Mr. Davis wrote, "finally, there seemed to be some economic and social justice in the world. The Yankees didn't win a World Series for 16 years—from 1979–1995."[56] But then the Yankees went back to their winning ways, which led Lanny Davis—via Underdogma—back to hating the Yankees. And then a "miracle" happened: he found himself rooting for the Yankees against the Philadelphia Phillies in the 2009 World Series. What finally tipped him over the edge? It was when the scales of power tipped against the Yankees.

> "First, they [the Yankees] hadn't won the Series for eight straight seasons—from 2001-2008 [championing of the underdog].
> "Second, the Phillies had won the year before and they were described as the 'favorites' by a lot of sports writers"
> [scorn for the overdog].
> —"Ok, I Surrender—Yeah for the Yankees!"
> Lanny Davis, *Huffington Post*, November 9, 2009

Thanks to Mr. Davis, the New York Yankees now have a blueprint for breaking the generational cycle of Under-

[56] "Ok, I Surrender—Yeah for the Yankees!" Lanny Davis, *Huffington Post*, November 9, 2009

dogmatist scorn. All the Yankees have to do is face more powerful opponents and, better yet, lose to them.

Field-Test #4: "Give Me Underdogma or Give Me Death"

Does Underdogma have the power to override our biological instinct to survive? Underdogma is a reflexive disdain for power and those who hold power, not a reasoned philosophical position based on logic, facts, or even the core beliefs or self-interests of its adherents. As we saw in Chapter 1—through the examples of the kidnapped Christian Peacemakers, the Dawson College shooting witness, and the chorus of anti-humanists—Underdogma is so compelling that it has led some people to put their desire to stand up for the little guy ahead of their own lives.

Like "Queers For Palestine."

North American gay and lesbian activist groups like Queers Undermining Israeli Terrorism (QUIT) and Queers For Palestine regularly rail against overdog Israel while taking the side of underdog Palestinians—even when they have no personal connection to the Palestinian cause. As Muslim/lesbian author Irshad Manji noted: "their [gays and lesbians] own identities are very much wrapped up in the struggle for Palestinian liberation"[57] because, as relative underdogs themselves, they feel an affinity for those who have less power (underdogs), while feeling a reflexive scorn for those who have more power (overdogs).

[57] "My Faith Is a Mess," interview with Irshad Manji, BeliefNet 2006

The problem with Queers For Palestine is that Palestine is not for "queers." In fact, Palestinians outlaw and murder "queers."

> "If you are queer and for Palestine it means that you are for the stoning of gay people. It means that you are for the torturing and disfigurement of gay people. You are for the brutal harassment and honor killings of gay people—because these are the things that Palestinians do to us."
>
> —Michael Lucas, gay activist and adult film director, September 24, 2009

In one case, Palestinian Authority police forced a gay Palestinian man "to stand in sewage water up to his neck, his head covered by a sack filled with feces, and then he was thrown into a dark cell infested with insects"[58] before they interrogated him, stripped him, and forced him to sit on a cola bottle. When he escaped his oppressive Palestinian homeland he found safe refuge in Israel, of all places, where he said that if he were forced to return to Gaza, "the police would kill me."[59]

The only country in the Middle East that welcomes gays is the very same country these gay activists demonize: Israel. In Israel, there are no anti-gay or anti-sodomy laws, gay organizations are free to operate openly, gay and lesbian issues are discussed on Israeli television and defended in the Israeli Parliament, Israel's annual Gay Pride parades are safe and well attended, Jerusalem played host to World

---

[58] *Israel, Palestine and Gays*, Paul Varnell, Chicago Free Press, August 28, 2002

[59] Ibid

Pride Day in 2006, and Israel's Prime Minister Benjamin Netanyahu, in his 2009 address to the United Nations, spoke out against radical Islam's treatment of gays.

Still, many gays and lesbians continue to side with those who would kill them, while heaping scorn on those who safeguard their way of life. Consider the gay and lesbian activists who donned T-shirts that read "QUEERS VISIT PALESTINE, NOT THE OCCUPIERS AND OPPRESSORS"[60] at a 2009 International Gay and Lesbian Travel Association event in Israel. The protesters were angry that some gays and lesbians were basing their travel decisions on facts, not on Underdogma—like the fact that gays and lesbians are generally well treated in Israel. Facts did not seem to matter much to these gay and lesbian protesters. They insisted that their fellow "QUEERS VISIT PALESTINE" (where they would perhaps get killed) so they could maintain their allegiance with powerless (and gay-killing) underdogs, while heaping scorn on powerful (and gay-friendly) overdogs. "Give me Underdogma or give me death?" These people put Underdogma ahead of their own lives, and the lives of their fellow gay and lesbian travelers.

On September 12, 2006, talk show host Rosie O'Donnell took to the air on ABC television and said, to thunderous studio audience applause, "radical Christianity is just as threatening as radical Islam in a country like

[60] "Tel Aviv's LGBT Tourism Conference Met with Protest," Indybay.org, October 14, 2009

America."[61] While many Underdogmatists chant slogans like "America is the real terrorist," Rosie took a more reasonable-sounding tone and put forth a moral equivalence argument, stating that "radical Christianity" is "just as" threatening as "radical Islam."

Well, is it?

For the sake of Rosie's argument, let us momentarily accept the ridiculous notion that the United States of America is under the control of "radical Christianity." Rosie O'Donnell is a lesbian. Presumably, the threat of "radical Christianity" to which she referred was American Christian opposition to gay and lesbian marriage. So, what negative effect has all this "radical Christianity" had on Ms. O'Donnell?

On February 26, 2004, Rosie O'Donnell married her longtime girlfriend Kelli Carpenter on American soil. She announced her wedding plans on ABC's *Good Morning America*. Her marriage ceremony was held in the office of San Francisco's mayor. Rosie and her new wife emerged onto the steps of City Hall, where they were serenaded by the San Francisco Gay Men's Chorus. Then, Ms. O'Donnell held a nationally attended press conference during which she called the President of the United States "vile and hateful."[62]

If Rosie O'Donnell was feeling threatened by "radical Christianity" that day, she was doing a great job of hiding it.

---

[61] *The View*, ABC Television, September 12, 2006

[62] "Rosie O'Donnell Marries Girlfriend in San Francisco," AP, February 27, 2004

How would Rosie's quest to marry her longtime girlfriend have fared under "radical Islam," which she said was "just as" threatening as "radical Christianity?" To start, no Muslim nations allow homosexuals to marry. Homosexual acts are outlawed in Pakistan, Qatar, Oman, the Maldives, the United Arab Emirates, and even the Gaza Strip, with punishment ranging from public whippings to jail time. Five Muslim nations (Iran, Saudi Arabia, Sudan, Mauritania, and Yemen) execute homosexuals for engaging in same-sex intercourse (it used to be six nations, until the "vile and hateful" President George W. Bush liberated Afghanistan).[63] Since 1979, the Islamic Republic of Iran has reportedly executed more than 4,000 people for engaging in homosexual acts.[64] Methods of execution range from public hangings to throwing homosexuals off the tops of buildings to burying homosexuals up to their necks and stoning them to death. True, the California Marriage Protection Act of 2008 (also known as "Prop 8") restricted the definition of marriage to opposite-sex couples. But then Prop 8 was struck down as "unconstitutional." Regardless, the state of California never tried to execute Rosie O'Donnell or her bride. California did not even nullify their marriage. Even when Prop 8 was in effect, the lesbian and gay couples of California could still get married in New Hampshire, Massachusetts, Connecticut, Washington, D.C., and Vermont. Or they could have had their civil unions recognized in Maine, New Mexico,

---

[63] Source: "State-sponsored Homophobia," May 2010, The International Lesbian, Gay, Bisexual, Trans and Intersex Association

[64] "Iranian Teen Fears Deportation Means Death," ABC News, March 8, 2008

New York, New Jersey, Nevada, Oregon, Rhode Island, Wisconsin, Washington, Hawaii, and even in California.

How could Rosie O'Donnell and others draw moral equivalence between "radical Islam," which executes homosexuals in town squares, and so-called "radical Christianity," which allows homosexuals to marry in town squares, to adopt children (Rosie has three), to live free lives, to have their own TV shows, and even to insult their "radical" Christian President on public airwaves without fear of retribution?

Rosie O'Donnell and other Underdogmatists cannot objectively look at the facts of how homosexuals are treated by so-called "radical" Christians in America, compare them to the torture, imprisonment, and public executions that homosexuals face at the hands of "radical" Islamists, and conclude that "radical Christianity is just as threatening as radical Islam."

But facts—and even the desire for self-preservation—are trumped by Underdogmatists' gag-reflex to power. Those who have less power—even those who would kill Underdogmatists if given the chance—are reflexively championed by Underdogmatists, while those who have more power—even those who protect Underdogmatists' rights and save their lives—are scorned.

For these people, Underdogma is a matter of life and death. For others—millions of others—Underdogma is a matter of right and wrong, as revealed in the next chapter: Chapter 3—THE POWER OF UNDERDOGMA: RIGHT, WRONG…IT DEPENDS.

3

The Power of Underdogma: Right, Wrong . . . It Depends

"It is the eternal struggle between these two principles—right and wrong—throughout the world. They are the two principles that have stood face to face from the beginning of time; and will ever continue to struggle."

—Abraham Lincoln, October 15, 1858

"Moral relativism has set in so deeply that the gilded classes have become incapable of discerning right from wrong. Everything can be explained away...Life is one great moral mush—sophistry washed down with Chardonnay."

—Ambrose Evans-Pritchard, 1997

UNDERDOGMATISTS BELIEVE THAT THOSE WHO have less power are automatically deemed righteous—regardless of their actions—simply because they have less power, and that those who have more power are to be scorned, simply because they have more power. By divorcing righteousness from behavior, actions, morality, character—even from laws and societal norms—Underdogmatists seek to overturn notions of right and wrong, which have stood, as Abraham Lincoln noted, since "the beginning of time."

Is it wrong for Underdogmatists to rearrange our notions of right and wrong? Find out in this chapter—and then visit the RIGHT OR WRONG THREAD at www.under-dogma.com to see (and contribute to) an ongoing list of issues, big and small, in which designations of "right" and "wrong" are based on which side has less or more power. Here are a few examples.

Example #1—Greenhouse Gas Emissions

Although the integrity of climate change science and climate change proponents is disputed, millions of people around the world firmly believe that "the debate is over" on climate change, that it is caused by greenhouse gases (GHGs), and that the biggest GHG culprit is carbon dioxide (CO_2). Global efforts to reduce greenhouse gases have, therefore, largely focused on reducing emissions of CO_2. If more CO_2 is objectively bad, then it should follow that those who emit more CO_2 are also bad. Right?

The answer, according to Underdogma, is: it depends on who is doing the emitting.

Things were simpler in the early days of the global warming debate. Back then, the world's No. 1 emitter of greenhouse gases (America) was also the world's No. 1 power. If scorn for U.S. emissions was somehow bundled together with scorn for U.S. power, it would have been hard to tell for sure, since both were locked together in the No. 1 slot. That changed in 2006, when China—which opens an average of one new coal-fired plant each week—overtook the U.S. to become the world's No. 1 emitter of greenhouse gases. Now, American CO_2 emissions are No.

2 (and dropping), and Chinese CO_2 emissions are No. 1 (and rising).

> "It had been known, but disputed, for a year that China was the new king of carbon, having pumped more of the heat-trapping gas into the atmosphere annually than the United States. Now, with a new analysis from the Netherlands, the rise of China's polluting power has been confirmed."
>
> "It [China] now emits 14% more than the United States every year, and that figure is expected to grow."
>
> —"China Alone Increased Worldwide CO2 Pollution 2% Last Year," *The Daily Green*, June 16, 2008

If CO_2 emissions are bad, then concern for the environment should lead environmentalists to heap *more* scorn on China (which emits more CO_2) and *less* scorn on the United States (which emits less CO_2).

That is not happening.

Therefore, something other than actual amounts of CO_2 emissions must be the determining factor when it comes to doling out environmental scorn.

First, a good percentage of people reading this page have not yet heard that China has overtaken the U.S. as the No. 1 emitter of greenhouse gases. Which brings us to the first telltale sign of Underdogma: underreporting the inconvenient truths about underdogs' bad behaviors. When China surpassed the United States as the world's biggest polluter in 2006, the news fell like a lone tree in the forest; heard by few, ignored or unknown by most. If you did not happen to pick up a newspaper on the one or two days this news was reported, you could have easily missed the fact that the balance of power at the center of one of the world's most pressing issues had dramatically shifted from one side of the world to the other.

Those who did manage to catch a glimpse of this brief media coverage were treated to one of the most dazzling displays of Underdogma yet seen. Not only did Underdogmatists stand up for underdog China by shielding the truth of its actions from the public, they actually *defended* the world's biggest polluter with outrageous "per capita" arguments:

> "At current projected growth rates, China's per capita emissions in 2030 still will be only one-third those of the West."
>
> —Faith Birol, International Energy Agency, *LA Times*, June 21, 2007

Those who believe that greenhouse gas emissions cause global warming must, by extension, also believe that more greenhouse gases are objectively bad—regardless of how many people it took to pump those gases into the air. Not according to Underdogmatists, who excuse underdog China by pointing out that China's "per capita" emissions are lower, even though China pumps more *actual* CO_2 into the atmosphere than any other nation on Earth.

The Associated Press (AP) and Greenpeace went even further—within the very first news cycle after China surpassed America's CO_2 emissions—and actually *blamed the overdog West for causing China's pollution.*

> "Developed countries are hypocritical for criticizing China's greenhouse gas emissions while buy-

> ing products from its booming manufacturing industry."
>
> —"China to West: Don't Criticize Our CO2 Emissions While Buying Our Products," AP, June 21, 2007

> "Greenpeace UK said responsibility for China's soaring emissions lay not just in Beijing, but also in Washington."
>
> —"China is Worst for CO2 Pollution," *Metro UK*, June 20, 2007

If America is to blame for China's greenhouse gas emissions, because America buys products from China, then Canada should be blamed for America's greenhouse gas emissions, because Canada is America's No. 1 trading partner. Canada, therefore, needs to be scorned immediately by Greenpeace, the AP, and the world community because its gluttonous, relentless hunger for American products has forced a helpless United States to pump tons of greenhouse gases into the atmosphere in order to satiate its ravenous neighbor to the north. Has such a story ever been printed? Has such a point of view ever been advanced by Greenpeace or the AP or others? If not, why?

Perhaps the reason why No. 2 emitter America is scorned by environmentalists while No. 1 emitter China is defended is because China treats its environmentalists far better than America treats its environmentalists.

Actually, quite the opposite is true.

> "Wu Lihong, named one of China's top 10 environmentalists in 2005, was arrested in April [and sentenced to three years] on what his wife and

> friends say were charges concocted by local officials who were embarrassed by Wu's whistle-blowing.
>
> "Three of his ribs were broken."
>
> —"China environmental activist imprisoned," *USA Today*, August 10, 2007

Outside China, environmentalists are given the Academy Award and the Nobel Peace Prize. Inside China, environmentalists are beaten and jailed.

Not satisfied with simply hiding the truth about the world's No. 1 polluter, China (underdog), or shifting environmental blame to No. 2 polluter, America (overdog), Underdogmatists went full circle and actually championed China for its "Environmental Renaissance." The following excerpts are from a detailed analysis entitled "China's Coming Environmental Renaissance," written by environmental group Worldwatch, which bills its research as "the gold-standard for sustainability analysis for decision makers in government, civil society, business, and academia."[1]

> "From the start of this millennium, China's central government has stepped up its commitment to the environment and resource conservation."
>
> ***Translation: China's commitment is quite recent.***

> "They [China] have not only set ambitious targets for energy savings and pollution control, but they have labeled these efforts as two paramount tasks for the government. Meeting these goals will naturally take time."
>
> ***Translation: Although China has set "ambitious targets,"***

[1] Source: Worldwatch Institute website "About Us" section

it has not come close to meeting them, and we should "naturally" give them more time.

"It will similarly take more than a few years for the country to achieve its goal of achieving a harmonious and sustainable economy."
Translation: When we said "more time" we meant to say "a lot more time."

"Increasing numbers of officials, including in Guangdong, Chongqing, and Shandong provinces, are working hard or vowing to promote the concept of 'greener development.'"
Translation: An unspecified number of officials ("increasing" might mean an increase from one to two) are "working hard or vowing to promote the concept of 'greener development.'" This means they are either "working hard" to promote a concept (not to actually deliver greener development) or they are "vowing to," at some unspecified time, promote the concept of greener development.

"With its expanding industrial base, increasingly skilled labor force, and geared-up R & D efforts, China brings hope—not despair—for a global leap forward in environmental stewardship."
Translation: Whereas America's shrinking industrial base, declining emissions, even more skilled labor force, and more advanced R & D efforts bring only despair—not hope—for the future of environmental stewardship.

—"China's Coming Environmental Renaissance,"
Worldwatch China Program Manager
Yingling Liu, November 29, 2007

Underdogma at its finest.

Example #2—Killing Innocent People

Can we at least agree that killing innocent people is wrong?

Not so fast. In the eyes of Underdogmatists, it depends on who is doing the killing, and how much relative power they hold.

On February 4, 2008, an innocent woman in her early seventies was killed in a shopping mall. On April 28, 2008, an innocent woman in her early forties was killed in her home. Two innocent women, killed within weeks and within miles of each other.

Which killing of an innocent woman was celebrated as "heroic," and which killing of an innocent woman triggered an apology and an investigation? As for the killers of these innocent women, which was scorned by the world community, and which continues to receive ongoing and unparalleled support from every corner of the Earth?

The answer can be found in Underdogma, which instructs us that the less powerful killer of innocent women should be excused and/or championed, and that the more powerful killer of innocent women should be scorned.

One killer was Palestinian, the other was Israeli. I ask the reader to stay focused on the issue at hand. This is not an examination of which side is right or wrong in the Israeli-Palestinian conflict. It is a look inside the mechanics of how we, who are not directly involved in this conflict, assign values of "right" or "wrong" to something that is, by all objective standards, wrong (the killing of innocent women).

Some details about the killings.

One killing was *intentional*. The other was *accidental*. While killing innocent people is never right, we do make legal and moral distinctions between premeditated killings (murder) and unintentional killings (manslaughter). In such cases, the killer's intent is important in drawing both legal and moral distinctions. So, let us examine the intents of these killers to see if the rules of civil society (intentional killing of innocents is wrong, unintentional killing of innocents is less wrong) or if the rules of Underdogma (whichever side has more power is wrong, whichever side has less power is less wrong, or even right) are in effect.

On February 4, 2008, Palestinian suicide bombers *intentionally* killed a seventy-three-year-old woman and injured eleven other people at a shopping center in Dimona, Israel. The military wing of Hamas proudly claimed responsibility for the killing, stating, "the Al-Qassam Brigades therefore congratulates our people on this heroic operation."[2] Afterward, rival Palestinian families fought over who got to claim "credit" for raising the "martyr" who killed the old woman, with "no fewer than four different families ... claiming credit for the attack."[3]

By contrast, when the Israeli Defense Forces (IDF) surrounded the hideout of a high-ranking Islamic Jihad terrorist in the West Bank and *accidentally* killed a woman who was inside the building at the time, the IDF immediately issued an apology and began an internal investigation into the incident.[4]

In both cases, an innocent woman was killed. Neither side is without blame. But one side does tend to get more

---

[2] "Hamas Militants Claim Responsibility for Israel Suicide Bombing," BBC, February 6, 2008

[3] "Our Son is a Martyr: Families Make Rival Claims to Bombers," *The Sunday Telegraph* (London), February 10, 2008

[4] "IDF Captures Terrorist, Thwarts Attack," Israel National News, May 1, 2006

of the world's blame (Israelis, who apologize for the deaths of innocents and investigate what went wrong), while the other side maintains its broad, worldwide support (Palestinians, who call the deaths of innocents "heroic" and celebrate what went right).

If logic or the norms of civil society were the driving forces here, both sides would—at the very least—be scorned equally, and perhaps the Palestinians would even be scorned to a greater degree because they *intentionally* killed an innocent woman and then *celebrated.*

Instead, the world community declares its solidarity with the underdog, regardless of its actions, and takes Underdogma so far as to observe a moment of silence at the United Nations to honor Palestinian suicide bombers.

> "In 2003 the representatives of over 100 member states stood along with the [United Nations] secretary-general, before a map predating the state of Israel, for a moment of silence 'for all those who had given their lives for the Palestinian people'—which include suicide bombers."
>
> —"One Small Step," Anne Bayefsky, *The Wall Street Journal*, June 21, 2004

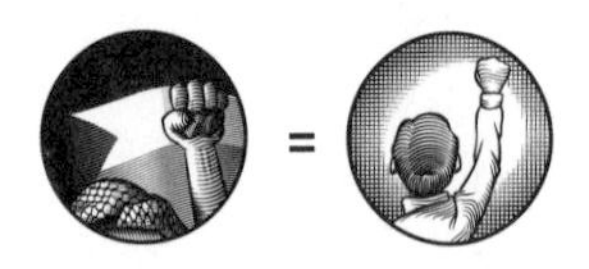

A University of San Diego/South Florida study set out to test if our perceptions of right and wrong—specifically when it comes to terrorist attacks—are affected by the relative power held by the terrorist attackers. The study's findings confirmed Underdogma.

The researcher who conducted the study, Joseph Vandello, summarized his findings for *Underdogma*.

A NOTE FROM JOSEPH VANDELLO

Participants read a fictional account of two countries involved in a long-standing conflict. The story described a violent episode (a bomb detonated at a military parade, killing seventeen soldiers) perpetrated by either the larger, more powerful country or the smaller, less powerful country.

There are basically four main findings of note:

When the violent act was committed by the low power group, 1) it was seen as more moral and justified, and 2) it was less likely to be seen as terrorism than when the same act was committed by the more powerful group. 3) Furthermore, reading about violence by the low power group (compared to the high power group) increased the favorability of participants' attitudes about aggression in the abstract. Finally, 4) reading about violence by the high power group also decreased people's beliefs in the legitimacy of social hierarchies (that is, they were less likely to endorse statements that suggested it was right and legitimate for some groups to be more powerful than others).

> "Participants sided with the less powerful group, giving it more sympathy and support, and seeing it as an underdog. In addition, the same violent bombing was seen as more justifiable, legitimate, moral, and necessary when committed by the weaker group. When people perceive a power imbalance, terrorism may be considered an equalizer for the disadvantaged."
>
> —"How Differences in Relative Group Power Influence Judgments of the Morality of Violent Actions," Joseph A. Vandello & Nadav Goldschmied

When underdog Palestinians *intentionally* kill innocent people and celebrate *what went right*, they somehow still continue to enjoy broad worldwide support, along with their own special body at the United Nations to champion their cause, and Palestinians continue to be the largest per capita recipients of international assistance in the world.[5] Israel, which apologizes when it *accidentally* kills innocent civilians and launches internal investigations to find out *what went wrong*, is berated on the world stage and threatened with extermination by its neighbors while "the United Nations and too many members of the international community have unfairly singled out Israel for condemnation."[6]

Logic or the norms of civil society are clearly not at play when it comes to choosing sides between more powerful Israelis (overdogs) and less powerful Palestinians (underdogs). Underdogma, however, is.

Example #3—Soldiers Behaving Badly

Is it wrong to humiliate terrorists? Is it wrong to rape starving children in exchange for food? The answer is: both are wrong. But are they equally wrong? Let us assume, for the sake of argument, that the humiliation of terrorists is equally as wrong as the rape of starving children. Both, therefore, should have received equal coverage in the media, and both groups of perpetrators should have been equally scorned by the world community.

---

[5] "Dollars and Diplomacy: Foreign Aid and the Palestinian Question," Scott Lasensky, August 2006

[6] Richard Goldstone, *Jerusalem Post*, October 19, 2009

That is not what happened.

First, humiliating terrorists. By now, you may have figured out that this is in reference to the American soldiers who stripped and taunted terrorist prisoners at Abu Ghraib prison from October to December of 2003. The reason you may have figured this out is because the prisoner abuses at Abu Ghraib generated massive, sustained, worldwide media coverage that included the front covers of *Time*, *Newsweek*, the *New York Times*, the *LA Times*, *USA Today*, the *Washington Post*, and virtually every other major newspaper around the world. It was the subject of repeated lead stories on the ABC, NBC, and CBS evening news broadcasts as well as cable news broadcasts, the BBC, CBC, profiles on *60 Minutes*, *Meet The Press*, *This Week*, *Fox News Sunday*, and others, as well as countless national and local radio news broadcasts. It was the focus of PBS, HBO, and other documentaries. It prompted Congressional hearings. And it spawned no less than nineteen books, numerous songs, and even an off-Broadway play. In total, a media search of "Abu Ghraib" at the time of this writing generated 121,000 hits.

We are all familiar with the results of the Abu Ghraib media coverage: America was scorned the world over, the American soldiers in question were investigated, put on trial, and jailed, and people around the world cited the abuses at Abu Ghraib as evidence of American evil and as justification for hatred and continued jihad against the United States.

> "If Osama bin Laden had hired a Madison Avenue public relations firm to rally Arab hearts and minds to his cause, it's hard to imagine that it

> could have devised a better propaganda campaign [than the Abu Ghraib prison scandal]."
>
> —"The Road to Abu Ghraib,"
> *Washington Monthly*, November 2004

Maximum coverage and maximum scorn for America's shameful behavior at Abu Ghraib.

So, how does it compare to the rape of starving children?

Between 2003 and 2009, United Nations peacekeepers have been implicated in the widespread rape of children in the Democratic Republic of the Congo, Ivory Coast, Sudan, Liberia, Burundi, and Haiti.[7] Some United Nations soldiers raped starving children in exchange for food, with CNN noting, "children as young as 6 have been forced to have sex with aid workers and peacekeepers in return for food."[8] Other UN soldiers made child pornography videos of the rapes.[9] Still more engaged in child prostitution while "peacekeeping" for the United Nations. The UN was aware of these problems, and at least one internal UN report documented the problem: "sexual exploitation and abuse, particularly prostitution of minors, is widespread and long-standing."[10]

> "A 13-year-old girl, 'Elizabeth' described to the BBC how 10 UN peacekeepers gang-raped her in a field near her Ivory Coast home.

---

[7] "Peacekeepers 'Abusing Children,'" BBC, May 27, 2008

[8] "Charity: Aid Workers Raping, Abusing Children," CNN, May 27, 2008

[9] "Sex Scandal in Congo Threatens to Engulf UN's Peacekeepers," *Times Online UK*, December 23, 2004

[10] "U.N. Sexual Abuse Alleged in Congo," *Washington Post*, December 16, 2004

> 'They grabbed me and threw me to the ground and they forced themselves on me...I tried to escape but there were 10 of them and I could do nothing,' she said.
>
> 'I was terrified. Then they just left me there bleeding.'"
>
> —"Peacekeepers 'Abusing Children,'" BBC, May 27, 2008

Although the United Nations became aware as early as 2004 that its blue-helmeted "peacekeepers" were raping starving children around the world, at the time of this writing, rape by United Nations "peacekeepers" continues (four-plus years of child rape, compared to three months of abusing terrorist prisoners at Abu Ghraib).

Whereas the United States was first to investigate and uncover the problem of its prison guards at Abu Ghraib (the earliest media coverage was about the U.S. military's internal investigation into the prisoner abuse), the United Nations' investigation of its soldiers' crimes against children has not gone as quickly or as smoothly, especially when the UN child rapists under investigation "threatened U.N. investigators...and sought to bribe witnesses to change incriminating testimony, a confidential U.N. draft report says."[11] As of March 2010, "more than six years after the United Nations implemented a zero-tolerance policy for sexual misconduct by its peacekeepers, the organization is still struggling to persuade member states to investigate and discipline accused soldiers."[12]

---

[11] "U.N. Sexual Abuse Alleged in Congo," *Washington Post*, December 16, 2004

[12] "U.N. Mum on Probes of Sex-Abuse Allegations," *The Wall Street Journal*, March 21, 2010

American officials prosecuted and jailed its soldiers who were directly involved in the Abu Ghraib prison scandal. By contrast, many of the United Nations' child rapists remain free, either going completely unpunished or getting suspended *with pay*.

> "No action has been taken against the soldiers."
> —"Peacekeepers 'Abusing Children,'" BBC, May 27, 2008

> "The latest disclosure comes as U.N. officials confirmed that a senior U.N. official in Congo was suspended from his job with pay in recent weeks pending an investigation into allegations of 'inappropriate conduct.'"
> —"U.N. Sexual Abuse Alleged in Congo," *Washington Post*, December 16, 2004

When "the UN rape-for-food"[13] program was uncovered, the *UK Times* reported that it could "become the UN's Abu Ghraib."[14] That forecast did not account for the power of Underdogma, which assigns virtue to whichever side has less power, *because it has less power*, and heaps scorn on whichever side has more power, *because it has more power*.

When a handful of U.S. soldiers abused terrorist prisoners for a period of months, the United States suffered massive worldwide scorn for years. When scores of United Nations soldiers raped starving children around the world for over four years, the United Nations sustained

---

[13] *The Rush Limbaugh Show*, July 20, 2006

[14] "Sex Scandal in Congo Threatens to Engulf UN's Peacekeepers," *Times Online UK*, December 23, 2004

little, if any, damage to its position as worldwide arbiter of right and wrong.

Perhaps it is because most people have never heard about the United Nations "child rape for food" program. This scandal has never appeared on the covers of *Time* or *Newsweek*. No PBS or HBO documentaries have been made about the United Nations child rapists. No songs have been sung, no books or off-Broadway plays have been written, and the United Nations' child rapes have generated less than 1.3% of Abu Ghraib's media coverage. At best, the public did not rise up against the United Nations child rapists because the UN's crimes were hidden from the public by Underdogmatists in the media. At worst, the public does know about United Nations "peacekeepers" raping starving children around the world, and yet still considers the United Nations to be a worthy arbiter of right and wrong.

When America pollutes, it is wrong. When Israelis kill innocents, it is wrong. When American soldiers behave badly, it is wrong. But just because China, Palestinians, and the UN have relatively less power than the U.S. and Israel does not make their pollution less polluting, does not make the people they kill less dead, and does not make the victims of their soldiers less victimized.

Right is right, wrong is wrong, and, to paraphrase Abraham Lincoln, we can only hope the "eternal struggle between...right and wrong" continues, and that it is not snuffed out by Underdogmatists who are bent on replacing age-old notions of right and wrong with a reflexive, non-thinking assignment of rightness and virtue to whichever side has less power.

Bonus Example #1—A Tale of Two Walls

When Israel built a wall to protect itself from Palestinian terrorists, Underdogmatists around the world were outraged, with many calling it "Israeli Apartheid."

In late 2009, Egypt started building a wall of its own, also in part to protect itself from Palestinian terrorists.

Two walls, in the exact same part of the world, to fence in the exact same Palestinian terrorists. Was the reaction to the two walls the same, or do we see evidence of Underdogma?

ISRAEL'S WALL	EGYPT'S WALL
"Roundly and bitterly condemned and protested—with comparisons to the Berlin Wall and even Nazi concentration camps." "Protested by the major powers in Europe and the U.S. government." "Protested personally by Barack Obama." —"A Tale of Two Walls," Joseph Farah, *WorldNetDaily*, December 13, 2009	"There is no word if the protesters will be confronting Egyptian soldiers in anti-fence activities along the Egypt-Gaza border." —IsraelNationalNews.com, December 21, 2009 "Not a word of protest in the U.S." "U.S. Army Corps of Engineers is helping Egypt build it." —"A Tale of Two Walls," Joseph Farah, *WorldNetDaily*, December 13, 2009

Bonus Example #2—Underdogma, Under God

God is great. Except, it seems, when certain groups of God's followers have more power than other groups of God's followers. To find out the different ways that Underdogmatists treat God in our public squares, in our schools, in our politics, and in our daily lives—based on how much relative power is held by different groups of God's followers—download the online exclusive Bonus Chapter—UNDERDOGMA, UNDER GOD at www.under-dogma.com.

In order for us to understand the effect of Underdogma in our world and in our lives today, we must first understand Underdogma's history. Which brings us to Chapter 4—THE HISTORY OF UNDERDOGMA.

4
The History of Underdogma

> "The oldest story of humanity is the story of someone who's had their power taken from them."
> —Tony Robbins, interview for *Underdogma*, April 6, 2010

> "Cain said to his brother Abel, 'Let's go out to the field.'"
> —Genesis 4:1-8

THE HISTORY OF UNDERDOGMA IS the history of power struggles. To understand how Underdogma came to exert such a powerful force in our world today, we must go all the way back to the beginning (literally, or biblically, depending on your beliefs). The first sons of Adam and Eve—Cain and Abel—each gave an offering to God. When God accepted Abel's offering and rejected Cain's, the balance of power between the first brothers tilted. Abel received more of God's blessings, and Cain received less. In that moment, equality vanished, jealousy and envy were born, and the seeds of Underdogma were sown.

Jealousy, envy, and Underdogma have their roots in our desire for equality. And although equality has eluded us since the day God bestowed unequal blessings on Adam and Eve's sons, it has not stopped us from trying to achieve equality.

In 350 BC, Aristotle observed that "all men think justice to be a sort of equality."[1] Aristotle and Plato had similar views on equality, but their idea of equality did not include, for instance, slaves; Aristotle felt that slaves were born as slaves just as beasts were born as beasts and women were born as women. Aristotle wrote that people's natures were assigned to them by birth, and he referred to them as "slaves by nature…It is better for them, just as in the cases mentioned [animals, etc.] to be ruled thus." He continued, "for there is one rule exercised over subjects who are by nature free, another over subjects who are by nature slaves."[2] In other words, because a slave was born a slave, Aristotle could write about equality and see no moral conflict with the fact that the slave could not rise up and achieve equality with Aristotle because, after all, the slave was a slave and Aristotle was not and that was the way each was born to be. Plato clarified this concept of equality by stating that equality was only meant to apply between those who were already of equal status: "the general method I mean is to grant much to the great and less to the less great, adjusting what you give to take account of the real nature of each—specifically, to confer high recognition on great virtue, but when you come to the poorly educated in this respect, to treat them as they deserve."[3] This is vastly different from today's concept of equality or egalitarianism, which seeks parity among all men (and

[1] "Politics," Aristotle, 384 BC–322 BC
[2] "Politics," Aristotle, 384 BC–322 BC
[3] Plato's *Laws*, VI, 757

women), and it is completely different from Underdogma, which reflexively scorns those who have power (because they have power) while canonizing the powerless (because they are powerless).

The Romans' concept of "Natural Law" gave all men access to a common code of behavior through the commonly held prism of reason. Since all men had access to reason, all men had access to Natural Law, which gave all men a certain level of equality. As Cicero wrote in *Laws*, "as all of us are to one another...Reason, which alone raises us above the level of the beasts...is certainly common to us all."[4] Atticus called reason "the gift of the gods [the] one principle by which men may live with one another, and that is the same for all, and possessed equally by all."[5] Still, this was not equality or egalitarianism, because Rome had a powerful Caesar at one end of the power scale and powerless slaves at the other. And this was not Underdogma, which would have reflexively demonized Caesar for being powerful while ascribing virtue to the slaves for being powerless. But it did put all men—at least theoretically—under the same tent of reason and Natural Law, even though the tent was perforated with contradictions and exceptions.

Continuing along this historical thread of equality and egalitarianism, we skip ahead to 1515, when Sir Thomas More wrote of a mythical egalitarian island called "Utopia, where every man has a right to everything" and "there is no unequal distribution." In 1776, the U.S. Declaration

---

[4] Cicero, *Laws*, 1515

[5] Thomas More, *Utopia*

of Independence stated the "self-evident" (and oft-misinterpreted) truth that "all men are created equal." Then, in 1859, Charles Darwin's *On the Origin of Species* threatened to derail egalitarianism with the notion of natural selection and survival of the fittest, but Darwin's work was quickly misunderstood and embraced by Karl Marx, who wrote: "Darwin's work is most important and suits my purpose in that it provides a basis in natural science for the historical class struggle."[6]

One of the first sparks of Underdogma, not equality or egalitarianism, can be found in the story of David and Goliath, in which the smaller, less powerful David triumphs over the bigger, more powerful Goliath. Though it is safe to say that David was firmly on the side of David, and Goliath was firmly on the side of Goliath, we, who view this story across the centuries and more as a metaphor, overwhelmingly regard the bigger, more powerful Goliath as the villain, and the smaller, less powerful David as the hero.

The story of David and Goliath (the way we view it now, as a metaphor) marked a fork in the road between equality/egalitarianism and the belief that would eventually become Underdogma. If the story of David and Goliath had been an egalitarian tale, a more appropriate ending would have been for the two combatants to put down their weapons, shake hands, and divide up their posses-

[6] Karl Marx, 1861

sions. Instead, the smaller, less powerful David with his smaller, less powerful weapon (a sling) triumphed over the bigger, more powerful Goliath with his bigger, more powerful sword and armor. That is what we cheer: the little guy standing up to the big guy—and *vanquishing* him.

The story of David and Goliath, however, is not a clear case of Underdogma because it lacks certain key elements: there is no reflexive assigning of virtue to David, and no reflexive demonization of Goliath. Yes, David is portrayed as brave and heroic, but it is not his weakness that we celebrate. We cheer him on because we want him to win. And we do not demonize Goliath for being big. We view him as a big and powerful opponent and, therefore, a bigger challenge for our hero David to overcome. Still, the story of David and Goliath does move us closer to Underdogma in that it takes us beyond man's desire for equality and egalitarianism and forges a new path with a new motive: the desire to see the weak *vanquish* the strong.

Jesus came close to articulating Underdogma by blessing the meek and declaring them inheritors of the Earth. Jesus also touched upon the second part of Underdogma (scorn for the powerful) by stating:

> "It is easier for a camel to pass through the eye of a needle than for a rich man to enter the Kingdom of God."
>
> —Matthew 19:24

But this was still not Underdogma. Jesus did not declare that those who had money were bad *because* they had money (money = power). He was merely answering a young, wealthy man who had asked, "what good thing must I do to get eternal life?" Jesus replied, "go, sell your possessions and give to the poor, and you will have a treasure in heaven."[7] The young man left in sadness because he felt he had too much money to give away. It was then that Jesus had the "camel through the eye of a needle" talk with his disciples. Jesus did not demonize the rich man for being rich. He simply stated that the price of admission for eternal life was to give away one's money. If Jesus had practiced Underdogma, he would have declared the rich man evil (or, in today's parlance, a "big, rich fat cat")—because he had money—rather than offering the rich man a path to salvation by giving away his money and getting into heaven.

In AD 1215, the Magna Carta shook up the "power haves" in that it "limited the king's authority by establishing the crucial principle that the law was a power in its own right to which the king was subject."[8] In this way, the Magna Carta marked an important shift in the balance of power between the governed (underdogs, power have-nots) and the governors (overdogs, power haves), by placing both overdog and underdog under the power of the same law.

This "Balance of Power" narrative weaves throughout the centuries. Sparta and the league of city-states united to offset the power of Athens. In the seventeenth century, the power of King Louis XIV was offset by an alliance that involved most of the rest of Europe. And, to balance power in the eighteenth century, "Prussia was first allied with France and Bavaria against Great Britain and Austria,

[7] Matthew 19:21

[8] British Library, "Treasures in Full: Magna Carta"

then later fought with Britain against Austria, France, and Russia."[9]

Still, these were not true examples of Underdogma, because their intent was to balance, offset, or fight the power of overdogs, not to glorify the weak for being weak while hurling philosophical slings and arrows at those who had power *because they had power*.

Karl Marx and Friedrich Engels circled around the concept of Underdogma in 1848 by combining scorn for the overdog (Bourgeoisie) with exaltation for the underdog (Proletariat) in *The Communist Manifesto*:

> "The history of all hitherto existing society is the history of class struggles. Freeman and slave, patrician and plebeian, lord and serf, guild-master and journeyman, in a word, oppressor and oppressed, stood in constant opposition to one another...Society as a whole is more and more splitting up into two great hostile camps, into two great classes directly facing each other—Bourgeoisie and Proletariat."
>
> —*The Communist Manifesto*, Karl Marx & Friedrich Engels, 1848

Marx and Engels, however, were not Underdogmatists. Yes, they exalted the underdog and scorned the overdog—but not based solely on the relative power each side held.

[9] History.com Encyclopedia

They scorned overdogs (Bourgeoisie) for *exploiting* underdogs (Proletariat), and they championed underdogs (Proletariat, workers) for working hard, even though the means of production were being withheld from them by big, powerful overdogs (Bourgeoisie, bosses). In other words, Marx and Engels were seeking to right some sort of wrong (perceived or real) arising from the *actions* of the powerful. Flawed as history has proven Marx and Engels to be, at least they demonstrated some sort of reasoning. Underdogma, on the other hand, operates more by reflex than by reason. It is an automatic reaction to lash out at those who have more power and to exalt those who have less power.

Underdogma's forward march gathered steam in the United States with the introduction of the Interstate Commerce Act of 1887 and the Sherman Anti-Trust Act of 1890. This "Anti-Industrial Revolution" wrote a "revolutionary new principle" into the law books: that "private greed must henceforth be subordinated to public need."[10] As former Federal Reserve Chair Alan Greenspan noted, the effect of these laws was an almost word-for-word recital of the second part of Underdogma:

> "The effective purpose, the hidden intent, and the actual practice of the antitrust laws in the United States have led to the condemnation of the productive and efficient members of our society *because* they are productive and efficient."
>
> —Alan Greenspan, *Antitrust*, 1961

[10] Best-selling history textbook *The American Pageant*, in print for more than fifty years, 2001

The Interstate Commerce Act and the Sherman Anti-Trust Act marked turning points on the road to Underdogma in that they contained scorn for the overdog—and a desire to *punish* the overdog—even though punishing the overdog would cause measurable harm to the underdogs whom these laws were presumably designed to protect. This is where Underdogma makes the all-important break from reason and self-interest and heaps scorn on the powerful simply for being powerful. Regardless of how much these so-called robber barons enriched themselves, they also enriched the lives of their customers by reducing the cost of shipping, oil, steel, and other essential building blocks of America. John D. Rockefeller reduced the price of oil from fifty-eight cents a gallon to eight cents a gallon. Carnegie Steel, headed by Charles Schwab, reduced the price of steel from $56 per ton to $11.50 per ton. And Cornelius Vanderbilt brought cross-Atlantic steamship travel within the grasp of everyday people by dropping ticket prices from $200 per person to $110 (for first class) and $75 (for steerage).[11]

> "No one can ever compute the price that all of us have paid for that Act which, by inducing less effective use of capital, has kept our standard of living lower than would otherwise have been possible."
> —Alan Greenspan, *Antitrust*, 1961

The central "wrong" that the government set out to right with the Underdogmatist Sherman Anti-Trust Act and the Interstate Commerce Act was the fact that these

[11] *The Myth of the Robber Barons,* Burton W. Folsom Jr., 1991

so-called robber barons had become rich and powerful by *lowering prices too much*. Who were the "victims" of lower prices? Certainly not consumers, who benefited by paying less for shipping, oil, steel, and other needed items. The wronged parties in these cases were the disgruntled competitors who could not compete with the robber barons on price or efficiency. How could the public allow itself to be turned into a pawn in an Underdogmatist war waged by less-capable industrialists against their more-capable competitors? A war that, if won, would cost the public money? With a little prodding by "muckraker" journalists like Ida Tarbell, who just happened to be the sister of W. W. Tarbell, who just happened to be the treasurer of the Pure Oil Company, which just happened to be the biggest competitor to Rockefeller's Standard Oil.

> "McClure's Magazine ran [Ida Tarbell's] History of the Standard Oil Company over the course of two years...it ignited a public fury and civic outrage that led the U.S. government to proceed against the Standard Oil Company."
>
> —Kathleen Brady, author of *Ida Tarbell, Portrait of a Muckraker*, 1989

The modern-day parallels to Ida Tarbell's anti-corporate screeds can be found in Chapter 12—UNDERDOGMA AND THE GLOBAL FINANCIAL CRISIS, in which the media—and even the President of the United States—play key roles in whipping up Underdogmatist scorn and aiming it at big, powerful overdog corporations and rich "fat cats." This kind of rhetoric is often called "Populism," and it finds its philosophical roots in the "Progressive" movement of the late 1800s and early twentieth century.

There is much debate about the nature and origin of Progressivism. In the book *Progressivism*, authors John D. Buenker, John C. Burnham, and Robert M. Crunden observed that "historians could no longer even agree whether or not there had been a 'Progressive movement' at all, when the era began or ended, or whether even the general concept of Progressivism was worth extended attention." Historians Arthur S. Link, Richard L. McCormick, and Harlan Davidson generally pegged the origins of the Progressive movement to "the profound economic and social changes of the last third of the nineteenth century [which] created the conditions to which the progressive reformers responded," namely a revolt against wealth and power in the midst of economic turmoil in which "common people—farmers, workers, and small businessmen—organized the progressive movement in order to recapture power from the railroads, large corporations, and party bosses who had plundered the United States during the Gilded Age."[12] History professor Burt Folsom, author of *The Myth of the Robber Barons* and *New Deal or Raw Deal*, wrote this description of the Progressive movement for *Underdogma*.

[12] *Progressivism*, Arthur S Link,Richard L. McCormick, & Harlan Davidson, 1983

A NOTE FROM PROFESSOR BURT FOLSOM

The Progressives wanted to centralize power and make government more efficient. They wanted a powerful executive to cure alleged abuses and fine tune the economy. The Founders believed that setting up freedom would produce inequalities of condition because people were unequal in ability, willingness to work, and in luck. As long as all had a right to life, liberty, and the pursuit of happiness (the pursuit of happiness, not a guarantee of it) society would function well. The progressives believed that by 1900 human nature had changed; we knew more; we could trust elected leaders with much greater power. They believed we could redistribute wealth and create greater equality of condition, which they deemed desirable. The original progressive income tax had a top rate of 7%. It was up to 25% by the 1920s; 63% under Hoover; 79% under FDR in the 1930s; and 94% at the time of FDR's death. In other words, envy and greed—the taxing of the few to capture the votes of the many—became a political exercise that prolonged the Great Depression, and would have sustained it after WWII if we had not cut taxes and increased freedom.

When large groups of Americans fell into poverty (powerlessness, inequality), and when their populist anger was stoked and aimed at rich and powerful fat-cat "robber barons" by Progressivists and muckraking journalists like Ida Tarbell, the Progressive movement emerged to offer "a new form of government able to engineer a better society, assuring equal outcomes."[13] In the "progressive classic" *The Promise of American Life*, New Republic founder Herbert Croly wrote that "centralization and elite control were

[13] "The Rediscovery of America," Dr. Matthew Spalding, Heritage.org, November 3, 2009

necessary to advance democratic ends because American constitutional government was based on 'erroneous and misleading ideas,' and 'the average American individual is morally and intellectually inadequate to a serious and consistent conception of his responsibilities as a democrat.'"[14] In other words, Progressives felt that the American people were not worthy of the power entrusted to them by the Founders, and therefore their power needed to be transferred to the state so that it could be redistributed more equitably.

This is the opposite of America's founding principles.

As Hillsdale College president Larry P. Arnn said in his interview for *Underdogma*, the Founders declared that, in America, "here, for the first time in history, sovereignty is located outside the government."[15] By seeking to concentrate power in the hands of the government (under the pretense of correcting power imbalances between individuals), the Progressives rejected America's founding principles, which declared that the proper role of government was to safeguard man's natural rights and resultant powers. As Professor Thomas G. West observed, the Progressive movement was "a total rejection in theory, and a partial rejection in practice, of the principles and policies on which America had been founded."[16]

---

[14] "The New Progressivism: Same as the Old Progressivism?" Peter Berkowitz, essay based on the November 2009 AEI Bradley Lecture, January 21, 2010

[15] Hillsdale College president Larry P. Arnn, interview for *Underdogma*, February 10, 2010

[16] "The Progressive Movement and the Transformation of American Politics," Thomas G. West, *The Heritage Foundation*, July 18, 2007

> "[Man's rights] are a gift of God and nature. Government is therefore always and fundamentally in the service of the individual, not the other way around. The purpose of government, then, is to enforce the natural law for the members of the political community by securing the people's natural rights."
>
> —"The Progressive Movement and the Transformation of American Politics," Thomas G. West, *The Heritage Foundation*, July 18, 2007

By declaring the self-evident truth that men are "endowed by their Creator with certain unalienable rights," and that the role of government was to secure those rights, the Founders set up the winning conditions for America to become the most successful—and most powerful—nation in world history. The Founders also set up the conditions for the eventual inequality of outcomes between men, because giving men the power to pursue their own happiness also gave them the power to succeed, or not to succeed, to gain wealth and power and to become rich fat-cat robber barons, or even to go broke. The Progressive movement sought to "correct" such power imbalances by rejecting America's founding principles and vesting power in the government, not in the people. In doing so, the Progressives took a big step toward Underdogma by focusing on power itself. The Progressives' remedy for power imbalances was to seize power for themselves and thus change the institutional and constitutional levers that had been carefully and specifically constructed by America's Founders to prevent such government power grabs in the first place.

The history of Underdogma until this point has largely been the history of people who tried to achieve what they felt were good goals, such as equality, fairness, or the joy of seeing the little guy triumph. The Anti-Industrial Revolution, with its vengeful scorn and desire to condemn the productive and efficient members of our society "*because* they are productive and efficient," as Alan Greenspan put it, was a bridge away from egalitarianism and to what would eventually become Underdogma. The Progressive movement went even further by seeking to reorder America's founding principles in order to correct power imbalances between the power haves and the power have-nots.

Underdogma is far different than egalitarianism or the desire to correct power imbalances. It is an irrational and sometimes hateful scorn for those who have more, and a reflexive and almost childish lauding of those who have less. This pure strain of Underdogma finds its roots in two events: the Berkeley student protests of 1964, and the rise in prominence of the United Nations. Berkeley and the UN are so crucial to the rise of Underdogma that each has been given its own chapter in this book: Chapter 5—FIGHT THE POWER (WHATEVER THE POWER MAY BE) and Chapter 6—THE UNITED NATIONS: INSTITUTIONALIZED UNDERDOGMA.

5
Fight the Power (Whatever the Power May Be)

"The young, upon whom the future of course would depend, were being given the American dream—and they didn't want it. More: they attacked it, with an innate challenge that reverberated through the entire society, striking at the premises and beliefs upon which it was founded. The Berkeley confrontation was a signal that a new generation had been born."

—*SDS: The Rise and Development of the Students for a Democratic Society*, Kirkpatrick Sale, 1971

UNDERDOGMA TOOK ROOT AT THE University of California, Berkeley, in September 1964 when school administrators banned political and social action groups from recruiting and raising funds on campus. Berkeley students and organizers ignored the ban. Then, on the morning of October 1, 1964, campus police arrested political organizer Jack Weinberg and put him in the back of a police car. Berkeley students rushed the police car, deflated its tires, and surrounded it on all sides, using their bodies to trap the cruiser in place.

> "There are almost as many claimants for the honor of being 'the first to sit down around the police car' as there were cities claiming to be Homer's birthplace, but in this case the explanation is different. People unacquainted with the civil rights movement believe that 'someone' must have launched the move, but in point of fact it is almost a ***reflex*** action among experienced civil-rights activists, of whom there were many within ten feet." [emphasis added]
>
> —*Berkeley: The New Student Revolt*,
> Hal Draper, 2009

As the crowd swelled to thousands, the students soon "realized that the roof of the captive car offered a perfect soap box."[1] For the next thirty-six hours, students took turns climbing on top of the police car and raising their fists against the so-called "power structure." One student, Mario Savio, "emerged as the voice of the movement, a figure who had in a few short hours captured the attention of the world."[2] Soon, the protest grew into "by far the most gigantic student protest movement ever mounted in the United States on a single campus."[3]

The Berkeley "Free Speech Movement" (FSM) of 1964 "launched a student revolt which would 'spread from campus to campus around the world, jumping like electrical sparks from terminal to terminal.'"[4] The revolutionaries'

---

[1] "From Atop a Police Car, A Revolution Was Born," *Berkeley Daily Planet*, October 1, 2004

[2] Ibid

[3] *Berkeley: The New Student Revolt*, Hal Draper, 2009

[4] *"The Bible of the Free Speech Movement": Hal Draper's The Mind of Clark Kerr Revisited*, Alan Johnson, 2000

lists of grievances ranged from social change to "a whole mode of arbitrary exercise of arbitrary power"[5] and eventually to the Vietnam War. But one thing remained constant: all fists were raised against those who had power, on behalf of those who did not.

> "The social turmoil of the sixties was really a battle over power."
>
> —*Berkeley at War: The 1960s*,
> W.J. Rorabaugh, 1990

> "The real issue is the seizure of power."
>
> —"What's Left at Berkeley," William Petersen,
> professor of sociology at the University of
> California at Berkeley, Spring 1965

> "Vietnam offered the key to a systematic criticism of America. During the last years, Vietnam has been stationed inside my consciousness as a quintessential image of the suffering and heroism of the 'weak.' But it was really America 'the strong' that obsessed me—the contours of American power, of American cruelty, of American self-righteousness."
>
> —Susan Sontag, quoted in *Useful Idiots*
> by Mona Charen, 2004

Before the Berkeley student uprising of 1964, protests were about more than just power. Case in point: the Civil Rights Movement. Professor John Searle—the first tenured

[5] Mario Savio, Sit-in Address on the Steps of Sproul Hall, December 2, 1964, The University of California at Berkeley

professor to join the Berkeley Free Speech Movement and the philosophy teacher of FSM student leader Mario Savio—noted, "the FSM was a kind of extension of the Civil Rights Movement. You will not understand the '60s and you will not understand the Free Speech Movement if you do not understand the role of the Civil Rights Movement."[6]

Rarely has such a clear moral choice presented itself along Underdogma's lines of power and virtue than in the American Civil Rights Movement of the 1950s and '60s. Black Americans were legitimate and historically-wronged underdogs, whose quest for equality was inextricably tied to America's founding documents and whose plight was voiced by one of the greatest orators in history, Martin Luther King Jr.

> "I have a dream that one day this nation will rise up and live out the true meaning of its creed: 'We hold these truths to be self-evident, that all men are created equal.'"
>
> —Martin Luther King Jr., Speech at Civil Rights March on Washington, August 28, 1963

The power of the Civil Rights Movement was not lost on "the spiritual leader of the Free Speech Movement" Mario Savio, "the messiah with waving hands...exhorting his followers from the police car's top."[7] Savio was quick to recognize that the legitimate plight of the Civil Rights Movement, and the growing sympathy it was building

---

[6] "Professor Recalls Pros, Cons of Free Speech Movement," CNN, January 9, 2004

[7] "Freedom's Orator: Mario Savio and the Radical Legacy of the 1960s," Robert Cohen, 2009

in the broader public through the courage and sacrifice of Rosa Parks, Martin Luther King Jr., and others, could be co-opted and used for other purposes. Only sixteen months had passed since Dr. King stood before hundreds of thousands on the National Mall in Washington, D.C., and delivered his famous "I Have a Dream" speech. Only five months had passed since the Civil Rights Act had become law. America was opening itself to the plight of the oppressed like never before. At Berkeley, "a *de facto* segregated school [where] only 2% of the Berkeley student body is Negro—in a city which is 22% Negro,"[8] student protesters decided to get in on the action. As Mario Savio himself admitted:

> "The [Berkeley] revolt began in the fall semester of 1964 as an extension of either vicarious or actual involvement in the struggle for civil rights. It was easy to draw upon this reservoir of outrage at the wrongs done to other people."
> —Mario Savio, Introduction to *Berkeley: The New Student Revolt*, by Hal Draper, 2009

When Mario Savio wrote that "what oppresses the American Negro community is merely an exaggerated, grotesque version of what oppresses the rest of the country," he demeaned and disrespected the black Civil Rights activists who risked everything—even their lives—to fight real oppression and to hold America to its highest ideals. The grievances of the Civil Rights Movement were legitimate and clear: racial discrimination—on buses, at lunch

[8] "The FSM: An Historical Narrative," Bettina Aptheker, published by the W.E.B. DuBois Clubs of America, 1965

counters, in ballot booths, and in schools—was morally and philosophically wrong and ran counter to America's founding principles. By contrast, the grievances of the Berkeley Free Speech Movement were not matters of life or death or even right or wrong. If the reader wishes to undergo the painful task of sifting through thousands of pages, and hours of audio and video, of FSM student protesters trying to articulate their numerous (and often incomprehensible) gripes in their own words, they are archived in the FIGHT THE POWER THREAD at www.underdogma.com. The rambling thoughts of the Berkeley student rebels were best summed up by *Newsweek*, which declared, "if they are rebels, they are rebels without an ideology…unable to formulate or sustain a systemized political theory of society,"[9] and by Ayn Rand, who wrote of the university student protesters, "in today's culture, it has always been safe to attack 'bigness.' And since the meaningless issue of mere *size* has long served as a means of evading real issues, on all sides of all political fences, a new catch phrase has been added to the list of 'Big Business,' Big Labor,' Big Government,' etc.: 'Big University.'"[10]

It is worthwhile to compare the speech that defined the Free Speech Movement ("Gears," delivered by Mario Savio) to the speech that defined the Civil Rights Movement ("I Have a Dream," delivered by Dr. Martin Luther King Jr.). Dr. King's "I Have a Dream" speech is a masterpiece from beginning to end, is readily available online in video, audio, and transcribed text, and I urge you read it, listen to it, or

---

[9] *Newsweek*, March 22, 1965, quoted in *Return of the Primitive* by Ayn Rand, 1999

[10] Ayn Rand, *Return of the Primitive*, "The Cashing In," 1999

watch it again. Its brilliance shines through the decades in its structure, content, delivery, and relevance.

By contrast, Mario Savio's defining speech (delivered one year later) is much harder to find, except for one paragraph near the end about "gears," and so I have reprinted the speech here in its entirety. A 1966 *New York Times* story observed that Mario Savio had "that rare personal gift, commonly found among good actors and politicians, of being able to utter the grossest vapidities and leave his audience feeling that it has listened to deep stuff."[11] Savio's "rare personal gift" was on full display when he delivered what became the speech that defined a generation. Here is the transcript:

> You know, I just wanna say one brief thing about something the previous speaker said. I didn't wanna spend too much time on that 'cause I don't think it's important enough. But one thing is worth considering.
>
> He's the—he's the nominal head of an organization supposedly representative of the undergraduates. Whereas in fact under the current director it derives—its authority is delegated power from the Administration. It's totally unrepresentative of the graduate students and TAs.
>
> But he made the following statement (I quote): "I would ask all those who are not definitely committed to the FSM cause to stay away from demonstration." Alright, now listen to this: "For all upper division students who are interested in alleviating the TA shortage problem, I would encourage you to offer your services to Department Chairmen and

[11] "A Cheer for Mario Savio," *New York Times*, December 6, 1966

Advisors." That has two things: A strike breaker and a fink.

I'd like to say—like to say one other thing about a union problem. Upstairs you may have noticed they're ready on the 2nd floor of Sproul Hall, Locals 40 and 127 of the Painters Union are painting the inside of the 2nd floor of Sproul Hall. Now, apparently that action had been planned some time in the past. I've tried to contact those unions. Unfortunately—and [it] tears my heart out—they're as bureaucratized as the Administration. It's difficult to get through to anyone in authority there. Very sad. We're still—we're still making an attempt. Those people up there have no desire to interfere with what we're doing. I would ask that they be considered and that they not be heckled in any way. And I think that—you know—while there's unfortunately no sense of—no sense of solidarity at this point between unions and students, there at least need be no—you know—excessively hard feelings between the two groups.

Now, there are at least two ways in which sit-ins and civil disobedience and whatever—least two major ways in which it can occur. One, when a law exists, is promulgated, which is totally unacceptable to people and they violate it again and again and again till it's rescinded, appealed. Alright, but there's another way. There's another way. Sometimes, the form of the law is such as to render impossible its effective violation—as a method to have it repealed. Sometimes, the grievances of people are more—extend more—to more than just the law, extend to a whole mode of arbitrary power, a whole mode of arbitrary exercise of arbitrary power.

And that's what we have here. We have an autocracy which—which runs this university. It's managed. We were told the following: If [university] President Kerr actually tried to get something more liberal out of the Regents in his telephone conversation, why didn't he make some public statement to that effect? And the answer we received—from a well-meaning liberal—was the following: He said, "Would you ever imagine the manager of a firm making a statement publicly in opposition to his Board of Directors?" That's the answer.

Well I ask you to consider—if this is a firm, and if the Board of Regents are the Board of Directors, and if President Kerr in fact is the manager, then I tell you something—the faculty are a bunch of employees and we're the raw material! But we're a bunch of raw materials that don't mean to be—have any process upon us. Don't mean to be made into any product! Don't mean—Don't mean to end up being bought by some clients of the University, be they the government, be they industry, be they organized labor, be they anyone! We're human beings!

And that—that brings me to the second mode of civil disobedience. There's a time when the operation of the machine becomes so odious, makes you so sick at heart that you can't take part! You can't even passively take part! And you've got to put your bodies upon the gears and upon the wheels, upon the levers, upon all the apparatus—and you've got to make it stop! And you've got to indicate to the people who run it, to the people who own it—that unless you're free the machine will be prevented from working at all!!

That doesn't mean—I know it will be interpreted to mean, unfortunately, by the bigots who run The Examiner, for example—That doesn't mean that you have to break anything. One thousand people sitting down some place, not letting anybody by, not [letting] anything happen, can stop any machine, including this machine! And it will stop!!

We're gonna do the following—and the greater the number of people, the safer they'll be and the more effective it will be. We're going, once again, to march up to the 2nd floor of Sproul Hall. And we're gonna conduct our lives for awhile in the 2nd floor of Sproul Hall. We'll show movies, for example. We tried to get Un Chant d'Amour and [they] shut them off. Unfortunately, that's tied up in the court because of a lot of squeamish moral mothers for a moral America and other people on the outside. The same people who get all their ideas out of the San Francisco Examiner. Sad, sad. But, Mr. Landau—Mr. Landau has gotten us some other films.

Likewise, we'll do something—we'll do something which hasn't occurred at this University in a good long time! We're going to have real classes up there! They're gonna be freedom schools conducted up there! We're going to have classes on [the] 1st and 14th amendments!! We're gonna spend our time learning about the things this University is afraid that we know! We're going to learn about freedom up there, and we're going to learn by doing!!

Now, we've had some good, long rallies. [Rally organizers inform Savio that Joan Baez has arrived.] Just one moment. We've had some good, long rallies. And I think I'm sicker of rallies than

> anyone else here. She's not going to be long. I'd like to introduce one last person—one last person before we enter Sproul Hall. Yeah. And the person is Joan Baez.
>
> —Mario Savio, Sit-in Address on the Steps of Sproul Hall, December 2, 1964, U.C. Berkeley

That was the "I Have a Dream" speech of '60s "messiah" and "spiritual leader" Mario Savio. He had a dream that, one day, his affluent and cloistered white brothers and sisters would no longer have to suffer the injustices of wet paint, teaching assistant shortages, or the inability to watch French art house films. It is little wonder why the students with raised fists who followed this "messiah" were unsure why their fists were raised.

> "You might say we're amoral and a-almost everything else."
>
> —"The New Student Left," *New York Times*, March 15, 1965

> "Our generation has no ideology."
>
> —Mike Rossman, Berkeley protester, June 14, 1965, CBS Television

Why did Underdogma appear in the 1960s, and not some other time? Why did it take root among young people, and not some other group? Why on a university campus, and not some other place? The answers to these questions all lead us back to power. The reason why young people had the power to propagate this new belief was because "for the first time in the nation's history they occupied a distinct and powerful position in society...there were more people below the age of twenty-five than ever before (27.2 million between fourteen and twenty-four in 1960, growing to 40 million by 1970)."[12] The reason that a university campus was the focal point for this new movement was because university "students were gathered together in greater numbers than ever before and—as the products of a university system which was now absolutely vital for the functioning of the nation—had more power than ever before. The sixties began with 3,789,000 people in institutions of higher education and ended with 7,852,000 enrolled. In the sixties, for the first time in the history of any nation, there were more students than there were farmers—indeed, in any year after 1962 there were more people engaged in formal studies than employed in transportation, public utilities, construction work, mining, or farming."[13] The reason why Underdogma took root in the mid-1960s and not some other time, again, leads us back to power. Because this generation of young people—concentrated in greater numbers than at any other time in the nation's history—were the first Americans to come of age in an America that was an international superpower.

In 1945, the United States of America—which was built on a spirit of achievement and the desire to be No. 1—became No. 1. A superpower. Every American who came of age after 1945, like Mario Savio and the Berkeley student protesters, came of age during a time of

[12] *SDS: The Rise and Development of the Students for a Democratic Society*, Kirkpatrick Sale, 1973
[13] Ibid

great "material comfort [which] enabled many students to look beyond the quest for security,"[14] a quest that had consumed the lives of previous generations. This material comfort gave the new generation the freedom to focus on other things, like American power and how it made them feel. Raising a fist against the power of one's own country is a luxury reserved only for those who live in powerful countries. The power, wealth, and abundance of America are what gave these affluent university students the time and freedom to protest, instead of plowing fields for sustenance like their ancestors and previous generations of less powerful Americans.

"The most widely distributed document of the American Left in the Sixties"[15] was the Port Huron Statement, written by the Students for a Democratic Society (SDS). It began with the words, "we are people of this generation, bred in at least modest comfort, housed now in universities, looking uncomfortably to the world we inherit."[16] The world they inherited was a world in which America, their country, was powerful. When the time came for their generation—as it does for every generation—to rebel against the generation that came before them, the target of their rebellion was "the establishment"—American power, and those who helped build American power. The SDS's Port Huron Statement concluded, and Underdogma

[14] *The '60s Experience: Hard Lessons about Modern America*, Edward P. Morgan, 1991

[15] "Rebels With a Cause," sdsrebels.com

[16] The Port Huron Statement, Introduction: Agenda for a Generation, SDS, 1962

began, with a call for university students to "consciously build a base for their assault upon the loci of power."[17]

The student protests of the '60s and '70s marked a turning point in our relationship with power. The age-old conflict between underdog and overdog—which had masqueraded throughout history under the guise of egalitarianism, righting past wrongs and injustices, and countless other "causes"—was distilled to its core. The enemy was no longer a monarch or an industrialist or the upper class in general—*it was power itself*. Those who had it were bad. Those who did not have it were good. "Fight the Power" (whatever the power may be). And so Underdogma was born.

> "Yet to a certain element, it's a rite of passage, a voyage into adulthood, an academic bar mitzvah. What worth is a college degree if you've never stood in front of the administrative building holding up a posterboard sign demanding some heinous wrong be righted by those who hold the power?"
>
> —"The Protest Culture," Nathan Finn, *Boundless*, 2003

In the years since the Berkeley protests, almost all pretenses of higher motives in the "Fight the Power" movement have fallen away. Today's "Protest Culture" is about fighting power. The power being fought often comes second, with causes being picked up and dropped like changing fashions. Members of this "anti" tribe are united

[17] The Port Huron Statement, Introduction: Agenda for a Generation, SDS, 1962

more by *how* they stand (generally with a raised fist) than by *where* they stand.

I should know. I used to be one of them.

The year was 1984. I was a fifteen-year-old protester, raising my fist to protest Ronald Reagan and his bloodlust to nuke the world. At least that's what I thought at the time. Strike that: I was not thinking at all. I just felt it in my gut. As did all my friends. We knew that Ronald Reagan was a warmonger. We knew that he would be the end of us. We knew that he was...the Antichrist. Ronald Wilson Reagan—six letters, six letters, six letters. Clearly, the mark of the beast. It sounds crazy now, but it was a common refrain back then. Search "Reagan 666" on the internet and see for yourself.

The problem was that—even as I raised my young fist and burned with rage over a man I felt was the devil—I had a lot in common with Ronald Wilson Reagan. In fact, his core beliefs were the same as my core beliefs. It was true then, and it is true now.

But I hated him. I was convinced that he was evil and that he was bent on destroying the world. Such is the power of Underdogma. And such is the danger of reflexively heaping scorn on those who have power. What was I thinking back then?

Nothing. Underdogma bypasses the rational mind.

The philosophically bankrupt seeds planted by the Berkeley protesters have born rotten fruit around the world. Their movement has grown into a fashion statement, an identity, and even self-satire—as demonstrated at the "How Berkeley Can You Be" parade, in which the "Protest Culture" is turned into a caricature of itself and protest is celebrated for the sake of protest. As the parade's official website declares, it is an opportunity for "the citizenry to look in the mirror and laugh." This now-cartoonish "Fight the Power" movement, which raises its fist for the sake of raising it, forms the foundation of today's underdog activism.

> "Anti-war? Anti-capitalism? Anti-everything? Don't worry about choosing one; you can finally mix and match your clothes just as you mix and match your causes...protesting is definitely fashionable."
>
> —"Protest Fashion Worth Fighting For," *The Georgetown Voice*, January 23, 2003

> "If this is a generation without a cause, the new activism fills that void. It offers something mere ambition cannot: the gratification of being part of something bigger than yourself."
>
> —*The Village Voice*, July 18, 2000

> "All of us need something beyond the self in which to believe; for those who do not find such an object of belief in traditional sources of spiritual wisdom, anti-establishment activism, or activist politics associated with the pursuit of social justice becomes a secular religion."
>
> —*Understanding Anti-Americanism*, Adam Garfinkle & Paul Hollander, 2004

In addition to finding something bigger than themselves in which to believe, today's underdog activists also find a sense of identity, community, peer recognition, and belonging: the "us" in "us versus them."

Photos courtesy of zombietime.com

MTV understood this need for peer recognition and belonging when it launched the online activism hub "Think MTV," which "was built to catalyze a sea change in youth activism and make rock stars out of those young people working to better themselves, their communities, and the world."[18]

Raise your fist. Fight the power. Be a rock star.

Visitors to the Think MTV website are presented with an elaborate social networking system that allows socially conscious members to create profiles, upload pictures and videos, tell people which issues are important to them, collect "badges" for good deeds, join groups, connect with other members, and hobnob with celebrities who take the same stances (which all seem to resemble Underdogma's raised fist against those who have power in the name of underdogs who do not).

Other online activist hubs practically do all the protesting for you. They allow Underdogmatists to pick and choose issues—à la carte—and to download talking points, action kits, and predesigned posters and flyers that help them "fight the power" with all the right accessories. Some notable

[18] MTV president Christina Norman, September 23, 2007

quotes at Protest.net include: "Right hand on mouse, left fist in the air!" "It's like finding the protest du jour," and, for the activist who is too busy to get personally active, "Do you wish you had more time to write letters protesting injustice? Check out the 'Progressive Secretary.' They'll write and send letters based on which issues you're concerned about."

Automated activism, if you will.

Some protest hubs have abandoned all pretext of standing for anything, and focus instead on the social aspect of being an "anti." Like "Act For Love," an activist dating site with the slogan: "Activist? Leftist? Take action, get action!"

Why should we care if Underdogmatists reflexively "fight the power," "stick it to the man," and rail against "the establishment" while championing the underdog? We should care because today's Underdogmatists will, if left unchallenged, become tomorrow's leaders. How do we know? Because yesterday's Underdogmatists have become today's leaders.

One of the architects of the "Fight the Power" movement was Saul Alinsky, who wrote the seminal Underdogmatist manifesto *Rules for Radicals*. It is a blueprint specifically designed to help the '60s student radicals Alinsky met "through all-night sessions on hundreds of campuses in America…create mass organizations to seize power."[19] *Rules* is "not an ideological book." In fact, it

[19] *Rules for Radicals*, Saul Alinsky, 1971

specifically warns against the dangers of holding any beliefs too strongly. It is a book of tactics separated from ideology—"written for the Have-Nots on how to take [power] away [from the Haves]."[20]

U.S. Secretary of State Hillary Clinton was a student of Saul Alinsky. She was offered a job by Saul Alinsky himself. As the *Washington Post* reported, "the job offer to 'Miss Hillary Rodham, Wellesley College' was dated Oct. 25, 1968, and signed by Saul D. Alinsky"[21] Hillary Clinton's senior thesis at Wellesley College was on Saul Alinsky: "There Is Only The Fight: An Analysis of the [Saul] Alinsky Model" (Hillary Clinton's Alinsky thesis is archived at www.under-dogma.com).

President Barack Obama was recruited by Saul Alinsky disciples and "stepped into the Alinsky tradition"[22] as a fellow Chicago "community organizer." As introduced in Chapter 1 (and fully explored in Chapter 10—POLITICAL UNDERDOGMA), Barack Obama has a complicated relationship with power. One of the most telling moments that revealed Underdogma's far reach into the Obama White House came from the woman about whom President Obama said, "I trust her completely...She is family." The President has further said that this woman is trusted "to speak for me" and has "a mind meld" with him; and, when asked "if he runs every decision by her, [Obama] answered without hesitation: 'Yep. Absolutely.'"[23] Her name is Valerie

---

[20] Ibid

[21] "For Clinton and Obama, a Common Ideological Touchstone," *Washington Post*, March 25, 2007

[22] Ibid

[23] "The Ultimate Obama Insider," *New York Times*, July 21, 2009

Jarrett. Here is the telling quote Ms. Jarrett let slip that revealed the Obama White House's stance on power (along with Jon Stewart's outraged commentary). That stance was a raised fist.

> "The administration has said very clearly...that we're going to speak truth to power," [Valerie] Jarrett told CNN.
>
> [Jon] Stewart stopped the tape. "Truth to power? You're the White House! *You're* the power."
>
> —"Jon Stewart Takes on Fox and the White House," NBC New York, Jere Hester, November 2, 2009

The White House is not the only seat of power that raises its fist against power. As you will see in the next chapter, there is a global institution, with growing power over the United States, which is dedicated to the worldwide advancement and proliferation of Underdogma.

6

THE UNITED NATIONS: INSTITUTIONALIZED UNDERDOGMA

"Thank goodness for this effort [*Underdogma*]."
—UN Ambassador John Bolton, author of
Surrender is Not an Option, 2007

UNDERDOGMA BEGAN IN THE BERKELEY student protests of the 1960s. The worldwide proliferation of Underdogma spreads, more than any place else, from the United Nations: the global institute for the advancement of Underdogma.

The United Nations Charter affirms the UN's "faith" in "the equal rights of men and women and of nations large and small."[1] But it appears the UN Charter was signed in bad faith when it comes to "nations large" because today the United Nations has firmly entrenched itself as the world's counterweight to power, the institutional champion of the underdog, with a self-declared mission to equalize "the global power imbalance that Kofi Annan identifies as one of the main challenges of our age."[2] Which is great for underdog nations—but not so great for a powerful overdog nation like the United States of America.

---

[1] United Nations Charter, Preamble, 1945

[2] Greeting at the 9th COSATU National Congress, 2006

> "Civil society plays the critical role of defending the underdog. All this, too, we must nurture."
> —United Nations High Commissioner for Human Rights Sergio Vieira De Mello, April 25, 2003

Former UN Secretary-General Kofi Annan said, "the UN's essential task is to protect the weak against the strong."[3] Protecting the weak may be a laudable goal, but it is not what the United Nations does. The UN acts—not to protect the weak[4]—but to *elevate* the weak and amplify their voices.

> "Within the various economic and social arenas of the United Nations, there is a distinct effort to ensure that the voices of the 'underdogs' are amplified."
> —"UN Voices: The Struggle for Development and Social Justice," Thomas George Weiss, 2005

The United States of America is the most powerful nation in the world. Therefore, all other nations in the world are less powerful. That is reality. The United Nations does not accept reality. Instead, the UN has created a false, alternate reality—based on Underdogma—that elevates underdog nations onto an artificially equalized plane, while scorning and diminishing and restraining America's power. Through the prism of the United Nations, America is

---

[3] Secretary-General Kofi A. Annan, Uppsala (Sweden), September 6, 2001

[4] To see how the United Nations not only fails to protect the weak, but how its peacekeepers have been implicated in raping weak and starving children around the world, read the "Soldiers Behaving Badly" section in Chapter 3

not—nor should it be—held in any higher regard than Zimbabwe, North Korea, or Cuba. And the most powerful cheerleader for this point of view is none other than the President of the United States, Barack Obama.

> "No world order that elevates one nation or group of people over another will succeed."
> —U.S. President Barack Obama, Address to the United Nations, September 23, 2009

A NOTE FROM UN AMBASSADOR JOHN BOLTON

Barack Obama is the first post-American president. And by this I don't mean he's anti-American. What I mean by post-American is suggested by a response the president gave to a reporter's question during a recent trip to Europe. The reporter asked about his unwillingness to discuss American exceptionalism—the notion that the United States has a unique mission, that it's "a shining city on a hill" as Ronald Reagan liked to say (echoing our pilgrim fathers). Mr. Obama responded that he believes in American exceptionalism in the same way that the British believe in British exceptionalism and the Greeks believe in Greek exceptionalism. Given that there are 192 member countries in the United Nations, I'm sure he could have gone on naming another 189 that believe in their own exceptionalism. But in any case, the idea that all countries believe themselves to be exceptional in the same way leads to the unmistakable conclusion that none are truly exceptional. In other words, the president's response reflects his belief that America is not so different from other countries.

What possible harm could come from the world's UN ambassadors trolling the streets of Manhattan in black limos, and strolling the cloistered halls of the United Nations, under the false—but internationally recognized—Underdogmatist belief that their nations are all equally exceptional?

At the time of this writing, the president's chair at the United Nations Security Council is held by the nation of Burkina Faso; a small, impoverished African nation with a lower GDP than North Korea, and with a military force of 6,000 men and nineteen operational aircraft. A few months previously, the UN Security Council was chaired by the United States, which has 1.5 million active duty personnel, 1.5 million reserve personnel, and 14,560 operational aircraft. The U.S. Navy alone has more *kinds* of planes than Burkina Faso has *planes*. But so what? At the United Nations (the international headquarters of Underdogma) everyone gets a chance to sit at the big kids' table. And Burkina Faso got to sit in the big chair at the United Nations Security Council for exactly the same amount of time in 2009 as the United States, Britain, Libya, and Uganda.

While all of this may seem about as quaint and harmless as children playing dress-up in their parents' clothes, the United Nations Security Council does wield tremendous power in the world. If, God forbid, a U.S. city were hit by a suitcase nuke or a chemical attack, the President of the United States would likely have to check in with the honorable member from Burkina Faso before mounting a response. If the U.S. President at the time happens to be Barack Obama, he might even bow down.

This is not funny. But it is ridiculous, and a danger to America's interests.

> "Whether one likes it or not, balance of power still functions in international politics. U.S. preponderance of power will certainly provoke the creation of a coalition [at the UN] to balance that superpower."
>
> —*The United Nations and Changing World Politics*, Foreword to the Fourth Edition, James O. C. Jonah, 2004

The United Nations seeks to "balance" American power by artificially elevating less powerful nations (the first part of Underdogma). But, for Underdogma to be truly present at the United Nations, the UN must go further and ascribe virtue and nobility to these underdog nations—*regardless of how barbaric their actions and/or characters might be*. Has that sort of thing ever happened at the United Nations?

UNDERDOGMA PART 1

The belief that those who have less power (regardless of their actions and/or characters) are virtuous and noble—because they have less power.

- MAY 4, 2004: The United Nations elevates Sudan to full membership on the UN's Commission on Human Rights. A *New York Times* story from the same year described Sudan's ethnic cleansing of Darfur as: "some 1,000 people are being killed a week, tribeswomen are being systematically raped, 700,000 people have been driven from their homes, and Sudan's Army is even bombing the survivors."[5]

- APRIL 21, 2006: The UN bestows the honor of "Champion of the Earth" on "Screaming Mary," the chief Iranian propagandist during the 1979 Iranian hostage crisis. When "asked by an ABC News correspondent whether she could see herself picking up a gun and killing the [American] hostages, she replied: 'Yes.'"[6]
- NOVEMBER 9, 2005: The UN hosts "International Day of Solidarity with the Palestinian People." A map at the head of the room—flanked by Palestinian and UN flags—shows Israel literally wiped from it. The gathered dignitaries (including the UN Secretary-General and the president of the UN Security Council) stand and observe "a moment of silence 'for all those who had given their lives for the Palestinian people'—which would include suicide bombers."[7]
- NOVEMBER 14, 2007: The United Nations praises Cuba as "a world model in feeding its population."[8]
- MARCH 18, 2008: Chinese soldiers slaughter Tibetan monks (who were seeking the very rights enumerated by the UN's Universal Declaration of Human Rights). The UN's

[5] "Will We Say 'Never Again' Yet Again?" *New York Times*, March 27, 2004

[6] "Top Woman in Iran's Government Once Spoke for Hostage-Takers," *New York Times*, January 28, 1998

[7] "One Small Step," *The Wall Street Journal*, June 21, 2004

[8] "UN Praises Cuba's Ability to Feed People," Global Research and AP, November 14, 2007

reaction? "U.N. Security Council members are carefully avoiding the subject, saying yesterday that the issue 'does not belong' in U.N. deliberations."[9] On June 19, 2008 (three months after China slaughtered Tibetan monks), the UN elevates China to full membership on the United Nations Human Rights Council.

- **JUNE 5, 2008**: Less than a year after Burma slaughtered thousands of monks and other pro-democracy campaigners, and less than a month after Burma allowed nearly 100,000 of its citizens to perish in the wake of a deadly cyclone, the United Nations elevates Burma to the post of vice president of the UN General Assembly.[10]
- **JUNE 16, 2008**: After the President of Iran calls its neighbor Israel a "stinking corpse" that will "soon disappear" and "be wiped off the earth's face,"[11] the United Nations praises Iran, saying, "we have long been witnessing humanitarian efforts graciously made by Iran to help its neighbors."[12]
- **JUNE 19, 2008**: The UN lends its, and UNICEF's, credibility to a Saudi-based charity linked to terror groups. "An Islamic charity with ties to Al Qaeda and the Taliban is now collaborating with an unlikely new partner:

---

[9] "U.N. Shirks Tibet, Despite Plea From Dalai Lama," *New York Sun*, March 18, 2008

[10] *The Irrawaddy News Magazine*, June 5, 2008

[11] Associated Press, June 2, 2008

[12] Fars News Agency, June 16, 2008

UNICEF, the United Nations' Children's Fund."[13]

- FEBRUARY 13, 2009: The United Nations Human Rights Council (UNHRC) institutes a "peer review" system for human rights issues. But, because more than half of UNHRC members "fall short of basic democracy standards,"[14] tyrants wind up reviewing tyrants. Like Iran, which praised China—"the world's biggest executioner" according to Amnesty International—for its "strong commitment to human rights."[15]
- APRIL 28, 2010: "Iran was elected, through a vote of acclamation, as a member on the [UN] Commission on the Status of Women (CSW)...an influential body comitted to promoting gender equality"[16] even though "women are not treated equally before the law in Iran and are especially vulnerable in the judicial system. A woman's testimony is worth half that of a man."[17] In Iran, women are stoned to death for the "crime" of adultery. Since a wife's testimony is worth less than her husband's, some "husbands turn wives in to get out of a marriage."[18] And, as reported by the Global Campaign to Stop

[13] "UNICEF Partners With Islamic Charity Linked to Terror Groups," Fox News, June 19, 2008
[14] UN Watch, March 31, 2009
[15] "Idiocy, United Nations-style," *Ottawa Citizen*, February 13, 2009
[16] "Iran wins seat on UN Commission on Status of Women," *Tehran Times*, May 1, 2010
[17] "Human rights activist tries to stop death by stoning for Iranian woman," CNN, July 5, 2010
[18] Ibid

> Killing and Stoning Women (SKSW), "most stoning sentences in Iran are issued not on the basis of testimony or confession but on the judge's 'knowledge' or 'intuition.' Article 105 of the Islamic Penal code of Iran allows a single judge to rule according to his personal opinion instead of hard evidence."[19]

The first part of Underdogma (the reflexive belief that those who have less power are virtuous and noble) appears to be alive and well at the United Nations, with the UN praising, elevating, and appointing to high positions: genocidal Sudan, "Screaming Mary" the hostage lady, suicide-bombing Palestinians, oppressive Cuba, Tibetan-monk-slaughtering (and "world's biggest executioner") China, Burmese-monk-slaughtering Burma, holocaust-threatening Iran, terrorist-funding Saudi Arabia and elects to the United Nations Commission on the Status of Women those who stone to death women on trumped-up charges and considers their testimony only half as valuable as a man's.

> "No one likes Goliath, and underdogs often gain our sympathy even when acting in a provocative manner."
>
> —*Taming American Power: The Global Response to U.S. Primacy*, Stephen M. Walt, 2006

[19] SKSW website, stop-stoning.org/node/9,"Frequently asked questions about stoning"

UNDERDOGMA PART 2

The belief that those who have more power (regardless of their actions and/or characters) are to be scorned—because they have more power.

> "Analyzing and refuting the common assumptions of anti-Americanism is a critical contribution to the global political debate. Thank goodness for this effort [Underdogma]."
>
> —UN Ambassador John Bolton, author of *Surrender is Not an Option*, 2007

> "It would be some time before I fully realized that the United States sees little need for diplomacy. Power is enough. Only the weak rely on diplomacy...the Roman Empire had no need for diplomacy. Nor does the United States."
>
> —Boutros Boutros-Ghali, Sixth Secretary General of the UN, "Unvanquished: a U.S.-U.N.-Saga," 1999

Although the United Nations was founded in America, is headquartered in America, and is largely funded by America, the UN has become a virtual factory of anti-American, Underdogmatist scorn.

One way to quantify this scorn is to track the UN's votes on American resolutions at the UN concerning issues like humanitarian relief, peace and security, terrorism, disarmament, economic and social development, and human rights. In 2005, the UN voted against America in non-consensus votes 75% of the time. The year before, it was

76.7%.[20] A 2007 study found that even "most recipients of U.S. assistance vote against the U.S. more often than they vote with the U.S,"[21] with 72.3% of the thirty largest recipients of U.S. aid voting against the United States of America.

The United Nations views American power as something to be restrained. And they view it as their job to restrain it.

> "[The UN] Council should serve to restrain strong nations."
>
> —Wangari Maathai, address to UN Secretary-General Kofi Annan at the launch of the United Nations Human Rights Council, June 19, 2006

> "America especially—must be domesticated. Their project is thus to restrain America by building an entangling web of interdependence, tying down Gulliver with myriad strings that diminish his overweening power."
>
> —"The Unipolar Moment Revisited," Charles Krauthammer, *The National Interest*, Winter 2002

But the United Nations goes beyond merely restraining U.S. power. It also delves deeply into the second part of Underdogma: heaping scorn on the powerful because they have more power.

When Venezuelan President Hugo Chavez addressed the United Nations General Assembly in 2006 and called the United States of America "a sword hanging over our

---

[20] 23rd Annual Report to the Congress on Voting Practices at the United Nations

[21] "U.S. Aid Does Not Build Support at the U.N.," Heritage Foundation, March 26, 2007

heads,"[22] he was cheered by the assembled dignitaries. When Iranian President Mahmoud Ahmadinejad stood at the same podium and declared that "certain powers" (read: America) "consider themselves the masters and rulers of the entire world and other nations as only second class in the world order,"[23] he was celebrated by the UN General Assembly. In 2008, the United Nations elected as president of the UN Assembly a zealous anti-Americanist (who said former U.S. President Ronald Reagan was "possessed by demons").[24] Between 2003 and 2009, the United Nations "human rights" system singled out the United States of America for criticism 216 times, which is more often than they criticized China, Afghanistan, Iran, and Pakistan, and more than double the number of times the UN sanctioned Saudi Arabia, Zimbabwe, and North Korea, and triple the amount of UN scorn levied on Rwanda, Cuba, and Yemen.[25] And when Ban Ki-moon became the eighth UN Secretary-General, and failed to show adequate scorn for the United States, his predecessor, Kofi Annan, scolded him for not upholding the UN's Underdogmatist tradition, saying, "I hope this perception that Secretary-General Ban is too close to the United States is a passing phase."[26]

---

[22] "Anti-Americanism Is a Big Hit at UN," *The Wall Street Journal*, September 21, 2006

[23] Mahmoud Ahmadinejad, speech to the UN General Assembly, September 19, 2006

[24] *New York Sun*, June 5, 2008

[25] Eye on the UN

[26] "Back at U.N., Annan Talks of U.S., Ban," *New York Sun*, March 21, 2008

The United Nations promotes and champions those who have less power (the first part of Underdogma), while scorning and restraining those who have more power (the second part of Underdogma). Through the various offices of the United Nations, Underdogmatists have the power to proliferate Underdogma on a worldwide scale. By making itself the referee between the world's "power haves" and "power have-nots," the UN has accomplished something remarkable: it has become powerful. Today, almost every major world issue—from wars to treaties to sanctions and international jurisprudence—flows through the United Nations. Ironically, by opposing power and practicing Underdogma, the United Nations is becoming the world's most powerful governing body, with jurisdiction over:

FOOD—FAO: Food and Agriculture Organization of the UN
SECURITY—UNSC: United Nations Security Council
HUMAN RIGHTS—UNHRC: United Nations Human Rights Council
ATOMIC ENERGY AND NUCLEAR PROLIFERATION—IAEA: International Atomic Energy Agency
FLYING—ICAO: International Civil Aviation Organization
FARMS—IFAD: International Fund for Agricultural Development
WORK—ILO: International Labour Organization
MONEY—IMF: International Monetary Fund
WATER—IMO: International Maritime Organization
PHONES—ITU: International Telecommunication Union
EDUCATION—UNESCO: UN Educational Scientific and Cultural Organization
INDUSTRY —UNIDO: UN Industrial Development Organization

DEVELOPMENT—UNDP: United Nations Development Program
DRUGS AND CRIME—UNODC: United Nations Office on Drugs and Crime
JUSTICE—ICJ: International Court of Justice
ENVIRONMENT—UNEP: United Nations Environment Programme
MAIL—UPU: Universal Postal Union
HEALTH—WHO: World Health Organization
INTELLECTUAL PROPERTY—WIPO: World Intellectual Property Organization
TOURISM—WTO: World Tourism Organization
WEATHER—WMO: World Meteorological Organization
CLIMATE—IPCC: Intergovernmental Panel on Climate Change

The United Nations seeks to dampen America's power by deploying Underdogma: elevating weaker nations onto an artificially equal plane, and restraining/seizing America's power and disbursing it through a tangled and unaccountable web of UN committees and councils. In its Underdogmatist quest to denigrate America's power while championing weaker nations, the UN has found a willing partner in U.S. President Barack Obama, who scorned American power and called for a leveling of the worldwide power playing field in his address to the UN General Assembly in September of 2009.[27]

At the center of all this power, the UN has influence over the ground we walk upon, the air we breathe, the water we drink, the food we eat, our health, money, commerce, security, international justice, the climate, and

[27] "No world order that elevates one nation or group of people over another will succeed." U.S. President Barack Obama, Address to the United Nations, September 23, 2009

nuclear proliferation, to name a few. Ceding that kind of power and control to a vast international bureaucracy may conceivably have some merit (in some people's minds) if the UN were a great bastion of morality and accountability. But the UN is neither moral nor accountable. Through the Oil For Food Scandal, "the UN rape-for-food"[28] scandal, the Procurement Scandal (which was called "just as bad as the gigantic Oil-for-Food debacle—or maybe worse"[29]), and various acts of nepotism,[30] bribery,[31] theft,[32] conspiracy,[33] and fraudulent climate science[34]—not to mention the aid and comfort and platform the United Nations has given to state sponsors of terrorism,[35] dictators,[36] former Nazis,[37] genocidal regimes,[38]

[28] *The Rush Limbaugh Show*, July 20, 2006

[29] "U.N. Procurement Scandal: A 'Culture of Impunity,'" Fox News, January 23, 2006

[30] "Nepotism Returns to the United Nations," *Canada Free Press*, October 22, 2007

[31] "Former U.N. Official Convicted of Taking Bribes," MSNBC/AP, June 7, 2007

[32] "Theft and Mismanagement Charged at U.N. Weather Agency," *New York Times*, February 9, 2005

[33] "The U.N.'s Spreading Bribery Scandal: Russian Ties and Global Reach," Fox News, September 7, 2005

[34] "Climategate: UN panel on climate change to investigate claims," *Telegraph UK*, December 4, 2009

[35] Iran and others

[36] Muammar al-Gaddafi, among others

[37] "Former UN Secretary General Kurt Waldheim has been on a watch list of unwanted people since 1987—when Justice Department probers found he 'assisted or participated' in Nazi deportations and the executions of Jews and soldiers in the Balkans during World War II." "UN Pays Former Nazi Waldheim 125G Annual Pension," *NY Daily News*, October 4, 2002

[38] Communist China, among others

nuclear proliferators,[39] and anti-Americans[40]—the United Nations has proven itself to be unworthy of the power it seeks to usurp from America.

Underdogma is a driving force in the power plays between countries and world bodies at the United Nations. But Underdogma is not limited to the international community. As you will see in Part 2 of this book, beginning with the next chapter (Chapter 7—PERSONAL UNDERDOGMA), Underdogma is alive and well and pulling our strings in our local communities, in our workplaces, and in our personal lives.

[39] Iran, among others

[40] See the UN's voting records, cited earlier in this chapter

PART TWO

Underdogma in Your Neighborhood

7
Personal Underdogma

"It is in the character of very few men to honor without envy a friend who has prospered."
—Aeschylus, 525 BC–456 BC

"No one was completely unhappy at the failure of his best friend."
—Groucho Marx, *Groucho and Me*, 1959

IMAGINE THAT I GAVE YOU a handful of money. Would you be happy? Now imagine that I gave your neighbors even more money. A lot more. Would it change the way you feel about the money in your hand? What if I gave you the chance to "burn" some of your neighbors' money and reduce their share? With one condition: every dollar of theirs you "burn" will cost you twenty-five cents. No matter what happens, if you go down this road and start burning your neighbors' money, you will reduce your own wealth, guaranteed.

A pair of economists at the universities of Oxford and Warwick conducted this experiment in 2001. The results surprised them.

> "Are people willing to pay to burn other people's money? The short answer to this question is: yes. Our subjects gave up large amounts of their cash to hurt others in the laboratory. The extent of burning was a surprise to us...Even at a price of 0.25 (meaning that to burn another person's dollar costs me 25 cents), many people wished to destroy other individuals' cash."
>
> —"Are People Willing to Pay to Reduce Others' Incomes?" Daniel John Zizzo & Andrew Oswald, July 2, 2001

This scorn for power (more money = more power) was so strong that it compelled *two-thirds* of test subjects to harm themselves (reduce their amount of money) in order to knock down others who had more. The researchers called this phenomenon "the dark side of human nature." I call it Personal Underdogma.

Scorn for "Big Box" stores. That stab of resentment over a co-worker's raise. Our neighbor's grass on the other side of the fence: always greener. The gap between worker and CEO pay. My kid's grades are better than your kid's grades. The rich guy at the end of the block—who does he think he is? Come to think of it, why does it have to be "he" all the time? Why not "she"?

Underdogma is alive and well in our personal lives and, it seems, in the personal lives of people around the world. In German, the word for "happiness at the misfortune of others" is Schadenfreude, and the word for "sadness at the good fortune of others" is Glückschmerz. In British English, they call it "taking the piss" (a puffed-up person getting knocked down a few pegs). The Chinese call it **幸灾乐祸**. Swedes call it skadeglädje. In Arabic, it's الشماتة. Czechs call it škodolibosti. Finns call it vahingoniloisia. In Hebrew it's **שמחה לאיד**. And, in Japanese, the phrase 他人の不幸は蜜の味 means "others' misfortunes are the taste of honey." Over twenty languages around the world have special words or phrases for the part of Underdogma that scorns those who have more power, and now American English has one: Underdogma.

If there is one trait that unites us as human beings, it appears to be our spite for those who succeed (overdogs) and a burning desire to knock them off their pedestals.

On the flipside of Underdogma, we also love to cheer for underdogs and ascribe to them nobility and virtue. The same Germany that gave us Schadenfreude and Glückschmerz also gave us *Cinderella*, a story that so embodies the plight of the underdog it has become the adjective we use to describe underdog stories. "Cinderella stories" can be found from ancient Greece to China to Persia, Japan, France, and Russia—on up to Disney's Cinderella in the movies, in theme parks; and on Broadway stages. Figurative Cinderella stories like *Rocky*, *Cinderella Man*, *Rudy*, and others are mainstays of our culture, as evidenced by the fact that *American Idol* is, at the time of this writing, the most popular show in America. We love underdogs so much that, in a given week, thirty to fifty million people tune in to *American Idol* to watch underdog amateurs sing (often poorly) in the hopes of winning a major record label deal, while an average of only 1.2 million people per week bother to buy the Top Ten albums *combined* on Billboard's Chart (produced by those who already have major record label deals). A more direct comparison is this: 2009 *American Idol* winner (and underdog) Kris Allen got more than fifty million votes during finale week to help him beat heavily favored front-runner Adam Lambert. But, after underdog Kris Allen became top dog, won *American Idol*, and landed his big record label deal, only 0.16% of those fifty million votes showed up to buy his debut album when it was released,[1] placing Kris Allen outside of the Billboard Top Ten chart. By contrast, the No. 1 album in America (and in the UK) that same week was from another underdog who sang her way out of obscurity and into our hearts on TV (*Britain's Got Talent*). Except this underdog had the good fortune to *lose* the competition, not win like Kris Allen did—and therefore she never relinquished the mantle of underdog. Her name is Susan Boyle, "the unlikely pop-star Cinderella story"[2] whose "I Dreamed a Dream" sold three million copies worldwide its first week, making it the best-selling debut album by any woman since SoundScan began tracking sales in 1991, and the biggest debut by any artist in the past sixteen years (the previous record was held

> To see how Underdogma is transforming the music industry (and education and journalism) visit www.under-dogma.com for the online exclusive Bonus Chapter—THE RISE OF THE UNDERDOG.

[1] First week sales.

[2] "Susan Boyle's 'I Dreamed a Dream' Tops U.S. Album Chart," *USA Today*, December 3, 2009

by Snoop Doggy Dogg, not an underdog). Billboard chart analyst Keith Caulfield credited Susan Boyle's success to her status as an underdog, noting that the decidedly unglamorous forty-eight-year-old spinster is "so moving to a lot of people, who see something of themselves in her. They like to see the underdog achieve. You may not buy it just for the music but for the whole story."[3]

The "whole story" is that there are two sides to Personal Underdogma. Sure, we cheer for these "rags-to-riches" underdogs and hope that our personal lives could someday be like theirs, but once we turn these underdogs into big, powerful celebrities, we tend to turn against them and feed them into the same Underdogmatist machine of tabloids and rumor mills that chews up and scorns the rich and famous celebrities we love to hate.

> "All these tabloids could as easily travel under the generic title of the National Schadenfreude, for more than half the stories they contain come under the category of 'See How the Mighty Have Fallen.'"
>
> —"The Culture of Celebrity," *The Weekly Standard*, October 17, 2005

If you are an underdog celebrity wannabe, be warned: with celebrity comes power, and with power comes the threat of facing Underdogmatist scorn. As Cary Grant once quipped, "above all, stop telling them [the public] you're happy. Because they're not in love and they're not happy…Just remember…people do not like beautiful

[3] "Susan Boyle's 'I Dreamed a Dream' Tops U.S. Album Chart," *USA Today*, December 3, 2009

people."[4] Big, powerful celebrities and their handlers—at least the smart ones—take great pains to head off this Underdogmatist scorn by cultivating and publicizing stories about celebrities' "humble roots" and charitable acts. Oprah Winfrey, the "most powerful woman in America,"[5] is a master of this craft and inoculates herself by making an affinity for, and a championing of, underdogs a central part of her public persona.

> "She's no longer an underdog herself, but she continues to affiliate herself with underdogs."
> —Professor Robert Thompson, "The Big O," *Chicago Tribune*, November 3, 2005

Perhaps Oprah's ability to play the underdog card and to connect with Americans on a personal level is what allowed her to make $260 million a year and be celebrated for it, while former Exxon Mobil chief Lee R. Raymond was hauled before the Senate—twice, during a Republican presidency, and two years before the Global Financial Crisis happened—to explain his "obscene" CEO pay ($69.7 million a year), which was less than a third of what Oprah made that year.[6]

Most of us will never have to face the kind of Underdogmatist scorn that is heaped upon the celebrities we love to love, then love to hate. But we certainly do experi-

[4] "The Culture of Celebrity," Joseph Epstein, *The Weekly Standard*, October 17, 2005

[5] Andrea Peyser, *New York Post*, January 25, 2009

[6] "Critics Question Exxon Executive Pay," Associated Press, April 15, 2006

ence Underdogma on a personal level—in our **neighborhoods**, in our **workplaces**, and in our **personal lives**.

NEIGHBORHOOD UNDERDOGMA

In our neighborhoods, Underdogma is all around us. We resent the perfect lawns of our neighbors —"the Joneses"— the brand-new cars in their driveways, the inground pools in their backyards. *London Times* writer Michele Kirsch had it worse than most. A friend of hers would call her each January to crow about the previous year's blessings: "her dream husband has got his dream job, she's got her dream promotion, and now they can buy their dream house. It is close to the great school that has given her gifted and talented child a full scholarship. Their child will have to fit studies around modeling work, as she was spotted by a talent scout at the shopping mall."[7] Having a friend or neighbor like that is enough to make an Underdogmatist think some downright un-neighborly thoughts.

Underdogma is not simply resenting what the Joneses have but scorning the Joneses for having it, while actively looking for ways to knock our overdog neighbors down a few pegs and, in the process, lifting ourselves (the underdogs) up. As clinical psychologist Simon Gelsthorpe described it, "you look at someone's big house and tell yourself that you wouldn't want it because it would be a fortune to heat. If you run it down, it doesn't

[7] "The Healthy Side to Envy," Michele Kirsch, *Times Online*, January 5, 2008

upset you."[8] Sociologist Gordon Clanton—who teaches an undergraduate course on jealousy and envy—went several steps further, saying that, although this kind of spiteful Underdogma is bad, "you can't stop me from sitting around and wishing my neighbor would crash his new Cadillac convertible."[9]

Keeping up with the Joneses is not just about the power or wealth or nice cars of our neighbors, but about the relative *spread* of power—the power imbalances—between the overdog Joneses and the rest of us in the neighborhood. Erzo Luttmer, an economist with Harvard University's John F. Kennedy School of Government, spent two years looking over the Joneses' fence in his study "Neighbors as Negatives: Relative Earnings and Well-Being." Luttmer's study found that "individuals' self-reported happiness is negatively affected by the earnings of others in their area" and that "people reported being less happy when their neighbors were richer,"[10] concluding that "the negative effect of neighbors' earnings on well-being is real."[11]

As real as neighborhood Underdogma is, it can vanish in an instant—and neighbors can come together—when an even bigger overdog tries to move into the neighborhood.

Like a Big Box store.

---

[8] "The Healthy Side to Envy," Michele Kirsch, *Times Online*, January 5, 2008

[9] Marija Potkonjak, "The Green-Eyed Monster Can Be a Deadly Sin or a Daily Motivator, Depending on Our Attitude," *East Valley Tribune*, November 8, 2005

[10] Ibid

[11] "Neighbors as Negatives: Relative Earnings and Well-Being," *Quarterly Journal of Economics*, Erzo F. P. Luttmer, 2005

When Big Box chain stores come knocking in our neighborhoods, many locals close ranks and reflexively heap scorn on these "predatory" retailers, while automatically siding with hometown underdog "Mom-and-Pop" stores. This phenomenon is not new. In his article "Big Box Panic: Americans have been afraid of chain stores for nearly a century…" Michael C. Moynihan reports that, "as early as 1922, the Los Angeles City Council tabled a resolution mandating that 'the number of chain stores in any community should be limited by law.'" In 1928, a *New York Times* story "warn[ed] readers of big business's domestic plot to 'displace the neighborhood store' through predatory pricing and sweetheart distribution deals. Beneath an image of a cigar-chomping capitalist casting a malevolent gaze over a map of America [the *New York Times* author] signaled the death knell of the neighborhood enterprise." Also, in 1928, "Sen. Smith Brookhart (R-Iowa) called on the Federal Trade Commission to investigate the 'chain menace.'" And, in 1938, Rep. Wright Patman (D-Texas) introduced an anti-chain store law that, had it passed, would have taxed chains that had more than ten stores so severely it would have put chain stores out of business entirely and sent their "cigar-chomping" owners to the poorhouse.

What if there was a Big Box, "predatory," "chain menace" retailer that did not displace any local, neighborhood "Mom and Pop" stores? And what if, inside that Big Box, there was nothing for sale at all? What if everything except the big company's "bigness" was stripped away? Would there still be Underdogmatist scorn in the neighborhood if the only thing to rail against was "bigness" itself?

In the summer of 2002, Nike opened an art gallery in a hip, bohemian neighborhood called Kensington Market.[12] Sandwiched between secondhand clothing stores and dilapidated fruit stands, the gallery sold no shoes and bore no trademark Nike swoosh. It was simply a welcome home to local artists, musicians, dancers, and DJs, described by curator Jeremy Bailey as "people who are young and don't have an extra $400 to rent gallery space."[13] Nike spent nearly $2 million to hire and promote local artists, musicians, and breakdancers, and to renovate the 3,000-square-foot gallery space (a vacant former electronics store in a less-traveled corner of Kensington Market). Nike invested millions in the neighborhood, sold no shoes, took no profit, and donated all door proceeds to the homeless shelter across the street.

All of this did nothing to stop the "blood"-wielding Underdogmatists.

Within days of its opening, protesters had barricaded the gallery's entrance with a mountain of garbage bags. Its façade was repeatedly defaced with paint. Sneakers soaked in bloodlike red paint were hung from its sign. Vandals struck nightly, forcing the gallery's curators to hire twenty-four-hour security teams. Many of the booked artists and musicians denounced the gallery and cancelled their performances. The street in front of the gallery was

[12] In downtown Toronto, Canada

[13] "Presto, You're Cool," Leah Rumack, *NOW Magazine*, July 4, 2002

shut down by a throng of chanting protesters. The day after the protest, Nike announced the gallery would close.

No Logo author Naomi Klein explained why Kensington Market was no place for a big overdog company like Nike:

> "Kensington Market might have seemed like a funky, indie neighbourhood, but what Nike might not have realized is that it's also ground zero for the activist community."
> —Naomi Klein, quoted in "Presto, You're Cool," Leah Rumack, *NOW Magazine*, July 4, 2002

What were these activists all activated about? Nike's labor practices around the world, perhaps? If these neighborhood Underdogmatists were so concerned about the plight of exploited workers in faraway lands, they could have spent the previous few decades hauling their buckets of blood-red paint one block east of Kensington Market, where one of North America's biggest Chinatowns had been selling the wares of slave labor since long before Nike sold its first shoe.

What actually "set pierced tongues a-wagging"[14] in this bohemian enclave was the feeling that Nike was "an impostor in the neighbourhood…a veritable wolf in sheep's clothing" that sought to "impose its agenda of aligning its product with the hip residents" who "remain vigilant against big businesses."[15]

The final confirmation that Underdogma, not principle, was the driving force in the Nike "bloodbath" came from

[14] "Presto, You're Cool," Leah Rumack, *NOW Magazine*, July 4, 2002

[15] "Expressive Culture, Locality and Big Business: The Case of Presto in Kensington Market," Naomi Fraser, 2004

local artist Matt Crookshank, whose art hung in the Nike gallery. Crookshank wanted to show his scorn for overdog Nike—not by pulling his art out of the Nike gallery, or by painting something disparaging about the world's biggest athletic shoe company—but instead by lending his artistic talents to promoting the world's *second-* and *third*-biggest shoe companies.

> "My first thought was, I would love to draw some Reebok or Adidas shoes—that would be nice and subversive."
>
> —"Presto, You're Cool," Leah Rumack, *NOW Magazine*, July 4, 2002

Reebok is a \$3.4 billion per year shoe company with a history of sweatshop issues. Adidas is a \$7.78 billion per year shoe company with a history of sweatshop issues. And yet both are deemed worthy of subversive support as a means by which to protest the bigger, more powerful Nike, a \$14.9 billion per year shoe company with a history of sweatshop issues.

Pure Underdogma.

WORKPLACE UNDERDOGMA

The workplace is a microcosm for Personal Underdogma, the setting where many of society's broader struggles between the power "haves" and the power "have-nots" play out in our personal lives.

Bosses have the power to hire us, fire us, promote us, and set our salaries (which gives them direct power over our quality of life). Bosses even have the power to control our most valuable, nonrenewable resource: our time. Bosses have bosses, too, who in turn must answer to another layer of bosses: regional managers, vice presidents, and so on. At each rung on the ladder, the balance of power is tipped against the underdog and the cycle of Personal Underdogma continues. Even the head of the company must answer to investors and shareholders who wield the power to fire CEOs and board members. And now there is another, more powerful overdog to answer to: the federal government and its various "czars," who hold the power to determine everything from salaries to bonuses to the modes of workers' travel.

> "[Pay Czar Kenneth] Feinberg acknowledged that his work is philosophically polarizing, noting that many people consider it 'a bad idea for the government to be determining pay for private companies.'"
>
> —*The Wall Street Journal*, September 30, 2009

> "Officials of the Obama administration called Citigroup about the company's new $50 million corporate jet and told execs to 'fix it.'"
>
> —ABC/*Huffington Post*, January 27, 2009

Even the Pay Czar himself felt the oppressive boot of Underdogma when he was tapped to become "the Obama administration's pay czar for no pay," noting that to say "no" to his new boss was not an option. "It's not easy saying 'no,' at least not to a request from the U.S. Treasury Secretary," said Feinberg. "Has anybody thought about saying no to the Secretary of the Treasury?"[16]

[16] Kenneth Feinberg, Reuters, November 17, 2009

Karl Marx and Friedrich Engels clearly understood that the workplace is where many of us experience power imbalances on a personal level. Their *Communist Manifesto* focused on power imbalances between workers and bosses, calling workers (Proletariat) the "slaves of the bourgeois class" while scorning the bosses (Bourgeoisie) for their "naked, shameless, direct, brutal exploitation" of workers. In the preface to the 1883 German edition of the *Communist Manifesto*, Engels wrote that "all history has been a history of class struggles, of struggles between exploited and exploiting, between dominated and dominating classes at various stages of social evolution." He also wrote glowingly of "workers [who] had again gathered sufficient strength for a new onslaught upon the power of the ruling classes [by] weld[ing] together into one huge army the whole militant working class of Europe and America."

One of the ways that workers "weld" themselves together to offset the power of ruling-class bosses is to organize into unions. Labor unions bridge the power gap between workers and bosses and promise to give "voice to millions of Americans who otherwise could not hope to match the power of corporations."[17] But, somewhere along the line, unions went beyond giving workers a "voice" and used their collective power to "transcend" the law and "wrestle power away from the bosses."

> "Solidarity transcends the law and power comes from unity. Power is not granted by the law…You have found your way around the law."
>
> —Remarks by John J. Sweeney, president of the AFL-CIO, AFLCIONOW blog, March 19, 2007

[17] Laurence E. Gold, AFL-CIO Senate Committee on Rules and Administration, April 12, 2000

> "Brothers and sisters, we've shown countless times that we can wrestle power away from the bosses at the bargaining table."
>
> —Remarks by Kenneth V. Georgetti, AFL-CIO Convention, Chicago, July 27, 2005

In addition to closing the power gap between bosses and workers, union Underdogmatists also seek to close the power gap between more productive workers (overdogs) and less productive workers (underdogs). How? By having unions determine workers' salaries through collective bargaining agreements, rather than basing workers' salaries on the unequal merits or skills of individual workers. In such an Underdogmatist worker's utopia, stronger workers are knocked down, weaker workers are raised up, and the power gap between the strong and weak workers vanishes in a puff of collective bargaining.

The problem with collective bargaining is that it eliminates incentives for the best, brightest, and most creative employees to work hard, to improve their skills, and to rise above the crowd ("rising above" would make them more powerful and more wealthy, which would turn them into overdogs). Under collective bargaining, a worker's value is whatever the union and corporate bosses say it is, based on a median, agreed-upon value between the most-productive workers and the least-productive workers. James Sherk, policy analyst in the Center for Data Analysis, asks, "would you want to work for a company that treats all workers exactly the same, no matter how hard they work?"[18] Only 7.2% of private-sector workers answer

---

[18] "Do Americans Today Still Need Labor Unions?" James Sherk, April 1, 2008

"yes" to that question, and "no" to merit-based pay, as reported by the Bureau of Labor Statistics in January 2010. The only holdouts against merit-based pay seem to have been government workers and teachers (public-sector employees: 37.4% unionized, teachers: 38.1% unionized, and local government employees: 43.3% unionized).[19]

Unions and collective bargaining aside, the workplace has often been the battleground where Personal Underdogma power struggles have been fought. Consider the women's movement. Before women ran Xerox, PepsiCo, the *New York Times*, Western Union, Archer Daniels Midland, Sunoco, Kraft Foods, DuPont—and even Congress—women waged battles for equality in the workplace.

Just a few years ago, the plight of women in the workplace was a major topic of discussion in America—not just among activists or opinion leaders, but in our popular culture as well. In 1980, the No. 1 movie at the box office was *The Empire Strikes Back*. The No. 2 movie that year was *9 to 5*, the story of three female office workers who, after being taken for granted and passed over for promotions by their sexist male boss, kidnap the boss and run the company themselves, sparking a sudden surge in productivity and a happy ending for all three women. Not only did the less powerful underdog women rise up in victory (and get away with kidnapping), their overdog male boss was scorned throughout the movie and was punished at the end by being kidnapped (again) by a tribe of Amazons in Brazil.

[19] Bureau of Labor Statistics, January 22, 2010

Before the 1980s, women had good reason to feel like underdogs in the workplace. According to the Bureau of Labor Statistics, prior to 1980 "the jobless rate for adult women tended to be higher than that for men."[20] Then things turned around for women. Since the early 1980s, "the unemployment rates for adult men and adult women have tracked quite closely"[21]—until 2010, when the unemployment rate for women actually dropped *below* the unemployment rate for men (9.7% for women, 11.7% for men).[22] As of February 2010, "women outnumber men in [the] American workplace for the first time in history."[23] And a study by salary data tracking company PayScale, which boasts "the world's largest database of individual employee compensation profiles,"[24] found that, when comparing women's and men's pay for specific jobs, women earn between 90% and 94% of the typical male worker's pay.[25]

Though the pay gap between male and female workers has been shrinking, the gap between bosses (overdog Bourgeoisie) and workers (underdog Proletariat) continues to grow—giving Underdogmatist politicians the fodder they need to stoke our scorn for the Bourgeoisie "big guy" bosses. If logic, reasoning, and even math were the driving forces here, workers and politicians would not care if the big guy makes millions more than the little guy. Case in point: the median salary for an executive assistant in the

---

[20] Bureau of Labor Statistics, 2006

[21] Ibid

[22] Economic Policy Institute, January 2010

[23] *New York Times*, February 6, 2010

[24] PayScale.com, "About Us"

[25] "Women Earn Less Than Men, Especially at the Top," *New York Times*, November 16, 2009

United States is $45,317. If the executive whom the executive assistant happens to be assisting makes $19 million a year, like Yahoo CEO Carol Bartz, or $13.4 million like PepsiCo chief Indra Nooyi—the executive assistant would still be making an average salary of $45,317 because that is what an executive assistant job pays. If the executive assistant wants to put in a few years of study and obtain a "Masters or PhD in Chemical, Mechanical Engineering or Chemistry"—plus a "minimum 8 years industrial or academic research," he or she can apply to become a "Technical Manager, Beverage Processing" at PepsiCo, at almost double the salary—because that is what *that* job pays.

But logic, reasoning, and math are not the driving forces here, nor do they have the power to stop the President of the United States from "whipping up public outrage" over "fat-cat" CEO "recklessness and greed,"[26] naming a "Pay Czar" to tame those fat cats, and—after doling out pitchforks to angry mobs of Underdogmatists—telling CEOs: "my administration is the only thing between you and the pitchforks."[27] I interviewed economics professor Walter E. Williams, a regular guest host on the *Rush Limbaugh Show*, and asked him what he thought about the government demonizing big businesspeople. He said: "politicians use so much demagoguery along these lines. I've said to people: Bill Gates is the richest man in the world. What can Bill Gates make me do? Can he force me to send my kids to a school that I don't want to send them to? Can he force me to use 1.8 gallons to flush my toilet...what can he do? But,

---

[26] UnionLeader.com, March 25, 2009

[27] "Inside Obama's bank CEOs meeting," *Politico*, April 3, 2009

by contrast, some lowly government employee can make my life miserable. So, when people talk about the power of the rich, and government has to protect us against the rich, that's BS."[28]

> "When it comes to Wall Street's bottom line, yes; if we do not see some reduction in profits at some of the largest financial institutions as a result of this Bill [the 'Dodd-Frank Wall Street Reform' Act], I've wasted a year."
> —Barney Frank, interview on WBUR.org (NPR), June 25, 2010

Rush Limbaugh, when asked about the effect of all this CEO and "rich fat-cat" hatred, said: "I want to know how that's improved your life. If all you're doing is sitting around saying, 'Yeah, man, yeah, man, you screw 'em,' is your life any better for that? How is that job search coming for you, by the way? So you gonna get a new job now because of this? You gonna get more money? You going to have a better life because Wall Street got screwed?"[29] For Underdogmatists, the answer is yes.

To see how Underdogmatists have used the Global Financial Crisis to whip up Underdogmatist scorn, and to mobilize angry hordes in a worldwide assault on wealthy people and free market capitalism, see Chapter 12—UNDERDOGMA AND THE GLOBAL FINANCIAL CRISIS.

---

[28] Professor Walter E. Williams, interview for *Underdogma*, January 2, 2010

[29] Rush Limbaugh, *The Rush Limbaugh Show*, October 22, 2009

PERSONAL UNDERDOGMA

> "Power is a very emotional word. People's responses to it are varied. For some people, power has a negative connotation."
> —*Unlimited Power*, Tony Robbins, 1986

> "In this country, you gotta make the money first. Then when you get the money, you get the power."
> —Tony Montana, *Scarface*, 1983

In his seminal 1937 book, *Think and Grow Rich*, Napoleon Hill warned readers about the "evil" of negative associations and thoughts regarding success, money, and power. "Men who accumulate great riches," wrote Hill, "always protect themselves against this evil! The poverty stricken never do! Those who succeed in any calling must prepare their minds to resist the evil." Napoleon Hill's ideas were revolutionary back in 1937, but they are almost common knowledge today: the understanding that we will likely not attain success, money, or power if we have negative ideas about success, money, and power. Negative ideas like:

- Money is the root of all evil.
- The rich and powerful are cold and heartless.
- You have to stomp on the "little guy" to get ahead.

- "Power tends to corrupt, and absolute power corrupts absolutely. Great men are most always bad men." —Lord Acton, 1887
- "Mo money, mo problems" —the Notorious B.I.G.
- "It is easier for a camel to pass through the eye of a needle than for a rich man to enter the Kingdom of God." —Matthew 19:24

Jack Canfield, best-selling author of the *Chicken Soup for the Soul* series, wrote in his 2004 book, *The Success Principles*, about the negative thoughts and conditioning around wealth and power that he had to overcome: "my father taught me that rich people got rich by exploiting the working classes. He constantly told me he wasn't made of money, that money didn't grow on trees, and that money was hard to come by…Somehow the rich were not to be trusted. They stepped on the little people. They took advantage of the common worker. To become rich would have meant becoming a traitor to my family and my class. I didn't want to become one of the 'bad guys.'"

Most of us do not want to become one of the "bad guys." And, in our culture today, the "bad guy" is the rich guy, the powerful guy. Underdogmatists—from the media to the movie theaters to the White House—barrage us each day with the messages that success, money, and power—and those who have them—are evil, wrong, and worthy of scorn. Ask yourself: when was the last time you saw a wealthy, successful, and powerful CEO portrayed as anything but hateful, vile, exploitative, cold, empty, mean-spirited, or evil in newspapers (outside of the business pages), in movies, in books, or on television? As *USA*

Today put it, "CEOs have been portrayed as villains since the dawn of silent movies and black-and-white TV,"[30] including those in: *Metropolis* (1927), Charlie Chaplin's *Modern Times* (1936), *Citizen Kane* (1941), *It's a Wonderful Life* (1946), *Scrooge* (1951), *Goldfinger* (1964), and *Network* (1976), in which a fictional CEO Arthur Jensen declared, "there is no America. There is no democracy. There is only IBM and ITT and AT&T and DuPont, Dow, Union Carbide, and Exxon. Those are the nations of the world today." And, of course, viewers will never forget the malevolent CEOs of *Wall Street* (1987), *The Insider* (1999), *Erin Brockovich* (2000), the twenty years of evil Mr. Burns on *The Simpsons*, or Michael Moore's documentary *Capitalism: A Love Story* (2009), which generated $14,363,397 at the box office (before adding in DVD sales, cable revenues, pay-per-view fees, in-flight movie revenues, and repertory cinema profits) by raising a fist against capitalism and CEOs.

> "About the only villains left are terrorists and CEOs—and terrorists will probably be portrayed as sympathetic long before CEOs."
>
> —Robert Thompson, director of the Center for the Study of Popular Television at Syracuse University, "America Loves to Hate Dastardly CEOs," *USA Today*, September 15, 2004

> "Obama Slams 'Fat Cat' Bankers."
>
> —*The Wall Street Journal*, December 14, 2009

---

[30] "America loves to hate dastardly CEOs," *USA Today*, September 15, 2004

> "[Obama] railed against greedy Wall Street bankers and lobbyists and shrieked about his dismay 'when I see reports of massive profits.'"
> —"Obama: Is His Presidency Close to Crisis?" *Telegraph UK*, January 22, 2010

When we are fed a steady diet of powerful and successful people depicted as evil, hateful overdogs—and when we consistently see the little guy portrayed as the plucky and honorable hero—it has an effect on us, personally. After all, who would want to be one of those nasty, power-hungry overdogs demonized by the President of the United States, by the anchors on the evening news, by our friends, our family, and by the characters in our favorite movies and TV shows? This incessant drumbeat of negative conditioning against wealth, power, and success leads many of us to believe that, if we become wealthy, powerful, or successful, people will hate us or reject us, too.

> "If you are top dog, you are a target of hostility. There's a very real possibility that others will reject you."
> —Julie Exline, assistant professor of psychology at Case Western Reserve University, *Psychology Today*, June 22, 2010

Millions of people fear what it would mean to become successful. They sabotage themselves before they achieve success and before they attain the power that comes with success. One man who understands this phenomenon better than anyone I know is entrepreneur, author, world authority on leadership psychology—and contributor to *Underdogma*—Anthony Robbins. Tony Robbins has spent more than three decades helping millions of people around the world identify and reverse their internal scorn for success and power through his multi-million selling books, CDs, and programs like *Personal Power*, *Unlimited Power*, and *Unleash The Power Within*.

> "If you find yourself resenting someone who is wealthy, what message does that send to your brain? It's probably something like 'Having excess money is bad.' If you harbor these feelings for others, you're subconsciously teaching your mind that for you to do well would make you a 'bad' person. By resenting others' success, you condition yourself to avoid the very financial abundance that you need and desire."
> —*Awaken The Giant Within*, Tony Robbins, 1992

In this chapter on Personal Underdogma, I would like to get personal. Twenty years ago, before Tony Robbins helped me with this book, he helped me realize that a childhood spent watching Disney movies had programmed me to believe that wealthy people were stuffy, cheap, cold, and bad (Mr. Banks in *Mary Poppins*) and that poor people (preferably covered in dirt) were good, lively, sang songs, danced, and generally got the girl (Bert, the chimney sweep, played by Dick Van Dyke). It sounds silly, but words and ideas mean things, especially to a young, impressionable child.

One of the most widely watched movies of this generation is *Titanic*, in which a dirty-faced poor boy from steerage (where they sang and danced) got the girl—while the rich, evil bad people in first class took all the lifeboats and left the nice poor people down in steerage to drown. The first wave of *Titanic* (the movie) survivors should be arriving on Tony Robbins' doorstep soon.

When I asked Anthony Robbins to contribute to *Underdogma*, he was profoundly generous with his time. I have no idea what Tony's political views are. It never came up. His observations on Underdogma, however, transcend politics and the headlines of the day and focus solely on his area of expertise: people. After helping more than fifty million people in one hundred countries over the past thirty-three years, Tony Robbins is a world leader in understanding people, and the universal patterns that drive people's behavior. Here are some of Tony's insights into the nature and origins of Personal Underdogma.

A NOTE FROM ANTHONY ROBBINS

My whole life has been focused on looking for universal patterns. There are two universal fears [and] they relate to *Underdogma* completely:

1. The fear that, at some level, we're not "enough"—we're not smart enough, we're not strong enough, beautiful enough, sexy enough, funny enough, rich enough—*something* enough. Because, the consequence that comes from feeling "not enough" is the deeper fear we have, which is;
2. If I'm "not enough," I won't be loved.

To be "not enough" is to basically be worthless. To be worthless and unloved is about as close to psychological and emotional death that a human being can get.

Universally, human beings around the world—regardless of the culture we live in—are born with one unique trait, different from virtually all other creatures or animals in the world except primates, and that is our unusually long dependency period on another human being for our survival. Many animals have a dependency period of six days, six weeks, six months—it's extremely unusual for most of the animal kingdom to have a dependency that goes beyond a year and a half. But human beings, left alone in the forest by themselves, don't have that evolutionary advantage of special teeth or nails or something else to protect themselves. Without someone to love them [they die]. So, it's not a trade: "I'll do this for you, as a child, if you do this for me." You take care of that child, you love them, you're committed to them in every way, shape, and form. And, because of that, we're able to survive as a species. Mother Nature has made sure that we have that same instinct. In fact, oxytocin is the specific chemistry, the specific biochemical change... [it] means that mother loves the way that child is.

We all have the experience of being "enough," and being loved, for doing *nothing*. We didn't have to *be* enough. We *were* enough. We were *born* as enough... You can scream, yell, throw things, not eat your food, go to the bathroom in your pants, you're fat, and you've got no teeth, no hair—and everybody thinks you're beautiful. But there's a day when the oxytocin wears off, and that's the day when fear is instilled in all human beings, and it relates directly to *Underdogma*.

Suddenly, you cry, you yell, you do something—and no one responds the same way. Suddenly, they *yell* at you for making those noises, or they *smack* you, or the scariest thing of all—they *ignore* you. And that's the moment in which fear is instilled in most human beings, and shows up in the pattern you see as this drive to be significant. Because, suddenly, we find out that we're *not* enough, we have to *do something* to be enough. So the baby might cry louder, and if the mother still ignores, the baby will yell harder. But if the baby, in the midst of crying, gets no feedback—in a panic—it'll try anything. Some people cry and scream and nobody comes, and they start to crawl and take their first steps and, all of a sudden, somebody says: "oh my God, Johnny or Mary is walking, look at this!" And everybody comes and cheers. And in that moment, an achiever is born. They find that the way to be significant is to *do* something significant, do something that impresses people. And suddenly you'll be "enough." You'll be enough and you'll get attention, you'll get connection, you'll get that love [which we all need to survive].

Now here's the problem: in order to get that love, [if] you're going to do it through achieving something, for example, you have to take risks. You have to try to walk and maybe fall. You have to try to start a business and maybe fail. You have to walk across the room and ask someone to dance, and they might say "no." Human beings want to avoid feeling insignificant, and feeling unloved, more than anything. So they have two choices: take the risks to be significant and do the difficult things and, if you fail, step back up and try again—which is scary. Or they rationalize, find a way to be significant *without* taking the risk. And the way to do that is to have a story about [how] "you're going to be more significant in the future." Or the easiest way to be significant—think about it—is not to take the risk yourself, but to *tear somebody else down*. If I tear you down, I look taller.

There are two ways to have the tallest building in town: either build the tallest building, or tear somebody else's down. Well, to build the tallest building, you have to take risks. You've got to go borrow the money. When everybody else goes to lunch you've got to keep building. But, to tear down somebody else's building, as we saw happen in New York [the attacks of 9/11], you can tear down something that took a decade to build in a few hours. Blow it up.

The most common pattern in human beings is this need for significance, the need to be certain that we can be *enough* and, as a result, be *loved*. And you've got two ways: take the risk, or tear something else down. So we all love when we see a story of someone who is insignificant and suddenly becomes significant. The example in this chapter, the woman from *Britain's Got Talent*, Susan [Boyle]—we all tune in to watch. *Rudy*, *Rocky*, etcetera etcetera. And the reason; it's a universal experience to have times in your life when you felt like you were not enough. And, to see somebody else who's not enough—you can identify with them—and when they succeed you feel that sense of success, even though you didn't have to *do* anything! You go into the hypnosis of "that's me." You identify with the character, and experience the emotion of that character as if it was you. So that's why we love it.

When people become successful, we root for them, at least in the beginning. But if they've been successful for a while [we tear them down]. Nike was a company everybody loved and, when they got really big, suddenly they're attacked *viciously*. And they weren't doing anything differently than their previous practices. They just became, now, this significant [company].

The basis of this [phenomenon], I believe, is in the structure of growing up for a child: this long dependency period that doesn't just go six months, a year, two years, three years, five years—how long are children dependent?—seven years, ten years, fifteen years, these days thirty-five years? That long dependency period makes us feel like someone else has power over us, because they *do* at some stage. And almost everyone has been at the brunt of that power at some point, where we felt out of control, which brings us to the second point I wanted to give to you, which is: ultimately, what these people are trying to do, by identifying with someone who has no power [an underdog], is say "I'm enough. I'm actually the powerful one, I'm the significant one, *I'm the meek that will inherit the earth.*" And, since the majority of people are not in a position of power in life, they assume that to try to [achieve power] would take huge risks, they may fail, and so the easier way is to develop an identity that says, "my problem, my pain, my weakness is my strength."

Again, there's only two ways... that you can convert the conditions of your life when they don't match how you think [they] should be. You either have to take risks to do something to change your life conditions, or you have to come up with a *story*—and someone to *blame*. You either blame your past, or you blame events, or you blame a person, or you blame yourself—that's what most people do. Your second choice is: change everything. Of course, that takes a lot of risk and a lot of challenges. Your third choice, of course, would be to change your expectations. But most people find "blame" to be the most effective tool. There's always got to be a villain. For there to be light, there has to be dark. The rich, the powerful, have always been that frame of reference.

The reason why we have to change what we associate to success is: if we link pain, negativity, crime, taking advantage to those who succeed, and we judge them without knowing who they truly are just to try to make ourselves feel better by contrast for having nothing—then the problem is: whatever we believe, we act on. And, if we believe success and money equals pain, we're going to act to avoid it and, as a result—ironically—we're going to suffer.

As Tony Robbins observed, many people deal with their own lack of power by heaping scorn on the powerful for being powerful. But, as you will see in Chapter 8—CONSPIRACIES: WAITING FOR "THE MAN," some other people take Underdogma even further—off the deep end—by believing that those who have power are not just powerful—they are *all-powerful*—with the power to shift and control global events by pulling the world's strings.

8

Conspiracies: Waiting for "The Man"

"Conspiracism serves the needs of diverse political and social groups in America and elsewhere. It identifies elites, blames them for economic and social catastrophes, and assumes that things will be better once popular action can remove them from positions of power."

—Frank P. Mintz, *The Liberty Lobby and the American Right,* 1985

"Conspiracism assigns tiny cabals of evildoers a superhuman power to control events [and] uses demonization to justify constructing the scapegoats as wholly evil while reconstructing the scapegoater as a hero."

—Political Research Associates, Public Eye

WHAT HAPPENS WHEN UNDERDOGMA RUNS amok, when those who hold positions of power are reflexively distrusted, feared, and ascribed almost supernatural abilities, when the world's problems are blamed on groups of elite and powerful overdogs who are bent on pulling the world's strings? Conspiracies abound, as do conspiracy theorists.

> "More than a third [of Americans] believe in a broad smorgasbord of conspiracy theories including the [9/11] attacks, international plots to rig oil prices, the plot to assassinate President John F. Kennedy in 1963 and the government's knowledge of intelligent life from other worlds."
>
> —Scripps Howard News Service/Ohio University poll, November 23, 2007

Conspiracy theorists view themselves as the underdogs; the good and noble champions of the little guy who have the courage to stand up to The Man. The University of East Anglia study "Critical Thinking about Conspiracy Theories" found that conspiracy theorists tend to "canonize" the victims of conspiracies (championing of the underdog) while "demonizing" the all-powerful conspirators (scorn for the overdog) and granting them "remarkable powers and properties, their wickedness clearly magnified."[1]

Which sounds a lot like Underdogma.

I asked Dr. Patrick Leman of Oxford and Cambridge, a researcher on the psychology of conspiracy theorists, if he knew of any conspiracies that did not feature a powerful overdog person or institution at the top, pulling the strings. "No," he replied, "all are powerful."

Big, powerful overdogs are essential to conspiracy theories. The Illuminati: a secret society that controls world events by controlling world governments. The Bilderberg Group: a powerful group working to build a "One-World Empire." Freemasons: bent on world domination since

[1] "Critical Thinking about Conspiracy Theories," Jerry Goodenough, University of East Anglia

the 1600s. The New World Order: a secretive and powerful global elite that conspires to rule the world. And, when conspiracy theorists fail to find big, powerful overdogs manipulating world events, they invent them, as Jerry Goodenough of the University of East Anglia wrote, by "*exaggerating the power and nature of organizations.*"[2]

One of the organizations whose power is often exaggerated by conspiracy theorists is the government: the all-seeing eye of Big Brother. Never mind the fact that Big Brother had a hard time keeping his all-seeing eye on tuberculosis carrier Andrew Speaker in 2007, in what was called "'an across-the-board meltdown' in border safeguards."[3] Mr. Speaker managed to pass through numerous airport security checkpoints and fly from the United States to Europe and back—and cross the Canada/U.S. land border "despite a lookout alert issued to all border posts"[4]—all without being detected by Big Brother's all-seeing eyes. Government conspiracy theorists must also avert their eyes from the fact that twenty-three-year-old terrorist Umar Farouk Abdulmutallab—whose own father put him on a "US watchlist of terror suspects"[5]—almost blew up a passenger jet over Detroit on Christmas Day 2009 after he "walked through airport security with explosives hidden on his body,"[6] unseen by Big Brother's big eyes. Despite all the evidence that Big Brother is either incompetent or that

---

[2] Ibid

[3] "TB Patient: No One Said I couldn't Travel," CBS News, June 6, 2007

[4] Ibid

[5] "Detroit Terror Attack: US Admits It Failed Over Terror Plot," *Telegraph UK*, December 28, 2009

[6] "Lonely Bomber Umar Farouk Abdulmutallab's Religious Angst Posted Online," *The Australian*, December 30, 2009

his all-seeing eye is blind, or both, millions of Underdogmatists continue to look at the government and think "Big Brother conspiracy"—from the belief that President Roosevelt had foreknowledge of the Pearl Harbor attack to the UFO "cover-up" at Roswell to the assassination of JFK to the moon landing "hoax" to the belief that the CIA manufactured AIDS and released it into the black community.

When Barack Obama's preacher Jeremiah Wright said, "the government lied about inventing the HIV virus as a means of genocide against people of color,"[7] he was preaching to a rather large choir. A 2005 study from Oregon State University and the nonprofit think tank Rand Corp. found that "a significant proportion of African Americans embrace the theory that government scientists created the disease to control or wipe out their communities," "nearly half" believed HIV was man-made, and a "majority said they believe that a cure for AIDS is being withheld from the poor."[8] I asked conspiracy researcher Dr. Patrick Leman about this phenomenon. His reply went straight to the heart of Underdogma and conspiracy theories when he spoke about the plight of the power have-nots in relation to big, powerful overdog conspirators.

A NOTE FROM DR. PATRICK LEMAN (OXFORD AND CAMBRIDGE)

The term [conspiracy] has almost been appropriated to commonly refer to nefarious activity by big, powerful or-

7 "Obama's Pastor's Sermon: 'God Damn America,'" FoxNews.com, March 14, 2008

8 "Study: Many Blacks Cite AIDS Conspiracy," *Washington Post*, January 25, 2005

ganisations. Psychologically, beliefs in conspiracy theories have an awful lot to do with power (or a sense of powerlessness). In terms of raw data, minority groups in the US show higher levels of belief in conspiracy theories ... I did just collect some data showing the same ethnic pattern in [the] UK. But, in the same study, I also found that beliefs were highest amongst those who rated their own income as below average—it was quite striking to find this strong link to the idea of power and being marginalised from decision-makers in society. One straightforward explanation is that, if you are not part of the decision-making process, you will always be left wondering what is going on inside the group.

Among those "left wondering what is going on inside the group" are conspiracy theorists known as the "9/11 Truthers," who believe that 9/11 was an "inside job." The "9/11 Truth" movement aims to spread the "truth" about what happened on September 11, 2001. What"truth"? An "awakening to the fraudulence of the 'official 9/11 story,'"[9] praise for the "heroes and heroines who have courageously faced that truth,"[10] (underdogs) and scorn for the U.S. government (overdogs), which used 9/11 to obtain "irresistible political power to increase inequality, repression [and] corporate domination."[11]

Praise for the underdog heroes, scorn for the power-hungry overdogs. It sounds a lot like Underdogma.

Are these "Truthers" relegated to the outer fringes of public discourse? Perhaps at first they were. But lately their ideas have begun to seep into mainstream culture. In 2006, "more than a third of the American public

[9] 911truth.org
[10] Ibid
[11] Ibid

suspect[ed] that federal officials assisted in the 9/11 terrorist attacks or took no action to stop them."[12] A year later, nearly *two-thirds* of Americans believed the U.S. government had "specific warnings of the Sept. 11, 2001, terrorist attacks on New York and Washington, but chose to ignore those warnings."[13]

The purpose of this book is not to disavow Truthers of their (actual) beliefs that the U.S. government somehow staged the 9/11 hijackings, intercepted the hijacked aircraft, removed all passengers, transferred them to new planes, impersonated their voices in fake phone calls back to their families, then flew them to their deaths in the Atlantic Ocean while taking the original planes and flying those, via remote-control, into their targets where the government had, over the previous months, tunneled through the interior walls of the World Trade Center buildings—without any of the office workers noticing—and planted thousands of pounds of explosives so they could be detonated to bring the Twin Towers down (which, if true, would make the whole airplane hijacking plot a bit unnecessary).

For those who accept the above theories as true (and they are actual beliefs held by 9/11 conspiracy theorists), there is no factual argument that can disavow them of their beliefs. Truthers already have all the evidence and facts they need to disavow themselves of such nonsensical beliefs right now, and yet they still believe these convoluted conspiracies anyway. Just for fun, here is another

[12] "Third of Americans Suspect 9-11 Government Conspiracy," Thomas Hargrove, Scripps Howard News Service, August 2, 2006
[13] Ibid

bit of truth for the Truthers to ignore. As someone who has spent more than a decade as a "government insider"—including time spent in the White House one month before the attacks of 9/11—I can tell you (not the Truthers, because they will never believe a word of it) that there is no possible way that government could have planned or executed a 9/11 "inside job." Why? Because the truth is that the government, and those who work in government, frankly lack the talent and creativity to come up with such a dastardly plan, and they especially lack the institutional competence to execute such a plan—perfectly and consistently, over long stretches of time, with not a single person involved leaking a word of it to anyone, ever. Then, these thousands of government conspirators would have to decide, independently of each other, that the biggest story of our time (which would have been damaging to George W. Bush) should be the one and only damaging story about George W. Bush that nobody ever leaked to anyone in the media. Then, the Obama administration (with "Green Jobs Czar" Van Jones on staff, who "signed a 2004 petition supporting the so-called'9/11 Truther' movement"[14]) would have to independently decide to join this conspiracy—an act that would destroy the Democratic Party's entire base of political support—in order to protect the reputation of George W. Bush, when barely a day went by in the first year of the Obama administration

Uncover the truth in Underdogma's CONSPIRACY THREAD at www.under-dogma.com.

[14] "Van Jones to Glenn Beck: 'I love you, brother,'" *Washington Examiner*, February 27, 2010

when it did not publicly scorn George W. Bush. As Richard A. Clarke, antiterrorism advisor to four consecutive U.S. Presidents, said, "anyone who's ever worked in government will tell you two things: that the government doesn't have the competence to do a large-scale conspiracy like this and, number two, it can't maintain secrecy. There's almost nothing that I know of, in thirty years of having top-secret clearances, that hasn't come out in the Washington Post and The New York Times."[15]

> "And what are the chances that an operation of such size—it would surely have involved hundreds of military and civilian personnel—could be carried out without a single leak? Without leaving behind a single piece of evidence hard enough to stand up to scrutiny in a court? People, the feds just aren't that slick. Nobody is."
>
> —"Why the 9/11 Conspiracy Theories Won't Go Away," *Time* magazine, September 3, 2006

But, as we have already discovered, truth and facts matter little to 9/11 Truthers (or to Underdogmatists). If truth and facts mattered to conspiracists, they would look at the examples of Big Brother failing to catch people on government watch lists as they passed through some of the world's most heavily monitored government checkpoints (airports) while carrying potentially deadly diseases and explosives. If truth or facts mattered, conspiracists would recall their own personal experiences with government incompetence and quickly realize that there is no way that the same government behind the DMV and the United States Postal Service

[15] "The Conspiracy Files," Richard A. Clarke, BBC, July 6, 2008

could pull off something like 9/11. Conspiracy theorists have an answer for that, too, with their impossible-to-reason-with argument that Big Brother government only *pretends* to be incompetent so that it can pull off government conspiracies without anyone suspecting the government. As the University of East Anglia study on conspiracy theories observed, "the more extreme conspiracy theories may argue that such organisations are only pretending to be inefficient, in order to fool the public about the true level of their efficiency. Such a position is, as [Karl] Popper would no doubt have pointed out, not open to refutation."[16]

This is why Underdogma helps us to better understand conspiracy theorists in general, and 9/11 Truthers in particular. Because Underdogma is a reflexive belief system, tied to power imbalances, which has the power to override truth, facts, and rational thought. Which is an apt description of the psychological profile of conspiracy theorists—and of Underdogmatists.

Why 9/11? What is it about the 9/11 attacks in particular that leads "hundreds of millions of people around the world [to] become convinced that the perpetrators of this monumental evil were not al-Qaeda terrorists, but elements within the U.S. government"?[17] I corresponded with *National Post* Managing Editor Jonathan Kay, who "embedded" himself in the 9/11 "Truther" movement for his book *Among the Truthers*. Kay observed that the American character itself, which is built on the narrative of an underdog revolution against powerful government forces,

---

[16] "Critical Thinking about Conspiracy Theories," Jerry Goodenough, University of East Anglia

[17] "Among The Truthers" website, Amongthetruthers.com, Jonathan Kay

makes Americans more naturally distrustful of powerful governments and therefore more susceptible to believing in government conspiracies.

> "There's a great tradition within America of ordinary, courageous heroes, rising up and speaking truth to power against the elites who control society—whether they're British, or whether they're Masons or whether they're bankers."
>
> —"The Unofficial Story," CBC Television, December 1, 2009

In his book *Empire of Conspiracy*, Timothy Melley finds further evidence that a part of the American character—tied to Underdogma's "Axis of Power"—makes Americans more susceptible to conspiracy theories. In his exploration of conspiracy theories, "Melley proposes that conspiracy thinking arises from a combination of two factors, when someone: 1) holds strong individualist values and 2) lacks a sense of control [aka power]."[18] No one holds stronger individualist values than Americans, with a Dutch study finding that "the United States ranks highest in individualism."[19] As Tony Robbins said in his interview for *Underdogma*, "self-esteem comes, to a great extent, from feeling like you have power over events, versus events and/or people have power over you."[20] Therefore, when something happens that causes strongly individualistic Americans to feel a profound lack of control (power)—like the 9/11 attacks—all the necessary elements are in place for a descent into conspiracism.

[18] "Paranoia, 9/11, and the Roots of Conspiracy Theories," *Psychology Today*, September 11, 2008

[19] MY SA News, November 28, 2008

[20] Tony Robbins, interview for *Underdogma*, April 6, 2010

> "When fervent individualists feel that they cannot exercise their independence, they experience a crisis and assume that larger forces are to blame for usurping this freedom."
> —"Paranoia, 9/11, and the Roots of Conspiracy Theories," *Psychology Today*, September 11, 2008

What is so bad about being distrustful of government power? After all, America was founded on a rebellion against government power. It feels good to raise a fist against Big Brother. Maybe these conspiracists are on to something. Is it such a leap of faith to think that Big Brother might be up to no good? As *Time* magazine observed, "there's something empowering about just exploring such questions...you feel as if you are participating in the great American tradition of self-reliance and nonconformist, antiauthoritarian dissent. You're fighting the power."[21]

Which sounds a lot like Underdogma.

If a small group holds fringe beliefs, why should we be concerned? Because this "small group" is no longer small. According to a Scripps-Howard poll, "36% of Americans consider it 'very likely' or 'somewhat likely' that government officials either allowed the attacks to be carried out or carried out the attacks themselves. Thirty-six percent adds up to a lot of people. That is not a fringe phenomenon. It is a mainstream political reality."[22] In hard numbers, 36% of Americans equals 109 million people. That means the constituency that believes that 9/11 was an "inside job"

---

[21] "Why the 9/11 Conspiracy Theories Won't Go Away," *Time* magazine, September 3, 2006

[22] "Why the 9/11 Conspiracy Theories Won't Go Away," *Time* magazine, September 3, 2006

is almost double the constituencies that voted for either Presidential candidate in 2008:

JOHN MCCAIN: 59 million supporters
BARACK OBAMA: 69 million supporters
9/11 WAS AN "INSIDE JOB": 109 million supporters

Underdogma has consequences. When America's reflexive affinity for the underdog and scorn for those who hold power is swept up in a national identity of individualism and rebellion against power, Americans put themselves at risk of getting swept away and abandoning their rational minds—as 36% of Americans have already done. By turning against their own country this way, conspiracy-minded Americans show America's enemies and attackers that they were right: it would only take nineteen men with boxcutters to strike the first blow. America would finish the rest of the job itself.

And, if you think America's enemies do not understand this dynamic, see Chapter 13—OUR ENEMIES DO NOT PRACTICE UNDERDOGMA.

But, before you read Chapter 13, would you be interested in buying a new car (Cadillac or Toyota)? Or perhaps a bottle of cola (Coke or Pepsi)? Or a pair of running shoes (Nike or its anti-branded shoe Blackspot)? The way you answer these questions has a lot more to do with Underdogma than you may think, as revealed in the next chapter: Chapter 9—SELLING UNDERDOGMA.

9

SELLING UNDERDOGMA

CADILLAC THEN

"The Leader is assailed because he is a Leader, and the effort to equal him is merely added proof of that leadership. Failing to equal or to excel, the follower seeks to depreciate and to destroy, but only confirms once more the superiority of that which he strives to supplant. There is nothing new in this, it is as old as the world and as old as the human passions envy, fear, greed, ambition, and the desire to surpass. And it all avails nothing. If the leader truly leads, he remains the leader. Master Poet, Master Painter, Master Workman; each in his turn is assailed, and each holds his laurels through the ages. That which is good or great makes itself known, no matter how loud the clamor of denial. That which deserves to live, Lives."

—Cadillac ad, "The Penalty of Leadership," 1915 (excerpt)

CADILLAC NOW

"I think some of [the problem with Cadillac/GM] is the David and Goliath syndrome. A lot of the time, I hear General Motors—even the name is somewhat unfortunate—dominates the car industry and is the goliath of the industry and these brave little start-up companies, the Japanese Honda and Toyota, they're so small and they're so humble and they're trying so hard, they just want to please people. And the American public loves that David and Goliath stuff. So automatically, we're cast in the role of the heavy and the brave little start-up companies from overseas are the giant killers and of course, now the shoe is on the other foot, but I don't think anyone has figured that out yet."

—GM VP Robert Lutz, January 22, 2009

IN THE YEARS THAT FOLLOWED its lone appearance in *The Saturday Evening Post*, Cadillac's "The Penalty of Leadership" ad was voted "the greatest advertisement of all time," and "Cadillac was inundated with requests for reprints."[1] The ad was an unapologetic declaration of Cadillac's greatness and dominance, and it displayed a clear understanding that "when a man's work becomes a standard for the whole world, it also becomes a target for the shafts of the envious few." Rather than stoop down to appease the "spiteful little voices" that nipped at its heels, Cadillac rose above "the little world;" confident in its own "genius" and "leadership."[2]

Fast-forward to the Cadillac (General Motors) of today, and we see "humility from a behemoth that has dominated the auto industry for most of its existence."[3] The *New York Times* trumpeted in a headline that the company was a "Symbol of America in Motion and Ascendancy, Now Humbled."[4] When the head of GM showed "arrogance,"[5] the President of the United States had him fired. Today, the "little world" expects from its corporate leaders "acts of contrition [and] corporate sacrifices to the altar of public opinion."[6] In this atmosphere, "auto executives are groveling, and angry taxpayers are picketing the homes of

[1] *The Mirror Makers: A History of American Advertising and Its Creators*, Stephen R. Fox, 1997

[2] All quotes from the full text of "The Penalty of Leadership"

[3] "GM Plays Follow the Leader," *US News & World Report*, June 12, 2005

[4] *New York Times*, May 31, 2009

[5] "The Auto Bailout: How We Did It," Steven Rattner, CNNMoney.com, October 21, 2009

[6] Entrepreneur.com, March 9, 2009

wealthy executives like French revolutionaries calling for Marie Antoinette's head."[7]

Marshall McLuhan said that "historians and archaeologists will one day discover that the ads of our times are the richest and most faithful daily reflections that any society ever made of its entire range of activities."[8] If archaeologists were to look at today's advertisements, they would see the reflection of a society far different than the original American audience for Cadillac's "The Penalty of Leadership" ad. In today's advertising landscape, less is more, big is bad, and the spotlight is on the little guy. "Consumers strongly relate to brands that they perceive as underdogs, according to a new study in the *Journal of Consumer Research*. The authors found that consumers identify with underdog stories because most people have felt disadvantaged at one time or another."[9] In the 2009 Super Bowl, "once the summit of advertising achievement [where] only the biggest and best could afford to advertise, and consumers expected only the biggest and best commercials to be shown,"[10] the award for best ad went to "two unemployed brothers from Batesville, Ind., whose [homemade] ad for Doritos [was] crafted for an online contest for amateurs."[11] The 2010 Super Bowl featured an ad from Miller High Life called "Little Guys on

---

[7] Ibid

[8] *Undressing the Ad: Reading Culture in Advertising*, Katherine Toland Frith, 1998

[9] ScienceBlog, July 20, 2010

[10] "Super Bowl Turning Into Spectacle of Waste for B-List Brands," BNET Advertising Blog, January 18, 2010

[11] "'Two Nobodies from Nowhere' Craft Winning Super Bowl Ad," *USA Today*, February 3, 2009

the Big Game," in which Miller handed over its thirty seconds of commercial airtime to "little guy" small businesspeople, stating, "you know who's getting all the help these days? Fat-Cat-Wall-Street-Muckity-Mucks. No one's helping out the little guy." Coca-Cola aired a Super Bowl ad that featured the rich, powerful, and hated Mr. Burns of *The Simpsons* losing all of his money and having his mansion foreclosed upon (to the mocking laughter of a news reporter). After Mr. Burns was stripped of his money and power, he was finally accepted by the Springfield townsfolk, who hoisted him on their shoulders while dancing to happy music. This led *Slate* magazine to recoil: "it was nice to see the Springfield gang's communitarian spirit, but I have to ask: Is America ready to feel sympathy for evil billionaires brought low?"[12] Meanwhile, traditional big advertisers like General Motors decided to pull their slates of Super Bowl ads entirely, lest they be accused of taking part in such a "Spectacle of Waste."[13]

The old axiom "As GM goes, so goes America" has come true. We are in the age of Underdogma. Gone are the days when a big, powerful company like Cadillac/GM could portray itself as big and powerful in advertisements like "The Penalty of Leadership." Today, "we love to hate big brands,"[14] and we revolt against big companies that have the audacity to advertise their "bigness." According to a study in the *Journal of Consumer Research*,

---

[12] "The Best and Worst Super Bowl Ads," *Slate*, Seth Stevenson, February 8, 2010

[13] "Super Bowl Turning Into Spectacle of Waste for B-List Brands," BNET Advertising Blog, January 18, 2010

[14] *Daily Telegraph*, May 11, 2008

today's "consumers strongly relate to brands they perceive as underdogs." That's why "many contemporary brand narratives highlight companies' humble beginnings and struggles against powerful adversaries. For example, Nantucket Nectars' label says the company started 'with only a blender and a dream,' while Google, Clif Bar, HP, and Apple emphasize that they started in garages."[15] Between Cadillac's 1915 ode to its own greatness and the Underdogma-driven advertising of today, something big changed. Advertisers began to "think small."

In 1959, Volkswagen appeared on the scene with its quirky, self-deprecating ad campaign: "Think small." Simple photos. Short, lucid copy. A hint of self-deprecating humor. A touch of irreverence. And not a whiff of overdog attitude. As VW ad copywriter Bob Levenson said at the time, "you want to talk to people, talk to them like they are people. *Don't* talk down."[16]

® Used with permission of Volkswagen Group of America, Inc.

In 1958, one year before the "Think small" campaign began, Volkswagen sold 150,601 cars in the United States. By 1963, VW was churning out one million cars per year.

[15] "The Underdog Effect: The Marketing of Disadvantage and Determination through Brand Biography," *Journal of Consumer Research*, February 2011

[16] *Think Small: The Story of Those Volkswagon Ads*, Frank Rowsome Jr., 1970

By 1965, VW sold its ten millionth car. A few years later, the Volkswagen Beetle passed the Ford Model T as the best-selling car of all time. When *Advertising Age* ranked the top 100 ad campaigns of the century in 1999, Volkswagen's "Think small" topped the list at No. 1, and Cadillac's "The Penalty of Leadership" (formerly No. 1) was knocked down to No. 49.

While Volkswagen started small, cultivated an underdog image, and grew big in the process, Detroit's "Big Three" automakers started big, acted big, and came crashing down to underdog status. How did they respond? They played the underdog card.

> "GM is the underdog now."
>
> —Mark LaNeve, GM's head of marketing, "Can Caddy's Driver Make GM Cool?," *Business Week*, September 20, 2004

> "Chrysler to stress status as 'underdog' to win U.S. buyers' loyalty."
>
> —Bloomberg News, June 14, 2007

> "The idea was for the company [Ford] to counter recent bad press and shake up buyers' perceptions by telling its own story, laying bare the automaker's vulnerability and portraying itself as an underdog."
>
> — "Desperate Measures," *Financial Post* magazine, January 1, 2007

When the VW Beetle passed the Ford Model T as the best-selling car of all time, Volkswagen found itself in the overdog position. Then VW plunged back down to underdog status when the Beetle was discontinued. VW rallied again with the launch of the New Beetle in 1998, and then tumbled once again in 2005, leading Volkswagen to fire its advertising agency. The president of VW's new ad agency admitted that Volkswagen was "in a difficult spot," but remained hopeful, saying, "we love being in the underdog position."[17]

Back in the 1960s, while Volkswagen was changing the culture of advertising from "That which is great makes itself known" to "Think small," the culture of America was changing, too. As shown in Chapter 5—FIGHT THE POWER, the Berkeley student protests of 1964 sparked a cultural shift in our attitude toward power with the birth of Underdogma: scorn for those who hold power and praise for those who do not. Power, in the 1960s, was something to be opposed, distrusted, and fought. Counterculture was fast becoming popular culture. It was a time for choosing sides. The smart money (and smart advertisers) chose the side of the little guy. And Volkswagen was perfectly positioned to ride the growing antiestablishment wave and transform its humble VW Beetle into the best-selling car of all time, using the principles of Underdogma. To this day, the Volkswagen Beetle and Volkswagen Microbus remain iconic symbols of the counterculture movement of the 1960s and '70s.

To see more ads from the VW "Think small" campaign, the original Cadillac ad "The Penalty of Leadership," and others, visit the UNDERDOG ADVERTISING THREAD at www.under-dogma.com.

[17] "With Sales Sagging, Volkswagen Gets a New Ad Agency," *New York Times*, September 6, 2005

The lessons of Volkswagen were not lost on the advertising industry, then or now. As Thomas Frank noted in *The Conquest of Cool*, "admen looked at the counterculture and saw...themselves."[18] And, rather than bristle at the sight of young hippies, these admen "hailed the young hipsters as comrades in a cultural revolution."[19]

> "American advertising took the side it did during the cultural revolution of the 1960s not simply because it wanted to sell a particular demographic, but because it found great promise in the new values of the counterculture."
>
> —*The Conquest of Cool*, Thomas Frank, 1998

In 1963, Pepsi got into the Underdogmatist game by launching an insurgent assault on "the near-universal hegemony of Coca-Cola"[20] with its counterculture-inspired "Pepsi Generation" campaign. The message was clear: Coke was the big, powerful overdog brand of "the establishment," and Pepsi was the underdog insurgent, "the choice of a new generation." While "the Volkswagen campaign had attacked the conventions of American car culture by punctuating its illusions and speaking to its skeptics, Pepsi cast doubt on the entire culture with which Coca-Cola was inextricably linked."[21] Tom Anderson of Pepsi's ad agency BBDO worried that Pepsi's stoking of Underdogmatist scorn was so effective that it may

---

[18] *The Conquest of Cool*, Thomas Frank, 1998
[19] "Business Culture, Counter Culture, and the Rise of Hip Consumerism," Eugene McCarraher, *Commonweal*, February 27, 1998
[20] *The Conquest of Cool*, Thomas Frank, 1998
[21] Ibid

have played a role in whipping up the fires of generational animosity in the 1960s and '70s.

> "I used to...especially in the late 60s, early 70s, started to go through the guilts of maybe having... contributed to some of the rebelliousness that was going on within the country. Yeah, I thought that it was that impactful, that perhaps we may have done something wrong."
>
> —Tom Anderson, 1984, quoted in *The Conquest of Cool*, Thomas Frank, 1998

A power gap has always existed between companies and their customers. Companies are often big, powerful, and wealthy and their customers are often not. When a company gets too big, or acts too big, its "bigness" can become a lightning rod for Underdogmatist consumer scorn.

"Big companies wield too much power"[22] screams one headline. "90% of Americans Believe Big Business Has Too Much Power"[23] heralds another. Yet another warns of a "public growing weary of inequality, corporate power."[24] And, of course, the Global Financial Crisis has unleashed Underdogmatist scorn for big business like never before (see Chapter 12—UNDERDOGMA AND THE GLOBAL FINANCIAL CRISIS). Even Hank Paulson, the former head of the U.S. Treasury Department—"the executive agency responsible

---

[22] CanWest News Service, January 2, 2008
[23] Harris Interactive Poll, December 1, 2005
[24] *Winnipeg Free Press*, January 9, 2008

for promoting economic prosperity"[25]—got in on the Underdogmatist game.

> "There's always been a tendency to dislike the big guy, and it has been intensified by concerns over global competition and the widening gap between the winners and the losers."
>
> —Henry M. Paulson Jr., (then) chairman of the Goldman Sachs Group, 74th United States Secretary of the Treasury, *New York Times*, December 9, 2005

In the world of Underdogma advertising and branding, "bigger is better" has become "bigger is bad." As the *Daily Telegraph* put it, "we love to hate big brands."[26] One of the big brands Underdogmatists love to hate is Wal-Mart. Although "it's hard to imagine Wal-Mart as a scrappy underdog...that's what it was in the 1960s and '70s. [Founder Sam] Walton was often heralded as a modern-day Robin Hood, building his retail discount chain for the cost-conscious masses."[27] The subject of Wal-Mart came up in a 2007 Democratic Presidential candidate debate, putting Hillary Clinton on the defensive: "In its earliest days, she said, it gave people in places like rural Arkansas the chance to stretch their dollars. However, now that the Wal-Mart business model of allowing everyone to stretch their dollars has made it the largest retailer in history, it has become bad."[28] Why was the subject of Wal-Mart's

---

[25] U.S. Department of the Treasury web page, "Mission," www.ustreas.gov/education/duties/

[26] *Daily Telegraph*, May 11, 2008

[27] *CIO* magazine, November 1, 2007

[28] "Underdog Upstages Duel of the Titans," *New York Post*, April 27, 2007

"bigness" elevated to the big stage of a Presidential candidate debate? Because Hillary Clinton had a skeleton in her closet—the kind that could spell political doom among hard-core liberal Democrats—a skeleton that Barack Obama pulled out of Hillary's closet. Hillary Clinton had spent time on the board of the biggest overdog company in the world, Wal-Mart.

> "While I was working on those streets watching those folks [underdogs] see their jobs shift overseas, you [Hillary Clinton] were a corporate lawyer sitting on the board at Wal-Mart [big bad overdog]."
>
> —Barack Obama, Myrtle Beach, South Carolina debate, January 21, 2008

The Democratic debate crowd roared and cheered. Hillary narrowed her eyes and shot icy daggers at candidate Barack Obama. If Mrs. Clinton had opened her eyes a little wider, she would have seen that—beyond the narrow confines of that room filled with hard-core liberal Democrats—most Americans do not demonize Wal-Mart the way Barack Obama did. True, a 2006 Pew Research study found that a majority (53%) of liberal Democrats had an unfavorable opinion of Wal-Mart, but it also found that 70% of moderate and conservative Democrats had *positive* impressions of Wal-Mart. The same study also found that, of those 53% hard-core anti-Wal-Mart Democrats, *74% admitted to having shopped at Wal-Mart in the previous year*, and 28% said they shopped there *regularly*.[29] This is the power of Underdogma: thousands of people ignoring their rational minds,

[29] Pew Research, August 30, 2006

cheering an Underdogmatist Presidential candidate who demonizes Wal-Mart, and then stopping at Wal-Mart on the way home to buy *The Audacity of Hope* at a good "rollback" price.

On July 16, 2010, after being savaged by the media like never before in the company's history, Apple CEO Steve Jobs was forced to humble himself and admit in the now-famous "Antennagate" press conference that the iPhone 4 had reception problems. The strange thing about this press conference was that Apple had reception problems with its iPhone dating back to 2008. What changed between 2008 and 2010? In May of 2010, Apple "surpassed Microsoft as the largest technology company in the world by market capitalization."[30] In other words: Apple got big. Apple got powerful. Apple became the overdog. And "Big Apple" became target of Underdogmatist scorn.

"When Apple (NASDAQ: AAPL) was the soft cuddly underdog, everyone loved them and rooted for the company's success," observed stock analyst Paul McWilliams. "While we could blame AAPL's recent decline on what the press has determined is a bad antenna design on its new iPhone 4 and, in doing so, we most certainly wouldn't be wrong, isolating only on that would be a mistake. What's happening in the larger picture is Apple has moved from being the cuddly underdog to become the new 'Evil Em-

---

[30] "Apple Dethrones Microsoft As World's Biggest Tech Company," *Huffington Post*, May 26, 2010

pire,' a title it has ironically taken from its old nemesis, Microsoft."[31]

At the Antennagate press conference, Steve Jobs tried to wrap his head around what had changed about the way people viewed his company. All he could come up with was, "maybe it's human nature—when you're doing well, people want to tear you down. I see it happening with Google, people trying to tear them down. And I don't understand it."[32]

One company that did understand the threats posed by Underdogma—but still got slammed by it anyway—is Japanese automaker Toyota. Before a series of high-profile recalls in 2009–2010 sent Toyota's stocks plunging and Toyota's president bowing and begging for forgiveness (more on that later in this chapter), Toyota worked overtime to steer clear of Underdogmatist backlashes against its growing size and power. While the former "Big Three" automakers dealt with their newfound status as underdogs, Toyota faced a different and more dangerous problem. In January of 2009, Toyota became the world's No. 1 automaker and, in doing so, faced the threat of being perceived as the overdog and of attracting Underdogmatist scorn. As *Newsweek* put it, "Toyota is experiencing what a Cadillac ad once called 'the penalty of leadership.'"[33] And, according to a leaked memo obtained by the *Detroit Free Press*, Toyota foresaw—back in 2007—the Underdogma implications of being No. 1.

---

[31] "Apple (NASDAQ: AAPL): Underdog To'Evil Empire'" by Paul McWilliams, iStockAnalyst.com, July 20, 2010
[32] "Live from Apple's iPhone 4 press conference" Engadget, July 16, 2010
[33] *Newsweek*, March 12, 2007

> "Toyota Motor Corp. is bracing for possible political and consumer backlash caused by its rapid U.S. growth, according to an internal report obtained by the *Free Press*."
>
> "'Toyota will be a scapegoat,' one slide says. 'And we need to position ourselves to respond to corporate image attacks.'"
>
> —"Toyota Fears U.S. Backlash Over Gains," *Detroit Free Press*, February 13, 2007

When I am not writing about Underdogma, I help companies and politicians deal with Underdogmatist scorn. Broadly speaking, there are two ways to do this: either mitigate Underdogma or embrace Underdogma. Before the 2009–2010 recalls, Toyota excelled at both.

Mitigate Underdogma

The first rule for big companies hoping to sidestep Underdogmatist scorn is to appear humble. When Toyota passed GM to become the world's largest automaker, Toyota spokesman Paul Nolasco kept his head down and said all the right things. "Our goal has never been to sell the most cars in the world. We simply want to be the best in quality. After that, sales will take care of themselves."[34]

The second rule is to extinguish small Underdogmatist brushfires before they can grow into raging infernos of public scorn. To continue the fire analogy, a company should also engage in "controlled burns" aimed at preemptively stripping away rhetorical fuel for Underdogmatists. In English, this means to carefully identify

[34] "Toyota 'World's Largest Carmaker,'" BBC, April 24, 2007

potential points of attack and engage in preemptive PR tactics to douse any possible Underdogmatist fires before they can flare up. In the case of Toyota, they knew that one likely point of attack would be a nationalist U.S. backlash against this powerful, foreign-owned company. Toyota's preemptive tactic was brilliant: build Toyota plants in America, hire American workers, and, most importantly, *advertise that fact to the American people*. Which is exactly what Toyota has done over the years. Toyota's 2009 national campaign "Beyond Cars" posed the question "What makes us an engine of the economy?" and answered with, "Plants across America," "Nearly 200,000 jobs created," and "Partnering with local communities."[35] In a truly inspired move, Toyota even hired 3,000 American workers who were laid off by General Motors.[36] Since 1990, Toyota—apparently at the behest of the Japanese government—has spent a great deal of time, money, and effort selling Americans on the idea that Toyota cares about them, cares about their families, and cares about their communities.

> "An official of the Japanese Government, who insisted on not being identified, said yesterday that Tokyo had been encouraging Japanese companies doing business in the United States to become more involved in their communities. 'It is something that has been neglected,' the official said.

[35] "Toyota Ad Campaign Stars Georgetown Employees," Kentucky.com, October 8, 2009

[36] "Toyota: The Reluctant King of the Road," *BusinessWeek*, February 23, 2007

> 'Japanese companies should take the opportunity to explain themselves and what they are doing.'"
>
> —"Toyota Effort Seeks to Show How It Cares About the U.S.," *New York Times*, October 2, 1990

In America, Toyota has sponsored livestock shows, partnered with Bass Pro Shops and lumber stores, funded a teacher program to send American teachers around the world, sponsored "National Public Lands Day," built a "National Center for Family Literacy," spent $1.3 million on a child-care center in Kentucky, and sponsored 4H2Online, "a community for youth to learn about water quality, water conservation and watershed issues." And, to help make sure that no good Toyota deed went unnoticed, Toyota spent millions of dollars advertising its community-minded good deeds to American citizens. Their message was clear: Toyota is on your side, and Toyota is good for the country.

> "In the past year, Toyota also has run TV ads and put up billboards touting its economic impact on the United States."
>
> —"Toyota Fears U.S. Backlash Over Gains," *Detroit Free Press*, February 13, 2007

The most dangerous group of Underdogmatists—meaning those who are most able to turn Underdogmatist scorn into harmful action against companies—are politicians. The public can heap a certain amount of scorn on large companies, but politicians can turn that populist anger into direct, legislative action that could devastate a company like Toyota with a stroke of a regulatory pen—

especially during an economic downturn, when politicians can harm powerful, foreign companies under the patriotic rallying cry of "Buy American." So, Toyota has spent upward of $5.9 million[37] a year tending to, and lobbying, Congress. In 2007, GM's head of global product development Bob Lutz bemoaned the fact that Toyota had "more congressmen and senators" than GM, and said "it is my considered opinion that Toyota has more clout in Washington than we do."[38] Leaving no stone unturned, Toyota has run numerous specialized ad campaigns designed to help keep Washington decision-makers feeling good about Toyota.

> "In Washington, subway stops frequented by policy makers are plastered with ads extolling Toyota's U.S. employment figures."
>
> —"Toyota Fears U.S. Backlash Over Gains," *Detroit Free Press*, February 13, 2007

Embrace Underdogma

The second way for companies to deal with Underdogmatist scorn is to embrace Underdogma by becoming smaller, behaving smaller, and, as Toyota has done, give its customers a way to distance themselves from the "bigness" of the "big company" by empowering customers to make the products of the "big company" their own. Doritos did this with its award-winning customer-created Super Bowl ads, and Toyota got in on the game with its niche line of "Scion" cars.

---

[37] "Auto Lobby Spends $70 Million," *Spinwatch*, January 5, 2008

[38] "G.M. Officer Says Toyota is Stronger in Washington," *New York Times*, January 10, 2007

Scion used an "innovative, consumer-driven process" to engage its customers, including the ability to "tweak" or customize cars for each buyer. In other words, they empowered their customers to make Scion cars their own. To further direct the spotlight away from the world's biggest automaker and onto its individual customers, the 2008 Scion advertising campaign, entitled "United by Individuality," featured billboards of Scion vehicles that were customized and modified by individual drivers. In 2009, Scion embraced Underdogma to an even greater degree by launching its "Brand Manifesto Campaign [which] Inspires Originality and Challenges Individuals to 'Become One of Us by Becoming None of Us.'"[39] This was Underdogma advertising at its most audacious: rebranding the act of buying a car from a big, powerful company into an expression of individuality and an act of rebellion against the big, powerful company that manufactured and sold the car.

Before the 2009–2010 Toyota recalls, the most important part of Toyota's firewall against Underdogma was the company's strategic decision to behave small and maintain a humble attitude, which was embodied by one of Toyota's internal slogans: "Run Scared." "Toyota is trying to shut out all the hoopla over its rise to the top," said Toyota Executive VP Tokuichi Uranishi. "What we are worrying about is if our employees become arrogant or compla-

[39] Toyota USA Newsroom, July 16, 2009

cent, assuming we are No. 1."[40] Toyota was right to "run scared." Arrogance got the head of General Motors fired by the President of the United States. By contrast, Toyota executive Katsuaki Watanabe was "obsessed with keeping Toyota safe from its own success," noting that "to be satisfied with becoming the top runner...is the path we must be most fearful of." Going down that path, he feared, could lead to "big-company disease."[41]

A mere twelve months after Toyota became the biggest, most powerful car company in the world, Toyota fell victim to "big-company disease."

In September 2009, Toyota announced a recall of four million U.S. vehicles due to the possibility that accelerator pedals could become trapped in floor mats and "[could] result in very high vehicle speeds and make it difficult to stop the vehicle, which could cause a crash, serious injury, or death."[42] In January 2010, Toyota expanded the recall "to fix potentially faulty accelerator pedals"[43] on approximately 2.3 million cars in the United States. Later that month, Toyota expanded the recall to Europe, and the term "Unintended Acceleration" entered the lexicon. How to fix the problem of "Unintended Acceleration"? *Car and Driver* offered this somewhat pithy and crass (but, as they put it, a "guaranteed") solution:

> "If your car starts accelerating unexpectedly, hit the brake (it's the one to the left of the gas) and

---

[40] "Comin' Through!" *Newsweek*, March 12, 2007

[41] "Katsuaki Watanabe: Fighting To Stay Humble," *BusinessWeek*, March 5, 2007

[42] "Timeline: Toyota's Recall Woes," *Guardian UK*, February 4, 2010

[43] Ibid

> shift into neutral. After you do this, the engine may race loudly but the car won't accelerate. Pull off the road, brake to a stop, shift to park, and shut off the car. This is a simple solution we guarantee will save your life in any car that suffers from unintended acceleration."
> —Mike Dushane, *Car and Driver*, February 2010

In February 2010, Toyota was dragged before U.S. Congressional hearings, just after U.S. Transportation Secretary Ray LaHood said, "we're not finished with Toyota"[44] and "sent Toyota's stock price into free fall…telling a House committee that Americans with cars made by the Japanese auto company should stop driving them."[45]

What does this have to do with Underdogma? After all, a safety recall is about safety—not the relative power held by the company issuing the safety recall, right? Not necessarily, when Underdogma is involved. If recalls are equal to outrage, then where was all the public outrage when Toyota recalled 55,000 cars in 1969? Or 145,000 cars for an accelerator problem in 1971? Or when hundreds of thousands of Toyotas were recalled in 1972, 1977, 1978, 1981, 1984, 1986, 1987, 1988, and 1989? Let us assume, for the sake of argument, that Toyota's hard-earned reputation for quality and safety began only recently. Then how does one explain the following pre-2009 Toyota recalls, and our strange lack of outrage for each of them?

---

[44] "Official: U.S. Had to Force Toyota into Safety Recall," *Detroit Free Press*, February 2, 2010

[45] "LaHood's Toyota Panic," StarTribune.com, February 7, 2010

- 1999—Toyota recalls 797,707 vehicles for "faulty suspension"
- 2000—Toyota Camrys are recalled because the rear axle shafts could fail or break
- 2001—Over 200,000 Toyota Celicas, Echos, and 4Runners are recalled for lighting and brake issues
- 2002—Toyota recalls "397,263 subcompact and mini-car vehicles…because of improperly designed brake fluid pipes"
- 2003—***"Toyota recalled cars in 2003 because of fears sliding floor mats would jam the accelerator pedal"***[46] (the same problem that sparked Toyota's 2009–2010 recall and attendant outrage)
- 2004—Toyota recalls 890,000 vehicles for defective airbags, steering wheels, and fuel tanks
- 2005—Toyota recalls more than 750,000 pickup trucks and SUVs for suspension and steering problems, 550,000 Camrys for door problems, 345,443 Sienna minivans "in response to complaints that in the event of a crash, a seat-belt malfunction could lead to injury," and 75,000 Prius cars "because their engines can stop due to an electrical problem"
- 2006—Toyota recalls nearly "1 million vehicles across the globe to replace faulty parts that could cause drivers to lose control of the steering wheel"

---

[46] "Toyota Floor-Mat Problems Arose in 2003," CBC News, March 23, 2010

- 2007—Toyota recalls 533,000 trucks for a "steering flaw," 470,000 cars for "fuel leaks," and ***"55,000 floor mats due to complaints of unintended acceleration caused by the mats sticking underneath the accelerator pedal"*** on Prius and other models (the same problem that sparked Toyota's 2009–2010 recall and attendant outrage)
- 2008—Toyota recalls 539,500 Corollas and Matrixs for faulty glass, 630,000 minivans due to defective fuel tanks, 90,000 Highlanders for faulty seat belts, and 420,000 vehicles fleetwide due to faulty engines

None of these ten million plus recalled Toyota cars, trucks, and vans—*including two recalls like the recall that triggered the 2009–2010 Toyota meltdown (floor mats jamming gas pedals)*—resulted in anything near the kind of public hysteria, media scorn, and political saber-rattling that was thrust upon Toyota in late 2009 and early 2010.

So what was different about Toyota, and the North American auto market, in 2009 and 2010?

One big difference was that, in 2009, the U.S. government took controlling interests in two of the "Big Three" U.S. automakers (GM and Chrysler). Does that mean there was some kind of coordinated government conspiracy to drag down Toyota in order to benefit the two competing auto companies that were owned by the U.S. government? As shown in Chapter 8—CONSPIRACIES: WAITING FOR "THE MAN," governments are not always adept at planning and executing well-coordinated conspiracies. But, as the *National Post* observed, "while it may be technically true that President Obama's team didn't explicitly reach a decision to target Toyota, nobody in this crowd needs a presidential order to turn the Japanese auto giant's Sudden Unintended Acceleration (SUA) problem into a national industrial advantage for the United States. The owners of union-dominated Government Motors can spot a strategic economic opportunity without waiting for the memo from head office."[47]

What is more likely than a coordinated government conspiracy, designed to siphon Toyota market share into the ledgers of government-controlled automakers? It is the more traditional threat that governments pose to big companies—a threat Toyota paid lobbyists millions of dollars to forestall in an "effort to prevent a Washington backlash against its success."[48]

> "The attack on Toyota, at this time of U.S. economic weakness and populist excess, is fast turning into a great American nationalist assault on a foreign corporation, an economic war."
> —"The War on Toyota," Terence Corcoran, *National Post*, February 3, 2010

"For most of their automaking history, [Toyota] were underdogs struggling against Detroit's juggernaut."[49] Then, in 2009, Toyota became the world's biggest and most powerful automaker. In doing so, Toyota became the focus of Underdogmatist scorn, something the previous

[47] "The War on Toyota," Terence Corcoran, *National Post*, February 3, 2010

[48] "Toyota Scrambles to Build D.C. Crisis Team," *The Wall Street Journal*, February 6, 2010

[49] "Toyota Recall Anxiety Accompanies Toyoda's Drive to President," Bloomberg.com, July 23, 2007

"top dog" automaker General Motors knew all too well. As one GM dealer noted, "it's tough to be the top-selling car company. A bright light is always shining on the top company, and things that smaller entities might have gotten away with suddenly take on greater importance. GM had to deal with being number one for 25 years and now Toyota has had that title for the last two years, and these things happen."[50]

In the wake of this crisis, "a Japanese Toyota executive said there is 'a lot of pent up frustration' among management over why Toyota's Washington office didn't see the warning signs of a backlash coming sooner."[51] If the people in Toyota's Washington office had read *Underdogma*, they would have seen the Underdogmatist backlash against Toyota coming from miles down the road. When Toyota became the biggest, most powerful automaker in the world, it became the target of Underdogmatist scorn.

The master practitioners of Underdogma advertising and branding are the companies that have turned hatred and scorn for big corporations into *central parts of their corporate cultures*. These are the so-called "*anti*preneurs," "business owners who have won both notice and profits by being overtly or covertly anti-big business and anti-advertising."[52]

---

[50] "Toyota's Rough Road," *The Chronicle Herald*, February 2, 2010
[51] "Toyota Scrambles to Build D.C. Crisis Team," *The Wall Street Journal*, February 6, 2010
[52] "Meet the Antipreneurs," *BusinessWeek*, June 20, 2008

In an Underdogmatist world, being anti-business is good business, but these antipreneurs should be cautious. If business gets too good for them, and they become big and powerful, they will face reflexive scorn from their Underdogmatist customers. As *BusinessWeek* observed, "antipreneurs walk a fine ideological line: they are pro-business and want their companies to grow, but they're against big business. They engage in global commerce while disdaining the machinations of globalization. They profit from the free market, but they criticize it, too."[53]

One company that has successfully walked this fine ideological line for the past twenty years is the "not for profit, anti-consumerist" magazine *Adbusters*, which gives the "antipreneur...movement much of its ideological weight."[54] Not only does the magazine rail against advertising and big corporations with its "Buy Nothing Day" and "Buy Nothing Christmas" campaigns, *Adbusters* jumps into the advertising and corporate game with its own brand of boots and running shoes called Blackspot. The Blackspot mission statement is a near word-for-word recitation of Underdogma: "Why buy your shoes from megacorporations? That kind of top-down, corporate-controlled capitalism has failed us; let's start over from the roots up. Let's go local, go indie, and put power back in the hands of the many."[55]

With revenues approaching $2.5 million, however, Blackspot would be wise to carefully monitor its own

---

[53] Ibid

[54] Ibid

[55] *Adbusters* Blackspot page, captured December 4, 2009

success, lest it find itself on the wrong side of the boot of Underdogma.

The people who are most attuned to the threats and opportunities posed by Underdogma are those whose job it is to seek power. Their stories are revealed in the next chapter: Chapter 10—POLITICAL UNDERDOGMA.

10

POLITICAL UNDERDOGMA

"Obama calls himself underdog."
—*Politico*, Mike Allen, October 16, 2007

"[Hillary] Clinton seeks to cast herself as underdog vs Obama."
—Reuters, Caren Bohan, February 10, 2008

"John McCain, Reprising the Underdog Role."
—*Washington Post*, Michael D. Shear, September 4, 2007

"I'm *way* the underdog."
—John Edwards, NBC, January 26, 2008

"Mitt Romney: I'm the Underdog."
—*New York Times*, December 13, 2007

"I like feeling like I'm an underdog."
—Rudy Giuliani, "Rudy Relishes Underdog Role," *MSNBC First Read*, January 26, 2008

THE MERRIAM-WEBSTER DICTIONARY DEFINES AN underdog as "a loser or predicted loser in a struggle or contest." So, if a politician's goal is to win elections (and, make no mistake, that is his or her goal), why do so many politicians clamor to portray themselves as underdogs?

A University of South Florida study, "The Advantage of Disadvantage: Underdogs in Politics," gave two groups of test subjects near-identical Barack Obama speeches. The only difference: one group's speech described Barack Obama as a front-runner, and the other described him as an underdog.

> "I know that I am not the favorite in this race [**I know that some early polls show that I'm the favorite in this race**]. As an underdog [**the front-runner**], my star is not quite that bright just yet [**there will be high expectations for my candidacy**]. However, I believe these serious times demand serious people who have real world experience in solving the challenges we face. I humbly believe I'm the best equipped to meet these challenges."
>
> —"The Advantage of Disadvantage," Nadav Goldshmeid & Joseph Vandello, 2009

The study found "the underdog label can reap benefits for politicians," "the underdog label is regarded positively," and "underdogs are seen as warmer and more likeable than frontrunners."[1] These findings are supported by earlier studies, including Fleitas (1971), in which voters demonstrated "a significant shift in favor of the underdog," and Ceci and Kain (1982), in which "participants who were told [Jimmy] Carter was leading in the polls were more likely to express a preference for [Ronald] Rea-

[1] "The Advantage of Disadvantage," Nadav Goldshmeid & Joseph Vandello, 2009

gan, while those exposed to a Reagan-lead poll aligned themselves with Carter."[2]

While academic studies are helpful, they pale in comparison to real, hands-on political experience. George Washington Plunkitt, one of the winningest politicians in history, said, "some young men think they can learn how to be successful in politics from books, and they cram their heads with all sorts of college rot. They couldn't make a bigger mistake."[3] As someone who has helped hundreds of politicians win elections over the years, I can tell you that the reason why so many politicians embrace the underdog label is because it works. This chapter will show you **why** it works, **how** it works—and give you a side-by-side **comparison** of two real-life underdog campaigns.

> "Of all our passions and appetites, the love of power is of the most imperious and unsociable nature, since the pride of one man requires the submission of the multitude."
> —*The History of the Decline and Fall Of The Roman Empire: Volume 1*, Edward Gibbon, 1806

WHY POLITICAL UNDERDOGMA WORKS

First, a warning: if you want to hold on to your belief that politics is about anything other than power, I recommend that you skip to the next chapter or put this book down. Politicians *require* power. An artist without an audience is still an artist. A politician without power is nothing. I have never met a politician who did not want to "do

[2] Ibid

[3] George Washington Plunkitt of Tammany Hall

good" while in power. But all of their good intentions will add up to nothing unless they get into power in the first place (by winning elections) and then stay in power (by winning re-election). This is the art and science of acquiring and holding on to power. An election is, at its core, a transfer of power from voters to politicians, from the people to the state. When politicians ask you for your vote, they are asking you to cede some of your personal power to them—power over your income, finances, taxes, your personal and national security, your child's education, your environment (including the air you breathe, the water you drink, and the land you walk upon), your retirement, your freedom (by empowering them to set and enforce laws and hand down punishment)—even power over your health, and your very life. If you do not believe that politics and elections are about power, you are not alone. More than half of the politicians I have helped lead to victory did not understand the basic nature of their chosen profession, which is to win and hold on to power. Whether you, or they, accept it or not does not make it any less true. Politics is about power.

The reason why Underdogma is so prevalent in politics is because Underdogma and politics are both about power. Few people understood this better than the man "who operated the most successful and long-running urban political machine in American history,"[4] George Washington Plunkitt of Tammany Hall.

---

[4] *Plunkitt of Tammany Hall*, William L. Riordon, 1963

> "Plunkitt is compellingly honest about the true lure of politics—first and foremost the desire to hold and wield power."
>
> —*Plunkitt of Tammany Hall*, William L. Riordon, 1963

Tammany Hall was the "political machine that dominated New York City politics from the mayoral victory of Fernando Wood in 1854 through the election of Fiorello LaGuardia in 1934."[5] If a week is an eternity in politics, then the eighty-year electoral reign of Tammany Hall was a heck of a long time. And the man in charge of Tammany Hall's Election Committee was its chairman, George Washington Plunkitt.

Plunkitt understood the power dynamic of politics. Politicians are in the business of asking everyday people to hand over a portion of their power. When engaged in transactions of power, politicians must understand how different the transaction looks—and how different politicians look—in the eyes of the people (the voters) who are ceding their power. Voters are not apt to hand their power over to people they dislike. And most voters dislike big, powerful overdogs. That is one of the reasons why politicians play the underdog card, because it gives voters the *perception* that the power gap between voter and politician has closed, or at least narrowed. The *actual* gap will always be there, but Underdogmatist politicians seek to narrow your perception of that gap by convincing you that they are "just like you."

---

[5] Eleanor Roosevelt National Historic Site

> "Make the poorest man in your district feel that he is your equal, or even a bit superior to you."
> —George Washington Plunkitt, *Plunkitt of Tammany Hall*, William L. Riordon, 1963

> "In order to become the master, the politician poses as the servant."
> —Charles de Gaulle

The truth is: politicians are not "just like you." You do not have handlers. Other people do not write your "spontaneous" remarks. You comb your own hair. You cannot raise tens of millions of dollars to promote a product that is you. And you are not in the business of seeking power. Politicians are not like you. But they work overtime to create the illusion that they are.

> "I grew up on Pinochle and the American dream."
> —Hillary Clinton TV ad "Scranton," 2008

Here is what CNN Money revealed about the 2008 Presidential hopefuls listed at the beginning of this chapter, all of whom played the underdog card, in a December 7, 2007, piece entitled "Millionaires-in-Chief."

PRESIDENTIAL CANDIDATE	NET WORTH
Barack Obama	$1.3 million
Hillary Clinton	$34.9 million
John McCain	$40.4 million
John Edwards	$54.7 million

PRESIDENTIAL CANDIDATE	NET WORTH
Mitt Romney	$202 million
Rudy Giuliani	$52.2 million
Average American	$11,000

A November 2009 Roll Call study found 125 millionaires in Congress, with the average wealth of its members pegged at $2.28 million (compared to the $11,000 net worth of the average American).[6] That means the average member of Congress has 207 times the net worth of the average American, and the six "underdog" 2008 Presidential candidates had 5,840 times the net worth of the average American. These are the same people who haul CEOs before Congress to explain the gap between CEO pay and worker pay, and who instituted a "Pay Czar" to limit executive earnings. When asked how politicians get away with such dizzying chutzpa, political scientist Eric Herzik replied, "that's the art of politics."[7]

The "art" of Political Underdogma, in addition to helping politicians close the perceived power gap between themselves and voters, also gives politicians numerous tactical advantages at election time.

- **GET OUT THE VOTE.** Underdog campaigns find it easier to get their supporters to vote, due to a built-in sense of urgency

[6] "Capital in the Capitol," Roll Call, November 30, 2009
[7] "Ibid

and insurgency (underdog supporter: "They need my vote") compared to front-runners, who tend to struggle in this area (overdog supporter: "They probably don't need my vote, they'll win anyway").

- REDUCE EXPECTATIONS. When a front-runner wins, it is expected. When an underdog wins, it is front-page news (AKA: free "earned media"). When a front-runner wins by a lower-than-expected margin, it is a setback. When an underdog loses, but comes closer than expected, it is a victory (see Bill Clinton's 1992 loss in the New Hampshire primary, after which he declared himself to be "the comeback kid" before riding a wave of momentum all the way to the White House).
- MEDIA FAVORS UNDERDOGS/MEDIA TARGETS FRONTRUNNERS. Media, like the rest of us, tends to side with underdogs. But that is not the only reason why underdogs get an easier ride from the press. Another reason is that underdog insurgencies are dramatic, which makes for good TV. Also, a close race creates more drama, which translates into higher ratings and is one reason why media tends to beat down front-runners and lift up underdogs. Underdogs are also seen as less threatening because they are farther away from the reins of power than more powerful front-running candidates (see the Ross Perot/Jesse Ventura comparison later in this chapter).

HOW POLITICAL UNDERDOGMA WORKS

In the power transaction we call "voting," one of the most important questions a voter asks before pulling the lever is: "which candidate is most like me?" The truth, as we have already established, is that none of them are like you. But, since voters tend to reflexively scorn big, powerful overdogs and reflexively side with less powerful underdogs, politicians must close the perceived power gap in order to create the illusion that they are just like you.

How? One of the best ways to learn how something works is to examine those times when it does not work. Like the time the elitist millionaire John Kerry tried, and failed, to close the power gap between himself and voters in order to convince Americans that he was "just like" them in the 2004 Presidential campaign. "Empathy is everything in modern politics," observed Chris Cillizza of the *Washington Post*, "and there is no better way for a politician to show it than fluency in the language of local food...John Kerry's request for Swiss cheese rather than Cheez Whiz on his cheese steak at a stop in Philadelphia during the 2004 campaign cemented the public's view of him as an out-of-touch Brahmin."[8] Candidate John Kerry also tried (and failed) to appear "just like" Ohio sportsmen, but he was jeered when he put on a fake backwoods accent and asked a local store owner, "can I get me a hunting license here?"[9] He even tried to appear "just like" black people by saying that he would like to become America's

[8] "Me? I Vote For the Cheez Whiz," *Washington Post*, September 3, 2006

[9] "When Johnny Went A-Huntin,'" *Washington Times*, October 23, 2004

second "black president"[10] and by professing his love for hip-hop.

> "President Clinton was often known as the first black president. I wouldn't be upset if I could earn the right to be the second."
>
> —John Kerry, quoted in *Talon News*, March 9, 2004

> "I'm fascinated by rap and by hip-hop. I think there's a lot of poetry in it."
>
> —John Kerry, MTV's "Choose or Lose" forum, as reported in *Time* magazine, April 5, 2004

The problem for John Kerry and Underdogmatists is that their underdog-loving "Player-Hater" rhetoric is directly at odds with the philosophical core of hip-hop. One might even say they are as different as black and white.

KERRY (UNDERDOGMATISTS)	RAPPERS
SCAPEGOAT THE RICH	CELEBRATE THE RICH
"They [Republicans] have catered to the wealth of the richest instead of honoring the work of the rest of us." —2004 Democratic Platform	"Ohhh money, you my honey Money is my bitch Ohhh money, money, money, Yeah yeah that bitch treat me like a trick Ohhh money you my honey, she says without her I can't be rich." —Nas, "Money is my Bitch," 2004

[10] John Kerry on the American Urban Radio Network, March 1, 2004

KERRY (UNDERDOGMATISTS)	RAPPERS
AGAINST GAS-GUZZLING SUVS (SPECIFICALLY HUMMERS) "We need to repeal the outrageous one hundred thousand dollar tax break for the purchase of luxury gas-guzzlers like Hummers." —John Kerry, Environmental Policy Address, University of New Hampshire, October 20, 2003	FOR GAS-GUZZLING SUVS (SPECIFICALLY HUMMERS) "26-inch chrome spokes on the Hummer This heat gon last for the whole summer Running your bitch faster than the Road Runner." —Lloyd Banks, "On Fire," 2004
ARROGANCE IS BAD "Arrogance and pride stand in the way of common sense and integrity." —John Kerry speech, Washington D.C., September 30, 2003	ARROGANCE IS GOOD "Now I could let these dream killers kill my self-esteem Or use my arrogance as the steam to power my dreams." —Jay-Z & Kanye West, "Last Call," 2004

continued on following page . . .

continued from previous page . . .

KERRY (UNDERDOGMATISTS)	RAPPERS
AGAINST GUNS	FOR GUNS
"I would rather be the candidate of the NAACP than the NRA." —John Kerry statement, November 1, 2003	"D-R-E! A mutherfu*#er who's known for carryin' gats And kick raps that make snaps. If you see me on the solo moves best believe that I'm strapped. 44, .38 or AK 47." —Dr. Dre, "A Nigga Witta Gun," 2001
WOMEN AND MEN ARE EQUAL	WOMEN AND MEN ARE UNEQUAL
"He [John Kerry] made women's issues part of the debate and established his commitment to the fight for equality and justice." —National Organization for Women (NOW) press release, October 14, 2004	"Back in the day, I use to like bitches But I'll tell you now days, Bitches ain't $hit." —Nate Dogg, Lil Jon, "Bitches Ain't $hit," 2004

CNN's Candy Crowley summed up John Kerry's inability to bridge the power gap with voters when she recalled a breakfast she had with Kerry at the Holiday Inn in Dubuque, Iowa.

> "'I'd like to start out with some green tea,' Kerry told the waitress, who stared at him for a moment before responding, 'We have Lipton's.'
>
> 'There were many green tea instances [Crowley said]. There's a very large disconnect between the Washington politicians and most of America and how they live. Bush was able to bridge that gap, and Kerry was not.'"
>
> —*Palm Beach Post*, November 16, 2004

While some politicians fail spectacularly at playing the underdog card, other politicians succeed in convincing you that they are "just like" you. Here are some of the ways they do it:

- INTRODUCING YOU TO THEIR FAMILIES. According to the U.S. Census Bureau, 78% of Americans live in "families"[11] of some sort, which gives politicians a 78% chance of forging some kind of connection with you by demonstrating themselves to be "family people."
- SURROUNDING THEMSELVES WITH PEOPLE WHO LOOK LIKE YOU. Campaign event coordinators work hard to ensure that the faces in their candidate's "human backdrops" look like you. Occasionally, this tactic backfires, as it did for the Obama campaign when Obama event planners were caught tweaking the racial mix of their human backdrop

[11] Family Status and Household Relationship of People 15 Years and Over, by Marital Status, Age, and Sex: 2009

and were overheard saying, "get me more white people, we need more white people."[12]

- DRESSING LIKE YOU. Politicians wear blue jeans in rural areas, hardhats in factories, and roll up their sleeves, just like you, when it's time to "get the job done."
- TALKING LIKE YOU. Political operatives spend millions of dollars on focus groups to test the resonance of language and slogans on people who are "just like you." Sometimes, they even pluck their winning language and slogans from the mouths of everyday people in these focus groups. This, too, can backfire horribly, like the time Hillary Clinton affected a cringe-worthy southern drawl while speaking at a church in Selma, Alabama (see the video at www.under-dogma.com).

Scott Brown, the underdog Senatorial candidate from Massachusetts, shocked the world in January 2010 by snatching "Ted Kennedy's seat" away from the big, powerful, "machine" Democrat front-runner Martha Coakley. Brown was so much of an underdog that few people across the country knew that the Republicans even had a dog in the race, let alone a chance of winning, until a few weeks before election day. Scott Brown did not run a traditional underdog campaign, but his ads did follow the four Political Underdogma "just like you" techniques described in this chapter. He introduced voters to his family, especially to his two daughters—one of whom was an underdog contestant on *American Idol*. His TV ad "Hey Dad" featured

---

[12] *The Tartan*, April 7, 2008

Scott Brown driving his "just like you" GM pickup truck (with 200,000 miles on it) to meet voters (who probably drove nicer vehicles). He surrounded himself with people who were "just like you" in his "People's Rally" and in his commercials. He dressed just like you in most of his ads, wearing sweaters, well-worn jackets—even a silly "dad-style" Christmas tie in his Christmas video (which also featured his two dogs—another good "just like you" move, considering that "74 percent of people like dogs a lot"[13]). And Scott Brown certainly talked like you, right up until the end of his campaign and in his final TV spot, which featured the candidate talking *like* everyday people *to* everyday people:

> *"We're right here in the middle of Southie [South Boston], meeting and greeting."*
>
> *"Go get 'em."*
>
> *"Tell 'em I said 'hi,' huh?"*
>
> *"Thank you very much—and the dogs, too!"*

The political underdog insurgency of Scott Brown was so successful that, when he passed the once-powerful overdog candidate Martha Coakley in the polls, Coakley fought back the only way she knew how: she played the underdog card. Poorly and obviously.

> "Coakley casts herself as underdog, 'Rocky' theme and all: State Attorney General Martha Coakley embraced the ultimate underdog's theme song in

[13] "Do Americans Like Dogs or Cats Best? No Contest: Dogs Win, Cats are Most Disliked," Associated Press, January 7, 2010

> the final hours of her campaign: 'Gonna Fly Now,' the recurring soundtrack from the 'Rocky' movies."
> —*Washington Post*, January 18, 2010

The ultimate American political underdog was, of course, Bill Clinton, who played the underdog card perfectly. The "Man from Hope" talked more about his humble beginnings than about his education at Georgetown, Oxford, and Yale. He even turned a New Hampshire primary loss into an Underdogmatist victory that led him all the way to the White House by rebranding his loss to Paul Tsongas as an underdog victory and calling himself the "comeback kid." And when scandal broke (and broke, and broke), Clinton revived the underdog image to successfully weather the storms, painting himself as besieged on all sides by powerful adversaries (or, as his wife phrased it, a "vast right-wing conspiracy"). Bill Clinton's skills in this area were unparalleled, and he made two unique contributions to the politician's "just like you" arsenal:

> *"I feel your pain."*
>
> *"I stumble and fall, just like you, and then I apologize."*

POLITICAL UNDERDOG CAMPAIGNS—A COMPARISON

When I first met Governor Jesse Ventura in 2001, what struck me most was not that we were both in politics, nor that we had both met with the Dalai Lama (Ventura used his time with the Dalai Lama to ask him if he had ever seen *Caddyshack*). What I remember most was his answer to a question about Minnesota entrepreneurs. Governor Ventura chose to single out for praise Jimmy Jam and Terry Lewis (Minneapolis dance music producers for Janet Jackson, Michael Jackson, Prince, Mary J. Blige, and others). As a former dance music producer myself, I was the only person in the room who knew what the heck Jesse was talking about. The Governor was oblivious to the gap that existed between himself and the handful of business leaders in the room. This former Navy SEAL/flamboyant wrestler turned governor was the direct opposite of John Kerry. Instead of being above his audience, he was below them. A real-life underdog.

A few years earlier, in 1998, Jesse Ventura had surprised political pundits when he got elected as Minnesota's thirty-eighth governor. Six years before that, in 1992, Ross Perot went from outsider businessman to outright leader in a three-way race for the U.S. Presidency—a mere six months before the election. And yet only one of these political underdogs won—which makes their campaigns fertile grounds for studying Political Underdogma.

In the week before Jesse Ventura's surprise gubernatorial victory in November 1998, two separate polls showed Ventura languishing in third place behind his Democratic and Republican rivals. Ross Perot followed an opposite trajectory, achieving front-runner status even before he declared his candidacy, only to falter and come in third behind Democrat Bill Clinton and former President George H.W. Bush.

The Ventura and Perot campaigns are microcosms of what can happen when political underdogs become overdogs.

In June of 1992, less than six months before the Presidential election, Ross Perot led the polls with 39% of public support, a full eight points ahead of then-sitting President George Bush and fourteen points ahead of the Democratic challenger, Governor Bill Clinton. The underdog had chewed through his collar and was making a legitimate run for the Presidency. It was then that everything began to change for Ross Perot.

To see a growing library of political ads including Scott Brown's "JFK" ad, Jesse Ventura's "Action Figure" ad, Hillary Clinton's "Pinochle" ad and others, visit Underdogma's POLITICAL THREAD at www.under-dogma.com.

Republican and Democratic operatives unleashed wave after wave of negative attacks aimed squarely at upstart Perot. In today's world, these attacks seem tame. The ad that reminded voters that Perot once called African-Americans "you people" in a speech to the NAACP is a far cry from the multimillion-dollar ad campaign against George W. Bush in 2000, in which Bush was "tied directly to a vicious racist lynching."[14]

> "Over black and white video of a pickup truck dragging a chain, the daughter of Texas dragging death victim James Byrd declares, 'So when Gov. George W. Bush refused to sign hate crimes legislation, it was like my father was killed all over again.'"
>
> —Media Research Center, October 31, 2000

[14] "Liberal Dirty Tricks Ignored," Media Research Center, October 31, 2000

Sure, Ross Perot was an unstable candidate who had bad policies, lacked discipline, and was quick to anger. But so was his Reform Party brother, Jesse Ventura. And yet Jesse won. Why did voters abandon Perot? Part of the reason was simple: he broke the Underdogmatist covenant with his supporters. Ross Perot stopped being the underdog. Part of the reason why Jesse Ventura won is that he never stopped being the underdog. He never led in the 1998 Minnesota gubernatorial polls, which meant that those who rooted for the underdog had (they thought) a safe place to park their votes. As sixty-nine-year-old voter Jan Norstad explained, two weeks before the election:

> "I don't think there is a chance in hell that Jesse Ventura is going to win. I do want to show that he has support. If it was close, I would vote for [Democrat candidate Hubert H.] Humphrey."
> —*Minneapolis Star Tribune*, October 19, 1998

Letting Underdogma sway votes is one thing. But when it leads some human beings to call for the extermination of other human beings, Underdogma becomes serious and even deadly, as you will see in Part 3—Underdogma on the World Stage, starting with Chapter 11—TWO LEGS? TOO BAD!: ARE OVERDOG HUMANS A "CANCER" OF THE EARTH?

PART THREE

Underdogma on the World Stage

11

Two Legs? Too Bad! Are Overdog Humans a "Cancer" of the Earth?

> "Industrial society seems likely to be entering a period of severe stress, due in part to problems of human behavior and in part to economic and environmental problems. And a considerable proportion of the system's economic and environmental problems result from the way human beings behave."

A QUOTE FROM GREENPEACE? PETA? Al Gore? No. It is a line from the manifesto of Ted Kaczynski, also known as the Unabomber, the man who killed people with mail-bombs in defense of Mother Nature. Now, compare the mad bomber's words to those of World Wildlife Fund past president Prince Phillip, the Sierra Club's first executive director David Brower, and New York's City University professor Paul W. Taylor:

> "If I were reincarnated I would wish to be returned to the earth as a killer virus to lower human population levels."
>
> —World Wildlife Fund past president Prince Phillip, Duke of Edinburgh, Insiders Report, American Policy Center, December 1995

> "Childbearing [should be] a punishable crime against society."
>
> —The Sierra Club's first executive director, the late David Brower, quoted in Dixy Lee Ray's *Trashing the Planet*, 1992

> "It seems quite clear that in the contemporary world the extinction of the species Homo sapiens would be beneficial to the Earth's Community of Life as a whole."
>
> —Professor Paul W. Taylor, *Respect For Nature*, 1986

In their zeal to protect Mother Nature from the destructive overdog known as man (the most powerful creature on Earth), some eco-Underdogmatists have gone beyond being pro-nature (support for the underdog) to become antihuman (scorn for the powerful overdog). Does that mean a handful of mad bombers, princes, and professors will be the end of us? Of course not. But words and ideas mean things. And, as Malcolm Gladwell noted in *The Tipping Point*, ideas can spread like epidemics. Today, the Underdogmatist belief that powerful overdog humans are a "cancer" appears to be spreading like…cancer.

> "A cancer is an uncontrolled multiplication of cells; the population explosion is an uncontrolled multiplication of people…We must shift our efforts from

> treatment of the symptoms to the cutting out of the cancer...We must have population control...by compulsion if voluntary methods fail."
>
> —Paul Ehrlich, *The Population Bomb*, 1968

> "Humans have grown like a cancer. We're the biggest blight on the face of the earth."
>
> —PETA founder Ingrid Newkirk, as quoted in "PETA Still Is Horsing Around," *The Washington Times*, May 7, 2008

> "Human beings are a disease, a cancer of this planet. You are a plague."
>
> —Agent Smith, *The Matrix*, 1999

The Merriam-Webster dictionary defines cancer as "something evil or malignant that spreads destructively." Dr. William Hern said "the human species is an example of a *malignant ecotumor*, an uncontrolled proliferation of a single species that threatens the existence of other species in their habitats."[1] Are these antihumanist/Underdogmatists right? Are human beings a cancer of the Earth?

Thomas Malthus' seminal 1798 antihuman tome, *An Essay on the Principle of Population*, gave us the "Malthusian Catastrophe," which is "a strong constantly operating check on population" caused by an "inequality of the two powers of population and of production in the earth." (Note the recurring Underdogmatist theme of power inequality.) Malthus was not, however, the first to fret overpopulation. In AD 210 (when the world's population was

[1] "Why Are There So Many of Us?" Warren M. Hern, University of Colorado, April 5, 1989

a mere 190 million—roughly 2.8% of the world's population today), Roman philosopher Tertullian wrote:

> "What most frequently meets our view (and occasions complaint) is our teeming population. Our numbers are burdensome to the world, which can hardly support us...In very deed, pestilence, and famine, and wars, and earthquakes have to be regarded as a remedy for nations, as the means of pruning the luxuriance of the human race."

Paul Ehrlich's best-selling 1968 book, *The Population Bomb*, brought antihumanism into the mainstream. In it, Ehrlich stated "there are only two kinds of solutions to the population problem. One is a 'birth rate solution,' in which we find ways to lower the birth rate. The other is a 'death rate solution,' in which ways to raise the death rate—war, famine, pestilence—find us." As reported in July 2009, Paul Ehrlich co-wrote another book, *Ecoscience*, with "President Obama's 'science czar,' John Holdren [who] once floated the idea of forced abortions, 'compulsory sterilization,' and the creation of a 'Planetary Regime' that would oversee human population levels and control all natural resources as a means of protecting the planet."[2]

History has not been kind to the dire warnings and antihumanist/Underdogmatist plans of those who sought to correct the power imbalance between man and Mother Nature by eliminating man. As *Slate* editor Daniel Engber noted, "Ehrlich and his fellow Malthusians were

---

[2] Joseph Abrams, FOXNews.com, July 21, 2009

discredited,"[3] largely because reality failed to match up with their doomsday predictions of famines, plagues, and water shortages. As Paul Ehrlich himself admitted in 2009, "their failure to occur is often cited as a failure of prediction. In honesty, the scenarios were way off, especially in their timing (we underestimated the resilience of the world system)."[4]

Not only did the "population bomb" fail to explode, it may not have been a bomb to begin with. As someone who has driven across America several times and traveled to forty-three states and the District of Columbia, I can share with you an inconvenient truth that seems to have escaped these antihumanist/Underdogmatists: in America, one of the most developed countries in the world, trees and open space vastly—*vastly*—outnumber human beings. Anyone who thinks the world is suffering from overpopulation has obviously never been to Wyoming, Utah, New Mexico, Colorado—or even traveled half an hour west of New York City, where tree-covered rolling hills and open space dominate the landscape as far as the eye can see. Some of the most beautiful parts of America are so sparsely populated that hundreds of highway miles can pass before encountering a single A.M. radio station. Or a city. Or a restroom. And those are the places where interstate highways have been built. Not exactly "off the beaten path."

Contrary to the preaching of antihumanist/Underdogmatists, the world has more than enough space to

[3] "Global Swarming: Is It Time for Americans to Start Cutting Our Baby Emissions?" Daniel Engber, *Slate*, September 10, 2007

[4] "The Population Bomb Revisited," *The Electronic Journal of Sustainable Development* (2009), Paul R. Ehrlich and Anne H. Ehrlich

comfortably fit all of its most powerful indigenous species (human beings). As Professor David Osterfeld noted, "if the entire population of the world were placed in the state of Alaska, *every individual* would receive nearly 3,500 square feet of space, or about one-half the size of the average American *family* homestead with front and back yards."[5]

And yet the Underdogmatist myth of overpopulation persists, perhaps because so many of us experience overpopulation firsthand on a daily basis. Seventy-seven percent of Americans choose to live in cities or in suburbs,[6] shoulder-to-shoulder with other people. Is that an unnatural way for human beings to live? I had a conversation about this with the Honorable John Snobelen, past Minister of Education and Minister of Natural Resources in Ontario, Canada. By not demonizing humans, John managed to bring together people from the environmental community and the forestry community—even hunters and native tribes—to protect 9,200 square miles of natural land (which is almost the same size as Vermont or Massachusetts). John and I were talking about rowhouses, the type of semidetached homes favored by many suburban dwellers. I wondered aloud why people would want to live so close together, suggesting that maybe it was due to a lack of space. John Snobelen replied, "explain Venice then. Was Italy overcrowded in the Middle Ages? Was

---

[5] "Overpopulation: The Perennial Myth," David Osterfeld, September 1993

[6] Population Division of the United Nations Secretariat, World Urbanization Prospects: The 2001 Revision, Data Tables and Highlights (ESA/P/WP.173, 20 March 2002) via NationMaster

the world overcrowded? Maybe folks just like to live near other folks."

Human beings are social creatures. It makes sense, then, that folks would choose to live near "other folks." What makes less sense is that some human beings (programmed, as we are, with the biological instinct to survive, thrive, and reproduce) believe that we—the most powerful creatures on Earth (overdogs)—should *not* survive, thrive, or reproduce.

> "Oh, if we all just disappeared. According to *The World Without Us*, Alan Weisman's strangely comforting vision of human annihilation, the Earth would be a lot better off...Let's not wait for climate change, he says. Let's start depopulating right now."
>
> —"Global Swarming: Is It Time for Americans to Start Cutting Our Baby Emissions?" David Engber, *Slate*, September 10, 2007

> "We have become a plague upon ourselves and upon the earth...some of us can only hope for the right virus to come along."
>
> —David Graber, research biologist at the National Park Service, 1996

> "Save the planet, kill yourself."
>
> —Church of Euthanasia slogan

Antihumanist/Underdogmatists make an important distinction: not all life should disappear from Planet Earth, just the lives of its most powerful creatures—human beings. Plants and animals—even rats that leave urine trails in their wake—can stay. Human beings—even the ones who bring their own recycled shopping bags to grocery stores—must go. Why? Because, according to their school of thought, (underdog) nature has "intrinsic value" and (overdog) mankind does not.

> "We are not interested in the utility of a particular species, or freeflowing river, or ecosystem, to mankind. They have intrinsic value—more value, to me—than another human body or a billion of them. Human happiness, and certainly human fecundity, are not as important as a wild and healthy planet. I know social scientists who remind me that people are part of nature, but it isn't true. Somewhere along the line—at about a billion [sic] years ago and maybe half that—we quit the contract and became a cancer."
>
> —David Graber, research biologist at the National Park Service, 1996

Note the difference between "intrinsic" and "instrumental" value. Cows have "instrumental" value to humans because cows produce milk, meat, and leather for our use. In other words, they generate real, tangible items of value, which we humans can either use ourselves or trade for other items of value (money, a handful of beans, etc.). Conversely, to say that a cow has "intrinsic" value is to say that the cow has value simply because it is, because it exists, regardless of what it can do for us.

It is fairly easy to look at a cow and recognize its intrinsic value. A cow has pretty eyes, is covered in soft fur, is relatively peaceful, and its babies are remarkably cute. Same goes for the endangered Giant Panda. These bears are so cute that the World Wildlife Fund (WWF) has used the panda as its symbol since 1961. But, when it comes to quantifying the panda's value, the World Wildlife Fund starts to stutter. On its Giant Panda profile page, under the question "Why is this species important?" the best answer the WWF can muster is "The survival of the panda and the protection of its habitat will ensure that people living in the region continue to reap ecosystem benefits for many generations." They do not explain what they mean by "ecosystem benefits." But they do sell cute stuffed panda bears in their gift center.

What about the endangered species that are not as cute as pandas? Bradley's Spleenwort, for instance—an endangered fern native to the eastern United States—is decidedly uncute. There are no Bradley's Spleenwort plush toys on the World Wildlife Fund page. In fact, there is hardly anything to recommend this small, leafy, green nondescript plant at all. If all the Bradley's Spleenworts disappeared forever, few of us would notice, and even fewer of us would care. Antihuman Underdogmatists believe that (underdog) nature and all of its Spleenworts have intrinsic value, and that (overdog) mankind does not. The Illinois Mud Turtle has intrinsic value. Cate Blanchett does not. The Small Bladderwort has intrinsic value. Shakespeare does not. The Hairy Umbrella-wort has intrinsic value. Michael Jordan does not. Then these antihumanist Underdogmatists take one giant leap further and declare that (underdog) nature is intrinsically valuable and worthy of protection and that (overdog) mankind is a cancer that needs to be wiped from the face of the Earth. And this suicidal Underdogmatist belief is gaining more and more mainstream followers each day.

> "[*The World Without Us*] seems like a notion from the fringe, but Weisman's book has become a main-

> stream best seller. Could population control be the next big thing in green culture?"
>
> —"Global Swarming: Is It Time for Americans to Start Cutting Our Baby Emissions?" Daniel Engber, *Slate*, September 10, 2007

This is more than just rhetoric. It is a fundamental shift in how we view our place in the world. Antihuman Underdogmatists fail to recognize that the belief that we do not belong here, that (overdog) humanity is somehow a cancer that needs to be wiped out in order to save (underdog) nature—*goes against nature itself* by going against our biological instinct to survive. Human beings are an indigenous species on this planet. We belong here. And just because we are the most powerful life form to ever walk the face of the Earth does not mean that we need to be knocked down a few notches (at best) or exterminated (at worst) by Underdogmatists.

There is more than enough room in this world for plants, animals, *and* human beings—even those human beings who call for sensible solutions to real environmental concerns, like Bjørn Lomborg, director of the Copenhagen Consensus Center and best-selling author of *Cool It* and *The Skeptical Environmentalist*. I interviewed Mr. Lomborg for *Underdogma* and asked him about the antihumanist movement. Here is what he had to say:

> "I don't subscribe to that view myself. I think that mankind is worth preserving, I think people are worth preserving."
>
> "If you actually believe that people are a blight on the planet, it would seem logical in some way

that you would also make sure that you don't live yourself."

—Bjørn Lomborg, August 15, 2008

One group of people, considered by many to be a "blight on the planet" and long overdue for some Underdogmatist "population control," are the big rich Wall Street fat cats who brought the Global Financial Crisis crashing down onto the backs of poor, innocent, powerless underdogs. At least that is the version of events that we were told. But what if the Global Financial Crisis and its origins were far different than Underdogmatists would have us believe? Find out in the next chapter: Chapter 12—UNDERDOGMA AND THE GLOBAL FINANCIAL CRISIS.

12

Underdogma and the Global Financial Crisis

"You never want a serious crisis to go to waste—and what I mean by that is an opportunity to do things that you didn't think you could do before."
—White House Chief of Staff Rahm Emanuel, "The Wall Street Journal CEO Council 2008, Shaping a New Agenda," *The Wall Street Journal*, November 19, 2008

"Hillary Clinton: 'Never waste a good crisis.'"
—*Guardian UK*, March 6, 2009

"Obama: Crisis is time of 'great opportunity.'"
—Associated Press, March 7, 2009

THE PRESIDENT OF THE UNITED STATES, his Chief of Staff, and his Secretary of State have all said out loud what most politicians only say behind closed doors: that a crisis is a time of great opportunity for politicians to do things they otherwise could not. As the Associated Press reported, "Barack Obama is embracing the worst economic conditions in a generation as an opportunity to advance an audacious agenda that, if successful, could reshape the country for decades to come."[1] As President Obama himself admitted, the Global Financial Crisis provided him the opportunity to set the future direction of the country and of the world: "I think that we are at an extraordinary moment that is full of peril but full of possibility and I think that's the time you want to be president. I think there's a sense that right now we are having to make some very big decisions that will help determine the direction of this country—and in ways large and small the direction of the world—for the next generation."[2]

This chapter will show how Underdogma helped create the Global Financial Crisis of the early twenty-first century, and how Underdogmatists have tried to use the Global Financial Crisis to reorder the balance of power in America.

Although the Global Financial Crisis posed a "great opportunity" for Underdogmatists to bring about generational change, it also posed a problem: the Global Financial Crisis did not fit cleanly into the Underdogma narrative. Because the bad guy, in this crisis, was also the little guy—and those who stood up for the little guy.

Upon reading the above sentence, you may have felt a swelling of indignation in your belly. Not to worry. That was just residual Underdogma. Hopefully, by now, your remaining Underdogma can be cleared up by the facts.

---

[1] Liz Sidoti, Associated Press Writer, March 2, 2009

[2] President Barack Obama, *PBS Newshour*, February 27, 2009

Here, for your benefit, are the facts about the Global Financial Crisis—before Underdogmatists worked overtime to rebrand it into the Underdogmatist narrative of the "big, rich fat cats stomping on the little guy."

The first time that many people heard about the Global Financial Crisis was during the so-called "mortgage meltdown" of 2007–2008. What was the mortgage meltdown? In short, it was a lot of borrowers failing to pay their mortgages at approximately the same time, which set off wave after wave of foreclosures. But how could foreclosed homes in Arizona or California possibly affect the globe? This was, after all, the Global Financial Crisis.

The answer is: these mortgages were not your everyday mortgages. They were backed implicitly (and sometimes explicitly) by the U.S. government through institutions like the Federal National Mortgage Association ("Fannie Mae") and the Federal Home Loan Mortgage Corporation ("Freddie Mac"), which, at the time the Crisis began, held paper on 58% of U.S. mortgages. What does it mean that these mortgages were "backed" by the U.S. government? It means that, if borrowers failed to make their payments, their mortgages were "backed by an implicit guarantee of repayment by the federal government in case of default—to finance their congressional mandate of promoting home ownership."[3] Why would the government back mortgages, or feel that it had a "congressional mandate" to promote home ownership?

This is where Underdogma comes in.

---

[3] *The Sellout: How Three Decades of Wall Street Greed and Government Mismanagement Destroyed the Global Financial System,* Charles Gasparino, 2009

As we saw in Chapter 10—POLITICAL UNDERDOGMA—politicians love to be seen standing up for the little guy. Combine that with the powerful narrative of the "American dream" of home ownership, and you can see why "politicians from both parties have spent decades trying to subsidize the 'American dream' of home ownership."[4] Politicians of all stripes, under the guise of standing up for the little guy (and against the big, greedy banks), "transformed home ownership [from] something that must be earned into something close to a civil right."[5] A "right" that was backstopped by the U.S. government.

In backstopping home loans, the government did something remarkable. It shifted the risk of mortgages away from borrowers, away from lenders—even away from Fannie Mae and Freddie Mac—and placed the risk squarely on the shoulders of the U.S. government, which itself was backstopped by your taxpayer dollars. In addition, the federal government's Community Reinvestment Act (passed in 1977) "required banks with assets of more than $250 million to satisfy stringent tests gauging their banking services to low- and moderate-income residents."[6] In other words, they were forced, by law, to lend money to the little guy. But, as the *New York Times* reported, "the law lay mostly fallow until 1989"[7] and only took flight when the "Clinton administration's top housing official in the mid-1990s [Henry] Cisneros loosened mortgage restrictions so

---

[4] *LA Times*, October 13, 2008

[5] "Three Decades of Subsidized Risk," *The Wall Street Journal*, November 5, 2009

[6] "U.S. Set to Alter Rules for Banks Lending to Poor," *New York Times*, October 20, 2004

[7] "For Banks, A Big Nudge To Do More," *New York Times*, July 5, 1998

first-time buyers could qualify for loans they could never get before."[8] The Clinton administration's move to empower those in poorer communities "strengthened the hand of community groups [like ACORN] and contributed to big increases in banks' low-income lending."[9] From 1977 to 1991, lending commitments under the Community Reinvestment Act (CRA) totaled $8.8 billion. Between 1992 and 1998, banks—under pressure from newly empowered community organizers like ACORN, and under the threat of punishment from the federal government—made "lending commitments under the law [totaling] $875 billion [an increase of 9843%]."[10] As of December 2009, "CRA commitments currently exceed $6 trillion,"[11] which is nine times more money than the entire budget for the U.S. military.

> "'C.R.A. has become a volume-oriented game, with up being good and down being bad,' said Ms. Bessant of Nationsbank [in 1998]. 'I worry about crazy pricing and crazy credit as everybody tries to generate more loans in order to get a better [government] rating.'"
>
> —"For Banks, A Big Nudge To Do More," *New York Times*, July 5, 1998

By artificially removing risk from the system and by legislatively mandating that banks make risky loans to the little guy, the government empowered scores of

---

[8] "Building Flawed American Dreams," *New York Times*, October 19, 2008
[9] "For Banks, A Big Nudge To Do More," *New York Times*, July 5, 1998
[10] Ibid
[11] "Cash For Clunkers: Home Edition," *Forbes*, December 28, 2009

hopeful underdog homeowners, who "failed to understand that they couldn't afford a $500,000 home on a $50,000 salary,"[12] to borrow irresponsibly and without immediate consequences—even when they had "poor credit, small or no down payments, and often no proof of income."[13] Which, in turn, allowed "duplicitous mortgage brokers [to make] pots of money selling mortgages to people without the means to repay them."[14] Which, in turn, allowed investors to bet on "mortgages-backed securities and the business model of embracing risk,"[15] because virtually all risk had been assumed by government, which made these mortgages some of the least risky and most stable investments around.

Stability is a rare and treasured asset in the investment world. And investment firms quickly recognized that mortgages, backed by the U.S. government, could also be used to back other things. Like investments. And so began the "mortgage-backed securities" craze. Mortgage-backed securities are "essentially a pool of mortgages in which the investor is paid an interest rate that flows from the mortgage payments of home owners."[16] As long as homeowners kept

---

[12] *The Sellout: How Three Decades of Wall Street Greed and Government Mismanagement Destroyed the Global Financial System*, Charles Gasparino, 2009

[13] "Report Finds U.S. Mortgage Problems Increasing," Carolyn Said, *San Francisco Chronicle*, April 3, 2009

[14] *The Sellout: How Three Decades of Wall Street Greed and Government Mismanagement Destroyed the Global Financial System*, Charles Gasparino, 2009

[15] *The Business Insider*, Charles Gasparino, November 3, 2009

[16] *The Sellout: How Three Decades of Wall Street Greed and Government Mismanagement Destroyed the Global Financial System*, Charles Gasparino, 2009

paying their mortgages, investors in mortgage-backed securities would keep collecting their interest. What could possibly go wrong? The only thing that could topple a house of cards like that would be some unimaginable, far-off catastrophe in which millions of people would all default on their mortgages at approximately the same time and drag Fannie Mae and Freddie Mac down with them. You know, like the Congressional Budget Office warned could happen back in 2003.

> "The director of the Congressional Budget Office (CBO) said the nation's financial system has outgrown the need for government sponsored mortgage financiers. Continued government sponsorship of Fannie and Freddie poses the risk that taxpayers could be stuck with the bill in the unlikely event that either company defaulted on its debts."
>
> —"Freddie, Fannie Escape Action on Hill—for Now," *Washington Post*, November 17, 2003

Politicians brushed off the warnings, the government kept backstopping mortgages, and the securities that were backed by those mortgages—along with all their spin-offs and derivatives—remained stable. For a while.

What the government created was an artificially stable base upon which all kinds of other investments were built. Think of it as building additional floors on a house of cards; as long as the foundation remains steady and strong (and what could be steadier and stronger than the U.S. Treasury?), everything piled on top will be secure. This went on for years, piling thousands of investments—and investment firms, and banks, and investment vehicles—onto a seemingly strong foundation.

With of all its new add-ons and extensions, however, this house of cards began to feel the strain. As it turns out, way down in the foundation, many of the original mortgages were "adjustable rate" mortgages. What does that mean? Aside from being the first word in the term "adjustable rate," "adjustable" means "changeable." Which means those mortgage rates were subject to change.

Borrowers who planned ahead for this imminent and foreseeable change had no problem. In fact, at the time of this writing, more than 93% of American homeowners were managing to pay their mortgages on time, even in a steep recession. For those who failed to plan ahead, however, when the "adjustable" part of their "adjustable rate mortgage" adjusted, they had a problem. Their monthly payments went up, they suddenly found that they had bought more house than they could afford, and many of them defaulted. Rinse and repeat, and soon this house of cards found itself buckling under the weight of foreclosure. Which suddenly made all of those mortgage-backed securities, which were piled on top, less secure.

To recap: a worldwide financial house of cards was built on a foundation of mortgages that were backed by Fannie and Freddie who were, in turn, backed by the U.S. government—a government that legislatively mandated risky mortgages. When adjustable mortgage interest rates went up, many borrowers defaulted, which weakened the foundation of this financial house of cards, causing many of the upper floors to collapse. So the question is: who is to blame?

Here is where Underdogma kicks into high gear.

Logic would suggest that those down in the foundation, who failed to pay their mortgages and who set off this chain reaction, are to blame. After all, if they had just paid their bills, none of this—I repeat *none of this*—would have happened. Next in line for blame would be the United States government, since "almost two-thirds of all bad mortgages in our financial system were bought by government agencies or required by government regulations,"[17] namely the government's Community Reinvestment Act, which "pressed banks to make loans to unqualified borrowers."[18] As economist Thomas Sowell wrote in *The Housing Boom and Bust*, "lax lending standards used to meet 'affordable housing' quotas were the key to the American mortgage crisis." If "champion of the underdog" politicians and governments had simply stayed out of the mortgage business and had not artificially removed risk from the system, opportunists—from borrowers to bankers to subprime lenders to Wall Street investors—would not have taken advantage of the system the way they did, because there would have been consequences to their actions. "Did government policy make the rise of the subprime lenders possible?" asked the *New York Times*' Joe Nocera. "You betcha. The point is: the financial crisis might well have been avoided if we as a culture hadn't invested so much political and psychological capital in the idea of owning a home. After all, the subprime mortgage business's supposed raison d'être was making homeownership possible

[17] *The Wall Street Journal*, Peter J Wallison, October 15, 2009
[18] "Cash For Clunkers: Home Edition," *Forbes*, December 28, 2009

for people who lacked the means—or the credit scores—to get a traditional mortgage."[19]

So, why were deadbeat mortgage defaulters being painted as helpless underdogs who were forced by predatory lenders to take bags of cash against their will and to live in big, beautiful homes that were beyond their means? And why were the Underdogmatist politicians who helped create this crisis allowed to whistle past public outrage and paint themselves as champions of the underdogs whose eviction notices they practically signed?

Because Underdogma, not logic, was at work.

Rather than blame the deadbeat borrowers (underdogs) who took out loans they could not pay back, or Underdogmatist politicians who stood up for the little guy and mandated that such risky loans be made, Underdogmatists blamed the big, rich, fat-cat lenders (overdogs) for doing what politicians ordered them to do: lend money to poor, hapless underdogs.

> "Stop blaming the working poor for lenders' greed."
>
> —MiamiHerald.com, February 27, 2009

> "Today President Obama talked about predatory lending as a root cause of the country's financial

[19] "Wake-Up Time for a Dream," Joe Nocera, *New York Times*, June 7, 2010

> mess: 'Banks and lenders must be held accountable.'"
>
> —CNN, February 18, 2009

How can it be "greedy" and "predatory" to lend money to people who do not pay it back? Such is the logic-twisting power of Underdogma. Could such a bizarre line of argument actually gain traction? By a factor of more than two to one, the answer is "yes."

> "By 62–25 percent, voters blame lenders more than borrowers for the mortgage crisis."
>
> —Quinnipiac University national poll, March 4, 2009

Some Underdogmatists claim that "American-style capitalism" is to blame for the Global Financial Crisis. That narrative has proven to be such a populist winner that an April 2009 Rasmussen poll found "only 53% of American adults believe capitalism is better than socialism,"[20] a BBC poll found "only 11% of those questioned across 27 countries said that it [capitalism] was working well,"[21] and the U.S. Chamber of Commerce was forced to take the unusual step of buying television ads "to defend America's free enterprise values"[22] in a country that was built on free enterprise. The problem with this "blame capitalism" narrative, as with many Underdogmatist threads, is that it bears little relation to the facts. Here is what the complete arc of the Global Financial

---

[20] Rasmussen Reports, April 9, 2009

[21] "Free Market Flawed, Says Survey," BBC, November 9, 2009

[22] "Chamber of Commerce All That's Standing Between Us and Communism," Salon.com, June 10, 2009

Crisis would have looked like if free market capitalism was in effect, in a parable I like to call:

"Why Johnny Can't Borrow"

One day, Johnny woke up and decided to buy a house.

But Johnny did not have enough money to buy a house.

So he went to someone who did have enough money: Mr. Capitalist.

"Mr. Capitalist," asked Johnny, "could you please loan me the money to buy a house?"

"Do you have good credit?" asked Mr. Capitalist. "A down payment, or proof of income?"

"No," replied Johnny.

THE END

If free market capitalism was in effect, lenders would not lend money to people who could not pay it back. End of story. And end of the Global Financial Crisis. But free market capitalism was not in effect. At the heart of capitalism is risk. Risk of failure is what spurs capitalists to make better products, to streamline operations, to work harder, to do well, to satisfy their customers—and to not make stupid loans. Without risk of failure, there is no motive to do well because, without risk of failure, there are no consequences for bad behavior. As CNBC host Larry Kudlow said in his interview for *Underdogma*: "if you knew you could fail and go out of business, I think you have a much better discipline. When you take the failure out, what you're left with is private profit and taxpayer risk. That is the essence of what is ***not*** free market capitalism."[23] When Underdogmatists in the government legislated

[23] Larry Kudlow, interview for *Underdogma*, February 11, 2010

that banks make risky loans, and when they artificially removed the consequences of bad behavior by backstopping loans on behalf of little-guy borrowers, people behaved badly: borrowers, lenders, investors—all of them. When the "checks and balances" of risk and consequences were removed from the system, the system stopped being free market capitalism and became a playground for those who were expert at *gaming* the government-run, government-regulated, noncapitalist system.

> "This crisis was caused by a lack of capitalism, and the government just piled on by bailing out banks that should have been allowed to die."
> —John Tamny, *The John Batchelor Show*, December 13, 2009

The government tried to solve the problem with more government regulation, which is like the captain of the Titanic trying to solve his iceberg problem with more acceleration. These problems "came *not* from a lack of government regulation and oversight," writes Thomas Sowell, "but precisely as a *result* of government regulation and oversight, directed toward the politically popular goal of more 'home ownership' through 'affordable housing,' especially for low-income home buyers. These lax lending standards were the foundation for a house of cards that was ready to collapse with a relatively small nudge."[24]

As psychologist Abraham Maslow observed, "it is tempting, if the only tool you have is a hammer, to treat everything as if it were a nail."[25] Rather than learn their

[24] *The Housing Boom and Bust*, Thomas Sowell

[25] *The Psychology of Science: A Reconnaissance*, Abraham H. Maslow

lessons, the very same government regulators who triggered this crisis chose to use their hammers to build yet *another* flimsy house of cards on the same foundation of Underdogma.

> "This morning House Financial Services Committee chairman Rep. Barney Frank held a hearing on H.R. 1479, the 'Community Reinvestment Modernization Act of 2009.' The bill's purpose is **'to close the wealth gap in the United States' by increasing 'home ownership and small business ownership for low- and moderate-income borrowers** and persons of color.' It would extend CRA's strict lending requirements to non-bank institutions like credit unions, insurance companies, and mortgage lenders. It would also make CRA more explicitly race-based by requiring CRA standards to be applied to minorities, **regardless of income, going beyond earlier requirements that applied solely to low- and moderate-income areas**."
>
> —"Dems Push Expanded Community Reinvestment Act," *Washington Examiner*, September 16, 2009

The first part of this chapter showed how Underdogma helped create the Global Financial Crisis. The second part of this chapter will show how Underdogmatists used the Global Financial Crisis to reorder the balance of power in America.

> "Obama finds opportunity in crisis."
> —*Politico*, January 8, 2009

> "Obama sees the continuing financial crisis as usefully creating the psychological conditions—the sense of crisis bordering on fear-itself panic—for enacting his 'Big Bang' agenda to federalize and/or socialize health care, education and energy."
> — "The Great Non Sequitur," Charles Krauthammer, *Washington Post*, March 6, 2009

An unprecedented transfusion of power has taken place in America—draining power from the people to the state. The pump that drained your power away was the Global Financial Crisis. The opiate that kept many Americans from getting up off the gurney was Underdogma.

In the less than two years since the Global Financial Crisis began, the United States government took controlling interests in:

- "58 percent of all U.S. single-family home loans";[26]
- The world's biggest bank (CITI);
- The world's biggest insurance company (AIG); and
- The former world's biggest car company (GM).

In October of 2008, the U.S. government locked the heads of America's nine biggest banks in a room and

[26] (through the government's purchase of Fannie Mae and Freddie Mac) Reuters, February 8, 2009

"Forced [them] to Blink."[27] The banks "acquiesced under pressure,"[28] and let the government "take stakes in nine of the nation's top financial institutions...a far-reaching effort that puts the government's guarantee behind the basic plumbing of financial markets."[29] All told, the U.S. government has taken stakes in 706 banks (and counting).[30]

The President of the United States, his Chief of Staff, and his Secretary of State were right: a time of crisis "is an opportunity to do things that you didn't think you could do before." The government has used the "opportunity" of this crisis to acquire *new* powers that no U.S. government has ever held—over the banks, insurance, homes, and cars of Americans. The government also used this crisis to grow its *existing* powers by transferring record amounts of money (money equals power) away from the people and to the state. Between the first rumblings of the Global Financial Crisis and February 2009, the U.S. government "spent, lent, consumed, borrowed, printed, guaranteed, assumed, or otherwise committed"[31] $14 tril-

To see an up-to-the-minute list of government takeovers and new government powers, visit Underdogma's GOVERNMENT POWER THREAD at www.under-dogma.com.

[27] "At Moment of Truth, U.S. Forced Big Bankers to Blink," The *Wall Street Journal*, October 15, 2008

[28] "U.S. to Buy Stakes in Nation's Largest Banks," The *Wall Street Journal*, October 14, 2008

[29] "Ibid

[30] ProPublica, Eye on the Bailout

[31] *The Big Picture*, Barry Ritholtz, June 18, 2009

lion[32] of your taxpayer dollars, under the guise of combating the crisis. How much money is $14 trillion? The inflation-adjusted cost of the Marshall Plan, the Louisiana Purchase, the Race to the Moon, the S&L crisis, the Korean War, the New Deal, the Iraq invasion, the Vietnam War, and NASA's entire budget since its inception—combined—is only $3.92 trillion.[33] If you add to that the entire inflation-adjusted cost of World War II ($3.6 trillion)[34] it would only add up to $7.52 trillion—which is about *half* of what the U.S. government has confiscated from taxpayers in the wake of the Global Financial Crisis. The government has also increased its Domestic Discretionary Spending by 80%[35] between 2008 and 2009 and spent its way into a $1.4 trillion budget deficit.[36] The U.S. government also used this time of crisis to remake America's education, health, energy, and trading sectors on the assumption that "the American people, jarred by a financial crisis they were routinely told was 'the worst since the Great Depression,' would race into the protective arms of Washington."[37] As of March 2010, the Obama administration has taken a controlling interest in higher education (student loan program, see chart on pages 189–191),

[32] *Bailout Nation: How Greed and Easy Money Corrupted Wall Street and Shook the World Economy*, Barry Ritholtz, 2009

[33] Ibid

[34] *The Big Picture*, Barry Ritholtz, November 25, 2008

[35] 2009 Federal Budget Backgrounder, The Heritage Foundation, March 16, 2009

[36] *BusinessWeek*, March 18, 2010

[37] *Time* magazine, December 14, 2009

America's energy sector (through EPA regulations[38]), and America's health-care system:

> "The [health care] proposal also has a populist appeal—Obama standing up to the big insurance companies."
>
> —"Obama Seeks Rate-Hike Control," *Politico*, February 21, 2010

> "'We are the party of the people again.' Those words uttered by a Democrat Party strategist the day after Barack Obama's healthcare *coup d'état*... The liberal left is delusionary—and willfully so... setting out to brainwash electorates. At the core of this liberal fantasy is a sentimentalised notion of 'progress,' of helping the underdog, of improving the world."
>
> —Gerald Warner, *Telegraph UK*, March 23rd, 2010

All told, the actions of the first half of the Obama administration mark the single largest transfer of wealth (power) away from the people and to the state in American history.

Former Vice President Al Gore wrote, "our ingrained American distrust of concentrated power [means that it is] power itself that must be constrained, checked, dispersed and carefully balanced."[39] If Americans are distrustful of concentrated power, why would Americans let

[38] "The Obama administration has long said it would attack greenhouse gas emissions with EPA regulation if Congress failed to pass a climate bill." "U.S. States Sue EPA to Stop Greenhouse Gas Rules," Reuters, March 19, 2010; "EPA Claim[ed the] Right to Cut Greenhouse Gases," *Washington Times*, December 9, 2009

[39] *The Assault on Reason*, Al Gore, 2007

politicians concentrate more and more power in Washington? Because politicians have learned to use Underdogma to co-opt and redirect this "ingrained American distrust of power." How? By picking big, powerful, third-party overdog targets, attacking them on your behalf (on behalf of the little guy), and then confiscating the big overdogs' power (in your name). Big banks, big CEOs, big oil, big pharmaceuticals, big health insurance—whichever big, powerful overdog enemy has caused you pain—the Underdogmatist politician will step in, "feel your pain," and lead the charge in your new shared battle against your new, common, and more powerful overdog enemy. President Barack Obama, the master of "community organizing, [the] old-fashioned, bare-knuckle politics for the little guy,"[40] "is now trying to strike a more populist tone to tap into anger many Americans feel about bailouts on Wall Street while Main Street is suffering…casting him as someone who will stand with the little guy."[41] Politicians, by standing with you, the "little guy," eliminate the power gap that once separated them from you, and place themselves firmly "on your side." Which empowers them to do something remarkable: it helps them take your power away.

> "Those who want to take our money and gain power over us have discovered the magic formula: Get us envious or angry at others and we will surrender, in installments, not only our money but our freedom. The most successful dictators of

[40] "What Obama's Community Organizing Experience Really Means," *Daily Kos*, July 30, 2008

[41] "Obama, With Defiant Tone, Vows to Push Agenda," *New York Times*, January 22, 2010

the 20th century—Hitler, Lenin, Stalin, Mao—all used this formula and now class warfare politicians here are doing the same."

—Thomas Sowell, *Ever Wonder Why?*, 2006

Here are a few examples of how the Obama administration **targeted** third-party "big" powerful enemies (overdogs), **attacked** those enemies on behalf of the little guy (underdogs), and used the Under-dogmatist rage they stoked to **transfer power** to the state.

TARGET	ATTACK	POWER TRANSFER
Big Health Insurance	"Speaker Pelosi prefers to demonize insurance companies as 'villains,' while President Obama rails at them for 'holding us hostage.'" —*National Review*, November 24, 2009	"President Obama's federal takeover of the U.S. health-care system... Liberals will try to blame insurers once again, but the public shouldn't be fooled. WellPoint, Aetna and the rest are from now on going to be public utilities, essentially creatures of Congress and the Health and Human Services Department." —*The Wall Street Journal*, March 21, 2010

TARGET	ATTACK	POWER TRANSFER
Big Banks	"The demonstrators in Chicago, beating drums and carrying signs, calling us [banks] 'bloodsuckers' and 'fascists,' apparently have been listening to Obama and his strident rhetoric, lumping all banks together to serve his political purpose." —Gerard M. Banmiller, president of First Colonial National Bank, November 10, 2009	The government took stakes in 706 banks (and counting).

TARGET	ATTACK	POWER TRANSFER
Big Lenders	"Today President Obama talked about predatory lending as a root cause of the country's financial mess: 'Banks and lenders must be held accountable.'" —CNN, February 18, 2009	"Almost two-thirds of all bad mortgages in our financial system were bought by government agencies or required by government regulations." —*The Wall Street Journal*, October 15, 2009

continued on following page . . .

continued from previous page . . .

TARGET	ATTACK	POWER TRANSFER
Big Insurance	"U.S. Seeks Expanded Power to Seize Firms. The Obama administration is considering asking Congress to give the Treasury secretary unprecedented powers to initiate the seizure of non-bank financial companies, such as large insurers." —*Washington Post*, March 24, 2009	"The government now owns about 80% of AIG [the world's biggest insurance company]." —*USA Today*, October 14, 2009
Big Student Lenders	"A bill that will go a long way to reform the student loan system…Ending this unwarranted subsidy for the big banks is a no-brainer… we're already seeing special interests rallying [to stop government]." —President Obama, September 21, 2009	"House Bill Shifts Student Loans to Gov't. Puts Government In Charge of Federal Student Loans, Pushes out Subsidized Private Lenders." —CBS News/AP, September 17, 2009
Big Wall Street "Fat Cats"	"Obama Versus the 'Fat-Cats.' President Obama has ratcheted up his rhetoric against Wall Street, calling them 'fat-cat[s]' and scolding them for not showing 'a lot of shame' about their behavior and outsized compensation." —CBS News, December 13, 2009	"A sweeping overhaul of Wall Street rules"[1] gave the federal government "near-total autonomy to write and enforce rules. The government would have broad new powers to seize and wind down large, failing financial firms." —*Washington Post*, June 25, 2010

TARGET	ATTACK	POWER TRANSFER
Big Oil	"Obama Looking for an 'Ass to Kick'" —ABC News, July 1, 2010 "'Kick-ass' Obama launches personal attack on BP chief Tony Hayward…a harsh personal attack on its chief executive from President Obama." —*The Times Online*, June 8, 2010	"President Obama's successful move to force BP to establish a $20 billion compensation fund that the company will have no voice in allocating… With that display of raw arm-twisting, Mr. Obama reinvigorated a debate about the renewed reach of government power, or, alternatively, the power of government overreach." —*New York Times*, June 17, 2010

TABLE FOOTNOTES
[1] "House, Senate Lawmakers Finalize Deal on Bank Bill," ABC News, June 25, 2010

> TOWN HALL QUESTIONER: "If they can do this, what can't they?"
> CONGRESSMAN PETE STARK: "The federal government, yes, can do most anything in this country."
> —Congressman Pete Stark's Town Hall Meeting, Hayward, California, July 24, 2010

There was a time in American history when a government power grab—a fraction of this size—sparked a revolution. In fact, that is precisely how American history began. The

American Revolution was a revolt against state power. America's founding documents were written specifically to limit state power. The American Constitution and the Bill of Rights are a series of checks, balances, and road-blocks designed to stop politicians from taking and exerting power over the American people.

> "In questions of power then, let no more be heard of confidence in man, but bind him down from mischief by the chains of the constitution."
> —Thomas Jefferson, Kentucky Resolutions of 1798

> "The essence of Government is power; and power, lodged as it must be in human hands, will ever be liable to abuse."
> —James Madison, December 1, 1829

The American spirit (rugged individualism, liberty, independence, self-reliance, free enterprise, revolution against state power) is a powerful societal narrative—one that transformed a wild, untamed colony into the most successful nation in world history. But the American spirit is at a practical disadvantage to Underdogma. Self-reliance is hard. Underdogma is easy and instinctive, drawing its strength from our shared human experience of being small and powerless underdogs in a world full of more powerful overdogs. Liberty, as Andrew Jackson said in 1837, requires "eternal vigilance…It behooves you, therefore, to be watchful in your States as well as in the Federal Government."[42] Underdogma does not re-

[42] Andrew Jackson, Farewell Address, March 4, 1837

quire "eternal vigilance" or watchfulness—only submission to the reflexive belief that the "big guy" must be cut down to size in the name of the little guy. And politicians who have learned how to *game* this power dynamic—Underdogma—use it to take your power away.

In exchange, Underdogmatist politicians give you the gratification of having big, demonized overdogs to hate—and more importantly, to blame—for the Global Financial Crisis.

There is a way to reverse this—an **antidote to Underdogma**—which you will find in the final chapter of this book. But first, why is it that **our enemies do not practice Underdogma**?

13
Our Enemies Do Not Practice Underdogma

"America is guilty and must atone for its sins by abandoning its power."
—"The Chorus of Useful Idiots," Prof. Bruce S. Thornton, *FrontPage Magazine*, November 1, 2002

"Team Obama still sees itself as an outsider and spouts counterculture nonsense [and] an eagerness to abdicate American power on the international stage."
— "Wobbly Prez Power-Trips Himself Up," *New York Post*, November 1, 2009

"[President Obama] seems embarrassed, even ashamed, by the power and greatness of his own country."
—*Telegraph UK*, September 23, 2009

AMERICAN UNDERDOGMATISTS HAVE BOUGHT INTO the notion that America's power is somehow wrong, that you are bad and arrogant for having it, and that the world would be a far better place if America were cut down to size. Who sold you this notion? The people who resent your power and aim to take it from you.

Many Americans, residing at the center of all this power, fail to understand how America is viewed by those who resent and covet America's power. It is a perspective that cannot be gained from the inside. Every American born since 1945 has spent every moment of his or her life as a member of the world's most exclusive club—the superpower club. Since the fall of the Berlin Wall in 1989, Americans have been the *only* members of the superpower club. What you take for granted, others around the world ache for. Those who live outside of America are reminded that they are not No. 1 almost every time they turn on a television, watch a movie, listen to the radio, read a book or magazine, fly in a plane, handle currency, conduct business, or drink a soda. While Americans' eyes are turned inward, or to each other, their eyes are fixed on you. America is the center of the world's focus, envy, and occasional rage. On the inside, Americans simply cannot understand this. From the outside, it is all that Underdogmatists can see. And now they have company. As *Newsweek* editor Jon Meacham observed, Barack Obama's formative years in the small, underdog foreign country of Indonesia made him "more conscious of what American power feels like on the receiving end than on the giving end."[1]

---

[1] "Morning View," NPR, October 29, 2008

The belief that those who have less power are virtuous and noble—*because* they have less power, and that those who have more power are to be scorned—*because* they have more power.

Since the beginning of this book, we have seen evidence of Underdogma in the clash between university students and Benjamin Netanyahu, in kidnap victims who champion their captors and killers, in human beings who call for the eradication of human beings, and in the world's most powerful man (the President of the United States) apologizing to the world for his nation's power.

We saw—through studies from the Universities of South Florida, Nebraska, Warwick, San Diego, and Oxford—that our underdog allegiances and scorn for the overdog have the power to bypass our rational minds and our self-interests.

We saw Underdogma's footprints throughout history, from David and Goliath to Christ's blessed meek to the Berkeley student protests to the rise of the United Nations. We saw the power of Underdogma unite American lesbians, Osama bin Laden, Jimmy Carter, and millions of others around the world in a common cause. We saw evidence of Underdogma in the attacks of 9/11, in the conspiracies that swirl around it, and even in our hatred for the New York Yankees.

We see Underdogma in the stories we tell, in our spite for Big Box stores, and in the power imbalances we feel in our neighborhoods, in our workplaces, and in our personal, internal struggles with power and success. And we see Underdogma as a driving force in politics, in the Global Financial Crisis, and in the way we distinguish between right and wrong.

But, up until now, we have only seen Underdogma from one side.

Underdogma is the reflexive belief that those who have less power are virtuous and noble—*because they have less power*—and that those who have more power are to be scorned—*because they have more power*. Described this way, Underdogma is a force that acts *upon* us, with enough power to bypass our rational minds, our self-interests—and sometimes even our biological instincts to survive.

But there is another side to Underdogma.

Not everyone goes through life under the control of a nonthinking, gut-level instinct to side with the little guy and to heap scorn on the big guy. I used to be an Underdogmatist. But years of observation, capped by the specter of university students smashing glass and spitting on Jews and stifling free speech on a university campus, opened my eyes to Underdogma. If my eyes were still closed, I could not have written this book. After reading this book, your eyes may be open, too.

But you and I are not the only ones who can see Underdogma for what it is. We are not the only ones who can see the awesome power that Underdogma has to control the behaviors of large groups of people. Yes, Underdogma has "true believers," people whose worldviews are shaped by reflexive Underdogma. Broadly described, these people are equality-seekers. When they see a power imbalance, it sets off their gut-level instinct to side with the underdog and to rail against the overdog in order to "set things right" along Underdogma's Axis of Power. But there is another group—a group that has learned to *use* Underdogma and to *manipulate* Underdogma's true believers in order to *acquire* power.

I call these two groups, respectively, the "**Useful Idiots**" and the "**Puppetmasters**."

The term Useful Idiot is largely attributed to Vladimir Lenin, who reportedly used it to describe Soviet sympathizers among the ranks of Western media and intellectual elites. Underdogma's Useful Idiots perform much the same function today.

> "Lenin called them 'useful idiots,' those people living in liberal democracies who by giving moral and material support to a totalitarian ideology in effect were braiding the rope that would hang them. Why people who enjoyed freedom and prosperity worked passionately to destroy both is a fascinating question, one still with us today. Now the useful idiots can be found in the chorus of appeasement, reflexive anti-Americanism, and sentimental idealism trying to inhibit the necessary responses to another freedom-hating ideology, radical Islam."
>
> —"The Chorus of Useful Idiots," Proffesor Bruce S. Thornton, *FrontPage Magazine*, November 11, 2002

Useful Idiot Underdogmatists are all around us. They are deeply embedded in our culture and often hold positions of great influence. Much of this book has focused on chronicling the words, deeds, and motivations of these

Useful Idiot Underdogmatists, from the countless American citizens who buy into the idea that "America is the real terrorist," to the Reuters News Service, which declared "one man's terrorist is another man's freedom fighter,"[2] to the *LA Times* writer who portrayed 9/11 mastermind Khalid Sheikh Mohammed as "thoughtful about his cause and craft" and "folksy,"[3] to the parade of American reporters who kowtowed to China during the 2008 Olympics. They praised the totalitarian regime for getting rich and "doing it the Communist way,"[4] and made the case to Americans back home that the Chinese are happier under communism than Americans are under democracy[5] (while neglecting to mention that the Chinese citizens' 86% happiness rating was, perhaps, influenced by the threat of being jailed or "disappeared" if they had answered otherwise) as the Western media helped China turn the 2008 Olympics into "an international triumph for Chinese authoritarianism."[6] A *New York Times* editorial, penned by a three-time Pulitzer Prize winner, even singled out for praise China's "one-party autocracy" and its "enlightened" rulers.

---

[2] Steven Jukes, global news head for Reuters News Service, internal memo cited by *Washington Post* reporter Howard Kurtz, September 24, 2001

[3] Josh Meyer, *LA Times*, March 16, 2007

[4] *CBS Early Show*, August 11, 2008

[5] Ibid

[6] "'Show of Power,' Indeed," Anne Applebaum, *Washington Post*, August 26, 2008

> "One-party autocracy certainly has its drawbacks. But when it is led by a reasonably enlightened group of people, as China is today, it can also have great advantages."
>
> —Thomas L. Friedman, *New York Times*, September 8, 2009

One of the "drawbacks" of having such an "enlightened group of people" running China is their unfortunate predilection for slaughtering Tibetan monks and jailing people for meditating in public, then cutting out their organs (without anesthetic) and selling them while the unwilling "donors" bleed to death.[7] I suppose it takes a Pulitzer Prize, or three, to call that brand of barbarism the work of "a reasonably enlightened group of people." Although Useful Idiot Underdogmatists in the media are dangerous in their ability to spread such damaging nonsense, I believe they are more misguided than evil. The truly evil ones are the Puppetmasters: the people who thirst for America's power and deploy Useful Idiot Underdogmatists to the front lines in a war to take America's power away.

While American Underdogmatists increasingly exalt the meek and apologize for their own power, Underdogma's Puppetmasters have something else in mind: "China intends to become the dominant global power"[8] and Islamists

---

[7] "Bloody Harvest: The Killing of Falun Gong for their Organs," David Matas & David Kilgour, 2009

[8] *China: The Gathering Threat*, Constantine Menges, 2005

want "the extension of the Islamic territory across the globe, and the establishment of a worldwide 'caliphate' founded on Sharia law and the temporal reign of ayatollahs and imams."[9]

> "In the traditional Chinese view, the world needs a hegemon—or dominant state—to prevent disorder. The Communist Chinese regime believes China should be that hegemon."
>
> —*China: The Gathering Threat*,
> Constantine Menges, 2005

> "If you would like to have good relations with the Iranian nation...bow down before the greatness of the Iranian nation and surrender."
>
> —Mahmoud Ahmadinejad, President of Iran,
> "Terrorists-In Their Own Words," The Claremont Institute, August 15, 2006

> "I am confident that Muslims will be able to end the legend of the so-called superpower that is America."
>
> —Osama bin Laden, *Time* magazine,
> January 11, 1999

> "[America] will be brought down...The conditions around the world are ripe for supporting our Islamic Revolutionary ideals and the messianic rule is close at hand."
>
> —Iranian President Mahmoud Ahmadinejad,
> Planet Iran, September 28, 2010

[9] *Telegraph UK*, July 20, 2005

America's enemies and competitors do not practice Underdogma. They value, respect, and covet America's power. And they are using Underdogma and its Useful Idiots to take America's power away—in a war of ideas, not military might. As General Sun Tzu wrote in The Art of War, "to subdue the enemy without fighting is the acme of skill." Today, America is preemptively subduing itself through the words and deeds of Useful Idiot Underdogmatists who are all too willing to cede America's power to its enemies and competitors.

> "No world order that elevates one nation or group of people over another will succeed."
>
> —U.S. President Barack Obama, Address to the United Nations, September 23, 2009

> "Obama has made a vivid display of his own trademark style—the diplomacy of deference."
>
> —"The Diplomacy of Deference," *Politico*, November 17, 2009

> "I pledge to you that we seek an equal partnership. There is no senior partner and junior partner in our relations."
>
> —President Obama to the Summit of the Americas, CBS News/AP, April 18, 2009

> "Reasonable people knew that Obama is a powerless man."
>
> —Osama bin Laden, "Osama bin Laden Calls Barack Obama 'Powerless,'" *Telegraph UK*, September 14, 2009

> "There was a time where no one dared to make one negative comment against the very existence of America but today, the Islamic Republic has

managed to defy America from within and there is nothing they can do about it."

—Iranian President Mahmoud Ahmadinejad, Planet Iran, September 28, 2010

President Obama has repeatedly bowed down to world leaders,[10] "offers a vision to the world of America diminished or constrained,"[11] and "arrived in China…as a fiscal supplicant, not the leader of the free world."[12] He badmouthed American power in Europe, then again at the Summit of the Americas, and again at the United Nations. He prostrated himself, and his nation, in Cairo before the Islamic world. He is "signaling weakness internationally in a very big way," says America's former UN Ambassador John Bolton, under the mistaken belief that showing "American weakness—reducing our nuclear capabilities—will induce others to become weaker as well."[13] "The Obama administration's massive deficit spending poses severe risks to American power"[14] as it shifts America's economic power, via sacks of borrowed money, to the other side of the world. And since "America will be even more starkly dependent on the world's new rising powers…China, the Gulf States and Russia…see this as an opportunity to tilt the balance of economic power further in their favour."[15] In the minds

[10] At the time of this writing, the list of world leaders President Barack Obama has bowed down to include: King Abdullah of Saudi Arabia, Japanese Emperor Akihito and Empress Michiko, Chinese Premier Wen Jaibao, Chinese President Hu Jintao, and King Harald of Norway.

[11] Charles Krauthammer, *Spiegel*, October 26, 2009

[12] *Times Online*, December 6, 2009

[13] Ambassador John Bolton, *The John Batchelor Show*, February 2, 2010

[14] "America The indispensable," *Forbes*, November 3, 2009

[15] "A shattering moment in America's fall from power," *Guardian UK*, September 28, 2008

of Useful Idiot Underdogmatists, this power shift is a good thing. And it is long overdue: "it's about time we were cut down to size! A 'weakened America' is an improvement because in their view—and Obama's—America has not been the solution to the world's problems. America is the problem."[16] As Andrew Breitbart noted in his interview for *Underdogma*, "the resurgent left, who used America at war after 9/11 as a means to organize and reassert itself…conspicuously ignore[s] radical Islam and its attempt for global domination."[17]

Photos courtesty of zombietime.com

Some Useful Idiot Underdogmatists in the West go even further. Beyond "conspicuously" ignoring the problem. Beyond anti-Americanism. Beyond ceding America's power to its enemies. Beyond cutting America down to size. These Underdogmatists cheer America's enemies on as they help bring down their own country.

[16] Rush Limbaugh, September 17, 2009

[17] Andrew Breitbart, interview for *Underdogma*, January 4, 2010

> "A box-cutter can bring down a tower. A poem can build up a movement. A pamphlet can spark a revolution."
>
> —Howard Zinn, foreword to *Dear President Bush*, 2006

What these Useful Idiot Underdogmatists in the West fail to understand is that, when they look through the prism of Underdogma and stand up for so-called "underdogs" like America's enemies while heaping scorn on overdogs like America, they are defending those who do not share their "fight the power" stance and who, in fact, crave and covet the very power that Underdogmatists scorn. As an added irony, the West's empathy for the underdog—leading some Useful Idiots in the West to tolerate, excuse, and even celebrate the violent actions of Islamic terrorists—is viewed by the Islamists they champion as despicable weakness and clear justification—even provocation—for violent jihad against the very Underdogmatists who stand up for them. In 1954, Winston Churchill said, "an appeaser is one who feeds a crocodile, hoping it will eat him last."[18] What Underdogmatists fail to understand today is that these particular crocodiles respond to appeasement by eating the Useful Idiot Underdogmatists first.

> To see more outrageous Useful Idiot photos, visit Underdogma's GALLERY OF USEFUL IDIOTS at www.under-dogma.com.

> "A falling camel attracts many knives."
>
> —Ancient Arab proverb

[18] *The Diplomat's Dictionary*, Charles W. Freeman Jr., 1994

Whether Underdogmatists like it or not, there will always be one nation in the world that has more power than others. What would happen if Underdogmatists got their way? What would the world look like if America were no longer No. 1?

> "Keep a cool head and maintain a low profile. Never take the lead—but aim to do something big."
> —Deng Xiaoping, former leader of the Communist Party of China

Next in line to usurp America's power is communist China, which is projected to overtake the United States economically by 2027.[19] In early 2010, a senior People's Liberation Army officer called for "China to abandon modesty about its global goals and 'sprint to become world number one,'" writing that "China's big goal in the 21st century is to become world number one, the top power."[20] What kind of "top power" would communist China be? China's totalitarian rulers and their policies have killed 73,000,000 of their own people since 1949.[21] That is six times more than the human destruction wrought by Hitler's Holocaust. The Chinese communist government detains between 250,000

[19] "Top Dog America Should Enjoy Its Last, Precious Years," Yahoo Finance, June 4, 2007

[20] "China PLA Officer Urges Challenging U.S. Dominance," Reuters, February 28, 2010

[21] *Mao: The Unknown Story*, Jung Chang & Jon Halliday, 2005; *China's Bloody Century* and other works by Professor R. J. Rummel, 2007; *China: The Gathering Threat*, Dr. Constantine Menges, 2005

and 300,000 human beings in "reeducation-through-labor" camps "on vaguely defined charges having never seen a lawyer, never been to a court, and with no form of judicial supervision."[22] Communist China also slaughters Tibetan monks,[23] "kill[s] Falun Gong practitioners so that their organs can be sold to transplant tourists,"[24] beats and jails environmentalists,[25] and imprisons or "disappears" people for typing the words "freedom" or "Dalai Lama" into search engines.[26]

After communist China, the next most likely inheritors of America's power are those who want to build a worldwide Islamic caliphate based on sharia law.[27]

> "In the fifth stage an Islamic caliphate will be declared. The balance of power will finally tip in the favor of the radical Islamists. Israel will no longer be able to defend itself. The sixth phase beginning in the year 2016 will be a phase of total confrontation. The caliphate will inaugurate an Islamic army and begin a final apocalyptic war with the

---

[22] Amnesty International report: "When in China: Encounters with Human Rights"

[23] *Times Online*, April 5, 2008

[24] "Bloody Harvest," an ongoing series of investigations and reports into Chinese organ harvesting by David Kilgour (former Canadian Member of Parliament and Secretary of State for the Asia Pacific Region) and David Matas (international human rights lawyer), 2009

[25] "China Environmental Activist Imprisoned," *USA Today*, August 10, 2007

[26] "If you write 'Dalai Lama' or 'Free Tibet,' they [the Chinese government] know who you are, where you are, they can come to your house and arrest you. You can be sent to jail and tortured. In china 62 people are in jail just for talking about democracy and human rights on the web," Emily Jacquard, Canadian officer of Reporters Without Borders, September 2005

[27] *Telegraph UK*, July 20, 2005

> unbelievers resulting in total victory in the year 2020."
>
> —Pulitzer Prize-winning author of *The Looming Tower*, Lawrence Wright, September 14, 2007

Imagine a world led by those who stone to death women for the "dishonor" of being raped,[28] who flew planeloads of innocent people into New York office towers filled with thousands of other innocent people, and who plan to "hasten the return of the Islamic messiah by ushering in [their] version of the apocalypse."[29] These people respect power and value strength—the polar opposite of the second part of Underdogma (scorn for those who have more power).

> "When people see a strong horse and a weak horse, by nature, they will like the strong horse."
>
> —Osama bin Laden, videotape claiming responsibility for the 9/11 attacks, December 13, 2001

> "There is no way to understand how the Middle East works without understanding the concept of the strong horse. It is not a moral judgment but a description."
>
> —*The Strong Horse: Power, Politics and the Clash of Arab Civilizations*, Lee Smith, 2009

Their beliefs are also the direct opposite of the first part of Underdogma (those who have less power are virtuous

[28] "Honor Killing Among the Palestinians," James Emery, *The World & I*, 2003

[29] *The Apocalypse of Ahmadinejad: The Revolution of Iran's Nuclear Prophet*, Mark Hitchcock, 2007

and noble), in that they view any sign of weakness as an open provocation for violent attack.

> "It was Osama bin Laden who said the perception of American weakness only inspired radicals to fight harder."
>
> —*Washington Post*, March 16, 2003

As Mark Steyn chronicled in *America Alone*, the Islamic world is ascendant and holds a demographic advantage over the West. "On the Continent and elsewhere in the West, native populations are aging and fading and being supplanted remorselessly by a young Muslim demographic. Time for the obligatory 'of courses': *of course*, not all Muslims are terrorists—though enough are hot for jihad to provide an impressive support network of mosques from Vienna to Stockholm to Toronto to Seattle."[30] Underdogmatists may brush off this threat, claiming that the number of radical Islamists is so small as to be inconsequential. But there are three problems with clinging to such a delusion:

1. It only took nineteen men to carry out the 9/11 attacks.
2. If only 1% of Muslims support a worldwide caliphate, that equals ten million people.
3. A 2008 survey of Muslims found that not 1%, not 2%, but "a third (33%) of respondents declared themselves supportive of

[30] "The Future Belongs to Islam," Mark Steyn, *Macleans*, October 20, 2006

> such a caliphate."[31] Was this survey conducted in Pakistan, Afghanistan, Iran, or Yemen? No. This survey was done on UK university campuses.[32] The study also found that 32% of UK Muslim students said that killing in the name of Islam was justified.[33] *And those are just the educated British Muslims who admitted to a survey-taker that they favor murdering in the name of Islam.* If the rest of the Islamic world openly favors sharia law and religious murder to the same extent as UK university students, that equals 502 million people worldwide. The entire U.S. population is only 307 million.

What do we know about these people, other than the fact that they want to usurp America's power and/or kill Americans? Not as much as what we will know after reading Chapter 14—UNDERSTANDING THE "THEM" IN "US" VS. "THEM."

[31] Islam on Campus: A Survey of UK Student Opinions, July 2008
[32] Ibid
[33] Ibid

14

UNDERSTANDING THE "THEM" IN "US" VS. "THEM"

"Yet, taught by time, my heart has learn'd to glow
for other's good, and melt at other's woe."
—*Odyssey*, Homer

WHILE COMMUNIST CHINA BELIEVES "it must either dominate the world or be dominated by the United States and its allies,"[1] President Obama took the occasion of his first visit to China to show "humility"[2] and to assure his Shanghai audience that "we do not seek to contain China's rise."[3] In his Cairo speech to the Islamic world, President Obama declared that "no system of government can or should be imposed upon one nation by any other."[4] In contrast to his audience, Barack Obama "is president of a country against which jihadis desiring an Islamic caliphate have declared war; meanwhile, Obama extends his hand and apologizes for his nation."[5]

---

[1] *China: The Gathering Threat*. Constantine Menges, 2005

[2] President Obama's China town hall, November 16, 2009

[3] "President Barack Obama in Shanghai," *People's Daily Online*, November 16, 2009

[4] Barack Obama's Cairo speech, June 4, 2009

[5] "Connecting the Dots," Claudia Rosett, Forbes.com, January 7, 2010

Why is it that America's enemies and competitors—specifically communist China and radical Islam—seem to be immune from Underdogma? Why do they lust after power while President Obama apologizes for America's power?

Full disclosure: for years, I have done pro bono work with the Chinese dissident community: Tibetans, Falun Gong, and others who have escaped Chinese totalitarian rule. One thing I have noticed during this time is the profoundly different character of those who were born and educated in communist China, compared to those of us who were born and raised in relative freedom. Aside from the small group of passionate and dedicated Chinese freedom fighters with whom I have had the pleasure of working, I have not often seen the level of passion and desire for freedom among Chinese expats that one would expect from one of the world's most ancient cultures, which, since 1949, has been usurped by a brutal communist regime that has killed tens of millions of Chinese.

I am not talking about the Chinese in China, who live under the boot of totalitarianism. If the penalty of speaking out against tyranny is death, it is understandable that people in China would avoid speaking out, especially after the Tiananmen Square massacre of 1989. But Chinese people who have escaped communist China and now live in North America, in freedom—why would they avoid speaking out against mass-murdering totalitarians who slaughter their fellow Chinese back home? Why is there such a desire among North American Chinese expats to "not make trouble"? And, when I speak to them about injustices suffered by their own people, why do so many of them reply with blank stares or, more strangely, anger and defensiveness—as if criticism of China's murderous totalitarian rulers equals criticism of them or of China?

Contrast their reactions to the way Americans react to real or even perceived injustices visited upon those with whom they have no personal connection. Think of all the times you have seen American Underdogmatists show solidarity and support for foreign, jailed terrorists who aim to slaughter American civilians. Now compare that to all the times you have seen Chinese protesters take to the streets—even the safe streets of America—to show their solidarity with the millions of their own people who have been jailed, tortured, and slaughtered back home. When American soldiers were found to be stripping and taunting foreign terrorists (who aimed to kill Americans) at Abu Ghraib, American Underdogmatists engaged in a years-long denouncement of their own government on behalf of these foreign terrorists. By contrast, when hundreds of thousands of innocent, nonterrorist Chinese people are jailed and tortured, as Amnesty International reports, "on vaguely defined charges having never seen a lawyer, never been to a court, and with no form of judicial supervision," the Chinese expat community is largely silent.

In these cases and others, American Underdogmatists seem to stand up for and champion the plight of disconnected foreigners moreso than Chinese expats stand up for and champion the plight of their own countrymen back in China—which can be frustrating for those of us who do stand up for the Chinese people. One day, my frustration boiled over and I turned to a leading Chinese dissident (a friend and colleague who was raised in China and escaped totalitarian rule) and asked her: why? Her answer was quick and matter-of-fact, as though it were an obvious truism or common knowledge among Chinese dissidents.

"Empathy," was her answer.

"What?"

"Empathy. The communist government systematically destroys empathy."

Underdogma is the reflexive belief that those who have less power are virtuous and noble—*because they have less power*—and that those who have more power are to be scorned—*because they have more power*.

Since every human being was born, every human being has a clear, personal understanding of what it feels like to be a small and powerless underdog in a world of more powerful overdogs. But that does not automatically make every human being an Underdogmatist. It only makes us susceptible to Underdogma, carriers of its dormant gene. Before Underdogma can be activated, there must be a *bridge* between our own personal experiences with powerlessness and the similar experiences of others.

That bridge is empathy.

> "A support motive for the underdog may be driven by the fact that people understand or empathize with the underdog's plight. Empathy is generally regarded as the ability to 'know another person's inner experience.' One who is empathetic should be more able to understand the plight of the underdog."
>
> —*Underdog Consumption*, Lee Phillip McGinnis & James W. Gentry, 2004

> "A strong correlation to underdog affection is empathic concern or empathy. People who can identify with being an underdog are more inclined to having empathy toward other underdogs."
>
> —Lee Phillip McGinnis, interview for *Underdogma*, December 5, 2009

Empathy allows us to take our own personal experiences, recognize those experiences in others, and forge an emotional connection between the two. Without empathy, we would not root for Rocky Balboa or The Little Engine That Could or the Star Wars Rebel Alliance. It would not matter to us if Rocky lost or if the Little Engine slid back down the mountain or if the Rebel Alliance was destroyed because, without empathy, we would not have an emotional connection to these underdogs.

So, does that mean our enemies and competitors lack empathy?

In May of 2008, *National Geographic* ran a special issue entitled "China: Inside the Dragon," featuring two articles by China specialist and *The New Yorker* correspondent Peter Hessler. In one story, Hessler wrote, "my [Chinese] students taught me that everything [in China] was personal—history, politics, foreign relations—but this approach creates boundaries as well...***For many Chinese, if a problem doesn't affect them personally, it might as well not exist***." [emphasis added]

I interviewed Mr. Hessler for *Underdogma* and I asked him to elaborate on this point. He said that "the tradition of Chinese collectivism" makes the Chinese less likely to take up the political causes of others, noting also that "in an individualistic society [like America], you are more able to put yourself in somebody else's shoes [whereas] the [Chinese] culture was always group-oriented and then they threw Communism on top of that. It's an unhealthy mix." In other words, those who do not focus on themselves as individuals have a harder time making the connection between "the self" and "the other," because they do not have a good grasp on "the self." Communism actively seeks to destroy the notion of "the self," therefore making it even more difficult to forge a connection between "the self" and "the other."

Hessler also noted that "the Chinese are often more generous with their families, and in particular they treat the elderly better than Americans and other Westerners. But they have a difficult time interacting with people outside of their known group. In an individualistic society, you are more able to put yourself in somebody else's shoes: how would I feel if that was happening to me?" Add to this the generational push from the Chinese communist party to indoctrinate children against feeling empathy for "the other," and the stage is set for the kind of horrific classroom scenes that took place during the cultural revolution:

> "Hanging from [the teachers'] necks were pails filled with rocks. I saw the principal; the pail

> around his neck was so heavy that the wire had cut deep into his neck and he was staggering... Greatly emboldened by the instigators, the other students also cried, 'Beat them!' and jumped on the other teachers, swinging their fists, kicking. There was nothing strange in this. Young students were ordinarily peaceful and well-behaved, but once the first step was taken, all were bound to follow."
>
> —*Red Guard: From Schoolboy to "Little General" in Mao's China*, Ken Ling, Miriam London, & Lee Ta-Ling, 1972

According to the Encyclopedia Britannica, "the People's Republic of China generally makes no distinction between education and propaganda or indoctrination. All three share the common task of changing man." What the Chinese communists are changing about man is his ability to put himself in others' shoes. According to my dissident colleague from China, "The communist government systematically destroys empathy"—which is a necessary ingredient for Underdogma. A recent newsletter from Chinese Children Adoption International (CCAI) featured a cover story about adopted Chinese children entitled: "Where is the empathy?" It gave examples of adopted Chinese children who failed to show empathy like their American-born siblings. The article noted that "empathy is a critical life skill, but it is also a learned skill." If empathy is learned, then it can be unlearned, or simply not taught—or people can be conditioned to not feel empathy for certain "enemies of the state." Just like the hundreds of millions of Chinese children and adults who have been conditioned to not feel empathy for Tibetans, Falun Gong practitioners, Uighurs, and countless dissidents whom the communist Chinese government has rounded up and killed or "disappeared."

So, what about the radical Islamists who also seem to be immune from Underdogma? Do they lack empathy, too? According to Barack Obama:

> "The essence of this tragedy [the 9/11 attacks], it seems to me, derives from a fundamental absence of empathy on the part of the attackers: an inability to imagine, or connect with, the humanity or suffering of others. Such a failure of empathy, such numbness to the pain of a child or the desperation of a parent is not innate; nor, history tells us, is it unique to a particular culture, religion or ethnicity. It may find expression in a particular brand of violence, it may be channeled by particular demagogues or fanatics."
>
> —"9-11 Happened Because Al-Qaida Lacks Empathy', Says Barack Obama," *WorldNetDaily*, July 21, 2008

Radical Islamists who preach that Jews are subhuman "descendants of monkeys and pigs"[6] certainly lack empathy for Jews. As do the Islamists who preach "educating the children to jihad and to hatred of the Jews"[7] while using

---

[6] "O Allah, destroy America as it is controlled by Zionist Jews...Allah will avenge, in the name of His Prophet, the colonialist settlers who are the descendents of monkeys and pigs." Ikrime Sabri, Mufti of the Palestinian Authority, *Voice of Palestine*, July 11, 1997

[7] "Saudi education system majors in 'Jihad'," Sheikh Majed 'Abd Al-Rahman Al-Firian, *WorldNetDaily*, December 24, 2002

puppets on children's TV to teach preschoolers to "wipe out the Jews."[8] Islamists who believe in stoning to death raped women for the "dishonor" of being raped show a considerable lack of empathy for women.[9] Islamists who declare that "homosexuals deserve to be executed or tortured and possibly both"[10] lack empathy for homosexuals. Islamists who believe America is the "Great Satan"[11] lack empathy for Americans. And the Islamists who flew planeloads of innocent people into the World Trade Center Twin Towers lacked empathy for the people on those planes and in those towers. What do all these people for whom radical Islamists lack empathy have in common? They are "the other," apostates, unbelievers, "kafir." Therefore, in the minds of radical Islamists, they are "fair game."

> "The 'other' [is] fair game as kafir (blasphemous; unbeliever in Allah). The 'other' covers a broad spectrum: the six billion or so people of the world who are not Muslims, including the Jews and Christians."
>
> —Amil Imani, May 25, 2008

> "Killing a Kafir for any reason, you can say it, it is OK—even if there is no reason for it."
>
> —Muslim cleric Abu Hamza al-Masri,
> BBC News, February 7, 2006

---

[8] "Anti-Semitic Hate Speech in the Name of Islam," *Spiegel*, May 16, 2008

[9] "Honor Killing Among the Palestinians," James Emery, *The World & I*, 2003

[10] "Gays Should Be Hanged, Iranian Minister," *Times Online*, November 13, 2007

[11] Ayatollah Khomeini of Iran

Declaring certain people or groups to be outcasts or "the other" is a time-tested way to dehumanize "the other" and to eliminate feelings of empathy for them within "the self." It also removes all possibility for the development of Underdogma. Once empathy for "the other" is removed, the bridge to Underdogma is severed, and anything is "fair game." A "kafir may be cheated, deceived, murdered, tortured, and raped."[12] As the *UK Times* reported, a "radical pamphlet believed to have emanated from London argues that Muslims are specifically prohibited from showing any sympathy for the victims of Islamic terrorism" and "such emotionless reaction has been displayed within recent weeks by Mohammed Bouyeri, the alleged killer of Dutch film maker Theo van Gogh, who in court last week looked the dead man's mother in the eye and said: 'I can't feel for you because you are an infidel.'"[13]

When Muslims declare certain other people to be kafir, they do not limit themselves just to non-Muslims. Some radical Muslims believe that other Muslims who are not *radical enough* are therefore not real Muslims, can be labeled kafir, and can be killed along with all the other kafir.

> "Extreme anti-Western jihadists for whom all non-Muslims are kafir (infidels) and therefore by definition enemies of Islam...according to the jihadist ideology, all Muslims allied or associated with the West in any way are themselves kafir. Consequently, it is acceptable collateral damage to

[12] Front-page interview with CSPI Director Bill Warner, May 7, 2008
[13] *Times Online*, July 24, 2005

> kill such innocent Muslims in order to obtain victory over the kafir."
>
> —"Underplaying the Threat of Terrorism Could Be a Fatal Mistake," *Sydney Morning Herald*, October 4, 2005

The Qur'an strictly forbids the killing of fellow Muslims, but some radical Muslim groups get around this by declaring non-radical Muslims to be not Muslim at all. Like the radical British Islamist group al-Ghurabaa, in a statement released after the London 7/7 bombings: "any Muslim that denies that terror is a part of Islam is kafir [an unbeliever]."[14] This is how radical Islamists who seek to kill fellow Muslims (in Middle Eastern suicide bombings, the World Trade Center, and elsewhere) get around the Qur'an's rule about not killing fellow Muslims. They declare their victims to be kafir, excommunicate them from Islam, and declare them to be "apostates" or no longer Muslims. It is a surgical cut that removes empathy for "the other."

Communist Chinese and radical Islamists were not born without the ability to feel empathy, but their beliefs and behaviors do have an effect on triggering or not triggering the "empathy switch." Since empathy is learned, it can also be unlearned, or simply not taught to children, or conditioned out of people's hearts and minds when it comes to certain "other" groups. If a culture, like communist China,

[14] *Times Online*, July 24, 2005

tends to be more group-oriented and focused on immediate, familial relationships, that certainly would have an effect on their capacity to feel empathy for "the other" and, by extension, their susceptibility to Underdogma. If they were raised their whole lives to hate Tibetans or Falun Gong or even the United States,[15] it follows that they would lack empathy for "the other," and therefore would be less susceptible to the empathy-based belief system Underdogma. Therefore, it should come as no surprise that, unlike the President of the United States and Western Underdogmatists, communist China does not apologize for its power, views itself as the "Middle Kingdom" (the center of the world), believes "the world needs a hegemon [and that] China should be that hegemon"[16] and, after President Obama visited in 2009 and said "we do not seek to contain China's rise,"[17] communist China took that for the sign of weakness that it was and quickly adopted a more strident and powerful stance on the world stage.

> "Chinese President Hu Jintao [unveiled an] ambitious agenda [for China to play a bigger role on the world stage] after US President Barack Obama's visit to China and before the Copenhagen climate change summit, two events that could become milestones in the Middle Kingdom's quest for quasi-superpower status."
>
> —"China Unveils Its New Worldview,"
> *Asia Times*, December 11, 2009

---

[15] "In China, it's a race war, with Americans the 'bad guys.' The children are taught hate songs, scream at any white as a 'dirty American,'" "Children Taught Hate Songs," *Herald Tribune*, September 26, 1965

[16] *China: The Gathering Threat*, Constantine Menges, 2005

[17] "President Barack Obama in Shanghai," *People's Daily Online*, November 16, 2009

When radical Islamists dehumanize Jews, women, homosexuals, Americans—and "the six billion or so people of the world who are not Muslims"—it is little wonder that radical Islamists are better known for murdering innocent people than for incubating empathy. And it should come as no surprise that their proverbs are a lot different than our proverbs.

THEIRS	OURS
"A falling camel attracts many knives." —Ancient Arab proverb	"Blessed are the meek, for they shall inherit the Earth." —Matthew 5:5

Author, classicist, and military historian Victor Davis Hanson observed that "the problem with all of these people in Washington is they feel that the more that they can show empathy, the more that these radical Islamists will lay off when, in fact, [Osama] bin Laden himself has said that magnanimity is essentially a sign of weakness, that we're the Shetland Pony and not the Strong Horse."[18]

But just because we can feel empathy does not automatically make us all Underdogmatists. True, empathy is a necessary *bridge* to Underdogma. But we have a choice about whether or not we cross that bridge. Empathy does not cause Underdogma any more than poverty causes crime. Saying that poverty causes crime is an insult to every poor person who chooses not to commit crimes. Yes, poverty ***can*** lead to crime, if a poor person who is hungry chooses to steal his dinner. But a poor person who is

[18] Victor Davis Hanson, *The Hugh Hewitt Show*, May 5, 2010

hungry can also choose to work hard and ***earn*** his dinner, and perhaps even elevate himself out of poverty and achieve a position of wealth and power. Yes, empathy ***can*** lead to Underdogma. But the times when empathy ***does*** lead to Underdogma is when empathic people choose to deal with power imbalances by demonizing those who have power and by deifying those who do not.

There are other ways for empathic people like myself, and perhaps you as well, to deal with power imbalances. We can celebrate those who have earned and achieved their power. We can inspire those who have not yet achieved power and urge them to reach for the top. We can write books that explain how to overcome the childish and non-thinking reactions we sometimes have to power imbalances, otherwise known as Underdogma. Or we can do what generations of Americans did when they fled to America to make better lives for themselves. We can climb the ladder. We can work hard. We can sacrifice. We can follow the American dream and make better lives for ourselves and for our children. A perfectly acceptable, and perfectly American, way to deal with power imbalances is to look at power imbalances as temporary, as challenges—even as motivations. Because, as the old American axiom goes, "in America, anyone can become President"; anyone can attain the highest seat of power in the land. Even someone like Barack Obama, who scorns American power.

There is an antidote to Underdogma, and I have already given part of it away. Find out what it is in the next, and final, chapter: Chapter 15—THE ANTIDOTE TO UNDERDOGMA.

15
THE ANTIDOTE TO UNDERDOGMA

> "The international arena remains a Hobbesian state of nature in which countries naturally strive for power. If we voluntarily renounce much of ours, others will not follow suit. They will fill the vacuum. Inevitably, an inversion of power relations will occur."
>
> —Charles Krauthammer, "Decline is a Choice," *The Weekly Standard*, October 19, 2009

AMERICA IS AT A PIVOT point in its history. Although the United States began this century as the world's lone superpower, its enemies and competitors are nipping at America's heels while American Underdogmatists try to appease them with offerings of your power. America's enemies are ascendant. American power is in decline. Underdogma is winning the battle.

Underdogmatists are taking every opportunity to heap scorn on American power and to give America's power away. American Underdogmatists—from the White House to the media to the angry hordes with "pitchforks" whose rage they kindle and stoke—are vilifying American exceptionalism. They are also attacking the American dream by demonizing wealth and those who have achieved positions of power. On campuses and in cities across the nation, American Underdogmatists regularly take to the streets to protest against American power, while championing and exalting America's power-hungry enemies. Scores of antihumanists/Underdogmatists believe that the modern, advanced, civilized, moral, and productive people of the United States are a "cancer" on the Earth that either need to be physically wiped off the face of the planet, or stripped of power and subjugated to international environmental and regulatory bodies. Millions of American Underdogmatists (9/11 Truthers) believe that American power is so malevolent that those who wield it either directly slaughtered thousands of people on September 11, 2001, and conspired to cover it up, or that the mere presence of American power was enough to provoke poor, sympathetic underdog terrorists into opposing America's power the only way they knew how (hijacking and murder) because "America is the real terrorist" and "America had it coming." And, as Charles Krauthammer said in his interview for *Underdogma*, the United States of America has, for the first time, a President who preaches to the world that "America is not intrinsically good, not intrinsically exceptional...that we've been corrupt since our beginning, so we necessarily would want to curtail the power of such a country."[1]

When Mikhail Gorbachev said that "Americans have a severe disease...called the winner's complex,"[2] he was right—but in a different way than he intended. When American

[1] Charles Krauthammer interview for *Underdogma*, December 2009

[2] "Gorbachev: 'Americans Have a Severe Disease'" ABC, Mikhail Gorbachev, July 12, 2006

Underdogmatists heap scorn on their own country for being too powerful, they do so from the safety and comfort of the world's most powerful nation. America's "winner's complex" means that every American born since 1945 has spent each and every moment of his or her life upon the world's loftiest perch of power. Disparaging the power of one's own country is a luxury reserved only for those who *have* power to disparage. Those who do not have that kind of power—like America's enemies and competitors—covet America's power and aim to take it away. And they may get it sooner than they anticipated.

In 2007, before the Global Financial Crisis took a bite out of America's power, you were told that "top dog America should enjoy its last, precious years,"[3] because China was set to "overtake the US by 2027"[4] and America's Unipolar Moment was winding down. Then, "the great shift in global power just hit high gear, sparked by a financial crash" at the precise moment an "American president in Obama… is prepared to take a conciliatory and concessive attitude towards America's decline."[5] At the time of this writing, the intersection of three historic events threatens to give Underdogmatists everything they could have hoped for:

> "First, the election of Barack Obama signalled a recognition by the US of the limitations of its own power and the need for it to co-operate with other nations. Second, China has reached a point where it is now clearly prepared, on the basis of

[3] "Top Dog America Should Enjoy Its Last, Precious Years," Yahoo Finance, June 4, 2007

[4] Ibid

[5] Martin Jacques, *The Guardian UK*, April 20, 2009

> the advances of the last three decades, to assume a more active global role. And third, the onset of the global financial crisis provides the context for the decline of American economic power and illustrates the extent to which it has become dependent on China for the continuation of its global financial hegemony."
>
> —Martin Jacques, *The Guardian UK*, April 20, 2009

At a time when American power declines and drains away to communist China, the President of the United States has chosen to show weakness to America's enemies in the Islamic world by bowing down to their leaders, badmouthing American power while traveling abroad, and calling for "a world without nuclear weapons"[6] while apocalyptic Islamists rush to arm themselves with nuclear weapons, and thus "testing the limits of U.S. power and influence, seeking to show that both are limited to hollow words and ineffective deeds." On April 6, 2010, "President Barack Obama unveiled a new policy...restricting U.S. use of nuclear weapons."[7] One month later, "Barack Obama declare[d] the 'War on Terror' is over" in his National Security Strategy, and "instead replaced it with a softer approach stressing 'new partnerships' and multilateral diplomacy,"[8] not the assertion or projection of American power. To quote directly from Obama's National Security Strategy:

---

[6] Remarks by President Barack Obama, Prague, Czech Republic, April 5, 2009

[7] Reuters UK, April 6, 2010

[8] Telegraph UK, May 27, 2010

- "We must pursue a rules-based international system that can advance our own interests by serving mutual interests."
- "We have an interest in a just and sustainable international order that can foster collective action to confront common challenges."
- "Empowering Communities to Counter Radicalization: Several recent incidences of violent extremists in the United States who are committed to fighting here and abroad have underscored the threat to the United States and our interests posed by individuals radicalized at home. Our best defenses against this threat are well informed and equipped families, local communities, and institutions. Government will invest in intelligence to understand this threat and expand community engagement and development programs to empower local communities. And the Federal Government, drawing on the expertise and resources from all relevant agencies, will clearly communicate our policies and intentions, listening to local concerns, tailoring policies to address regional concerns, and making clear that our diversity is part of our strength—not a source of division or insecurity."

No wonder "the Islamic Republic, in short, regards the U.S. as a washed-up world power that can no longer run the global show."[9] While America reduces its military capabilities, pulls troops back from the world, refuses to call its

[9] "Iran's New World Order," *The Wall Street Journal*, March 1, 2010

enemies by name, targets its own people, cedes America's power to the United Nations, and fights terrorism with community organizer techniques like "community engagement and development programs to empower local communities," radical Islamists are arming up and marching forward in their clearly stated plan to rule the world through an Islamic caliphate, in which "the balance of power will finally tip in the favor of the radical Islamists."[10]

> "We (Muslims) have ruled the world before, and by Allah, the day will come when we will rule the entire world again. The day will come when we will rule America."
> —Sheik Ibrahim Mudeiris, PA TV, May 13, 2005

Also on the march to usurp America's power is communist China, which seeks to take America's mantle as hegemon and to rule the world with a murderous, totalitarian fist from the Middle Kingdom.

America is in this situation, and its enemies are not, because Americans are susceptible to Underdogma—and its enemies are not. While America's enemies crave and covet your power, home-grown Underdogmatists apologize for America's power and give it away. Now, with the convergence of the Global Financial Crisis, the Presidency of Barack Obama, and the rise of communist China and militant Islam—Underdogmatists find themselves with the winning conditions they need to remake the world according to Underdogma.

---

[10] Pulitzer Prize-winning author of *The Looming Tower*, Lawrence Wright, September 14, 2007

WHY UNDERDOGMA IS WRONG

Reducing America's power is philosophically wrong. By all objective measures, the United States of America is the greatest, noblest, most honorable and charitable nation in world history. It is a beacon of freedom and opportunity to oppressed people around the world. "America is indeed exceptional by any plausible definition of the term and actually has grown increasingly exceptional over time."[11] America is powerful. Some say America is a hegemon. But even those who decry hegemony of any kind must agree that, as far as hegemons go, the United States of America is "as benign a hegemon as the world has ever seen."[12] As President Bill Clinton's National Security Advisor said, "we are the first global power in history that is not an imperial power."[13] America is the first global power or "hegemon" that seeks exit strategies instead of empires after American soldiers win battles. This is true in Iraq and Afghanistan, just as it was true in Germany, France, Japan, and elsewhere. America leaves behind sovereign states, not satellite states of the "American Empire," because America is not an empire-building hegemon. Even the most die-hard anti-imperialist Underdogmatists will have to admit that America is more benign a hegemon than the two hege-

---

[11] *Understanding America*, Peter H. Schuck & James Q. Wilson, 2009

[12] "Decline is a Choice," Charles Krauthammer, *The Weekly Standard*, October 19, 2009

[13] Sandy Berger, October 1999, quoted in "U.S. Foreign Policy after the Cold War: Global Hegemon or Reluctant Sheriff?," Fraser Cameron

mons waiting in the wings: communist China (the most murderous regime in world history) and militant Islam (which seeks to bring world history to an end).

> "Ahmadinejad's aggressive and destructive messianism is trying its best to speed up the apocalypse."
>
> —Radio Free Europe, December 9, 2009

When Americans—driven by Underdogma—seek to reduce America's power, it is not just philosophically wrong, it is also practically wrong. If Underdogmatists hope to placate less powerful underdog nations, and perhaps gain from them concessions or policy changes by bowing down and bringing America to its knees, such hopes have proven to be empty hopes in practical terms. As Charles Krauthammer noted, "unilateral American concessions and offers of unconditional engagement have moved neither Iran nor Russia nor North Korea to accommodate us. Nor have the Arab states—or even the powerless Palestinian Authority—offered so much as a gesture of accommodation...Nor have even our European allies responded."[14] And in China, where Obama bowed down to their communist Premier and apologized for America's power, the Chinese communists took the President's gestures as the signs of weakness they were, and quickly made "radical departures from late patriarch Deng Xiaoping's famous diplomatic credo of 'adopting a low profile and never taking the lead' in international affairs"[15] by unveiling China's

---

[14] "Decline Is a Choice," Charles Krauthammer, *The Weekly Standard*, October 19, 2009

[15] "China Unveils Its New Worldview," *Asia Times*, December 11, 2009

new "ambitious agenda"[16] to assume a more powerful stance on the world stage and "to become world number one, the top power."[17]

If the goal of Underdogmatists was not to gain concessions but to simply have underdog nations look more favorably upon the United States, then that has also been a failure in practical terms. In Cairo, where Obama rhetorically bowed down in his speech to the Arab world, only 27% have a favorable view of the United States. In Turkey, the site of another Underdogmatist badmouthing of America by the U.S. President, only 14% have a favorable opinion of America. And in the Palestinian territories, where they have rarely found a more vocal champion than in the Obama White House, 82% have an unfavorable view of the United States.[18] Why? Because they are not Underdogmatists. They value and respect power. They prefer, as Osama bin Laden said, the strong horse over the weak horse.[19] And, as Fouad Ajami pointed out, they look down upon those who look down upon themselves.

> "Steeped in an overarching idea of American guilt, Mr. Obama and his lieutenants offered nothing less than a doctrine, and a policy, of American penance. No one told Mr. Obama that the Islamic world, where American power is engaged and so dangerously exposed, it is considered bad form,

---

[16] Ibid

[17] "China PLA Officer Urges Challenging U.S. Dominance," Reuters, February 28, 2010

[18] "The Arabs Have Stopped Applauding Obama," Fouad Ajami, *The Wall Street Journal*, November 29, 2009

[19] Osama bin Laden, videotape claiming responsibility for the 9/11 attacks, December 13, 2001

nay a great moral lapse, to speak ill of one's own tribe."

—"The Arabs Have Stopped Applauding Obama," Fouad Ajami, *The Wall Street Journal*, November 29, 2009

"As an Iranian saying reads: 'A knife never cuts its own handle.'"

—Iranian President Mahmoud Ahmadinejad, May 3, 2010

THE CONSEQUENCES OF UNDERDOGMA

A December 2009 Pew Survey[20] found Americans "apprehensive and uncertain about America's place in the world" and, for the majority of respondents, the "U.S. [is] seen as less important, and China as more powerful." Meanwhile, the rise of Islam is "set[ting] the scene for a 'clash of civilizations,' which they welcome as a polarising device that will allow them to recruit from the much larger Muslim mainstream."[21] And, as the U.S. National Intelligence Council warned in November 2008, "the international system—as constructed following the Second World War—will be almost unrecognizable by 2025 owing to the rise of emerging powers, a globalizing economy, an historic transfer of relative wealth, and economic power from West to East."[22]

---

[20] America's Place In The World—Pew Survey, December 3, 2009

[21] *Pakistan Daily Times*, May 14, 2007

[22] "Global Trends 2025: A Transformed World," National Intelligence Council

At this pivotal moment in history, the United States of America is still the most powerful nation in the world. America is an exceptional nation, and its exceptionalism is the fountainhead of America's success and resultant power. But just because most of you have spent your entire lives in the freest, most open, most tolerant, and most powerful nation in world history does not mean that it will always be this way. Most of human history has unfolded at either end of the sword of tyranny. The brief flash of liberty that gave rise to the United States can disappear, and history's long, near-uninterrupted line of tyranny can resume. Underdogma is putting us on the road back to that long line of tyranny. China is poised to overtake America economically, the worldwide Islamic caliphate is set to overtake America demographically, and the President of the United States is ceding America's power rhetorically, economically, and strategically. If nothing is done to stop these trends, at some point in your future—likely in *your* lifetime—the American epoch will end.

If Underdogmatists cannot stomach having the freest country in the history of the world holding the No. 1 position of power, they may very well live long enough to see America's mantle of power handed over to a country that has racked up the biggest body count in world history (communist China: 73,000,000 dead and counting[23]), or a movement that wants to bring the world's history to an end (militant Islam, and its call for hastening the apocalypse).

---

[23] *Mao: The Unknown Story*, Jung Chang & Jon Halliday; *China's Bloody Century* and other works by Professor R. J. Rummel; *China: The Gathering Threat*, Dr. Constantine Menges

You can stop this from happening. America can lead again. America has done this before.

THE ANTIDOTE TO UNDERDOGMA

"Fundamentally, what are those who love America asking of her, if not to remain forever true to her founding values?"

—French President Nicolas Sarkozy, Speech Before U.S. Congress, November 7, 2007

"The United States of America is the greatest, the noblest and, in its original founding principles, the only moral country in the history of the world."

—Ayn Rand, "Philosophy: Who Needs It," 1974

"The American dream, defended and projected by American power, has transformed oppression and poverty into liberty and prosperity."

— Margaret Thatcher, Speech at the Hoover Institution, "A Time for Leadership," July 19, 2000

"For we must consider that we shall be as a City upon a hill. The eyes of all people are upon us."

—John Winthrop, 1630

"You and I have a rendezvous with destiny. We will preserve for our children this, the last best hope of man on Earth, or we will sentence them to take the last step into a thousand years of darkness."

—Ronald Reagan, "A Time For Choosing," October 27, 1964

Underdogma is the belief that those who have less power are virtuous and noble, and that those who have more power are to be scorned. Underdogma reflexively champions the weak and vilifies the strong. It rewards failure and punishes success. And it scorns those who embody the American spirit, who lift themselves up and who make something of themselves—*because they make something of themselves*—while ascribing nobility and virtue to those who have not—*because they have not*.

Underdogma is the opposite of the American spirit, a spirit that transformed a once rugged, untamed colony into the greatest, richest, freest, most powerful, and most culturally vibrant nation in world history. ***Underdogma is the opposite of The American dream***, which James Truslow Adams, the man who coined the phrase, defined as "a dream of being able to grow to fullest development as a man and woman, unhampered by the barriers which had slowly been erected in the older civilizations, unrepressed by social orders which had developed for the benefit of classes rather than for the simple human being of any and every class."[24] ***Underdogma is the opposite of American exceptionalism***, a concept that fueled Ronald Reagan's Presidency in a positive way and Barack Obama's Presidency in a negative way. As Charles Krauthammer told me, "if you listen to Obama's speeches, you'd think we're exceptional in how many sins and crimes we've committed through the ages—that's what makes us exceptional."[25] In Ronald Reagan's telling, American exceptionalism means

---

[24] "America's 93 Greatest Living Authors Present This Is My Best," James Truslow Adams, 1945

[25] Charles Krauthammer, interview for *Underdogma*, December 2009

that America is not just big and powerful, but that America is also special, a "shining city upon a hill," chosen by divine providence to be an exceptional nation with an exceptional mission in the world; to be a light of hope unto others. Hillsdale College president Larry P. Arnn took it one step further when he told me that "great power in a nation, assembled and sustained over long periods of time, likely indicates some virtue."[26] In other words, America's power is *evidence* of America's *virtue*—which is the opposite of Underdogma. ***Underdogma is the opposite of the "Self-Made Man,"*** an ideal put forth by Frederick Douglass, a man who was born into slavery and lifted himself up to become a brilliant orator, a best-selling author, and an advisor to President Abraham Lincoln. As Douglass said, "self-made men are the men who…have attained knowledge, usefulness, power and position…who owe little or nothing to birth, relationship, friendly surroundings; to wealth inherited…who are what they are, without the aid of any of the favoring conditions by which other men usually rise in the world and achieve great results [where] If they have ascended high, they have built their own ladder."[27] And the one place, more than any other place, where people can build their own ladders and ascend high—is in the United States of America.

"As [Alexis de] Tocqueville found, America is wide open. There is no other country in which almost any child can legitimately dream of becoming…anything."[28] America is

[26] Hillsdale College president Larry P. Arnn, interview for *Underdogma*, February 10, 2010

[27] *Self-Made Men*, Frederick Douglass, 1859

[28] *Tocqueville on American Character*, Michael A. Ledeen, 2001

the place where college dropouts can revolutionize computers (Bill Gates and Steve Jobs) and become billionaires, or revolutionize talk radio and be heard by millions each day (Rush Limbaugh), or revolutionize space travel and orbit the Earth (John Glenn). As radio host and author Hugh Hewitt told me, "[Alexander] Hamilton was right to enshrine 'ambition' as a noble virtue and to praise the ambitions of Americans to be successful." In doing so, he added, "every American is a Bill Gates in waiting."[29]

America is home to liberty and equal opportunity, where the pursuit of happiness is enshrined in the Constitution and where you are free to create, to succeed, and to enjoy the fruits of your labor. Americans invented manned flight, the mobile phone, jazz, and lunar travel. Americans pioneered hundreds of life-saving medical advancements, enjoy a remarkably high standard of living, and are a beacon of opportunity and freedom to people around the world who often find both in short supply. When disaster strikes around the world—earthquakes, tsunamis, floods—America responds with helicopters, supplies, and boots on the ground to save people's lives. The reason America can respond and help people in need is because America is powerful. Weak countries do not have the helicopters or resources to help others in need. America does. Because America is powerful. Power is what allows America to turn its empathy into action—and to save people's lives. When the world's huddled masses and persecuted people look for hope and freedom and better lives for themselves and for their families, they look to America. And although

[29] Hugh Hewitt, interview for *Underdogma*, January 3, 2010

Americans do not have the same equality as other, more socialist nations (which are more adept at making their citizens more equally poor and equally miserable), America is the place where those who want to lift themselves up, to "build their own ladders," and to make better lives for themselves face fewer barriers and have better access to more opportunities than in any other place in the world.

> "America is the land of the uncommon man. It is the land where man is free to develop his genius—and to get its just rewards. It is the land where each man tries to develop whatever quality he may possess and to rise to whatever degree he can, great or modest. It is not the land where one glories or is taught to glory in one's mediocrity. No self-respecting man in America is or thinks of himself as 'little,' no matter how poor he may be."
>
> —Ayn Rand, "Screen Guide for Americans," *Plain Talk*, November 1947

By not thinking of itself as "little," America has become big. And powerful. The most powerful nation in world history. America's power is not derived through conquest or plunder, but through the power of its ideas and founding principles: "Americans think America is superior because of what Americans believe. For this reason, Ronald Reagan was absolutely right to describe us as a beacon of freedom for the whole world. America has in fact created the freest, most socially egalitarian, and most racially integrated society in the world."[30] Now that America is

[30] "A Shining City On A Hill: American Exceptionalism and the Supreme Court's Practice of Relying on Foreign Law," Steven G. Calabresi, *Boston University Law Review 1335-1416* (2006)

powerful, those who covet your power (Puppetmasters) are using Underdogma to siphon your power away, while those who feel uncomfortable with American power (Useful Idiots) are ceding your power to America's enemies in the name of Underdogma.

America's Founders were well aware of mankind's love/hate relationship with power. The United States was founded on a revolt against state power, and America's founding documents are designed specifically to limit and balance state power. The Constitution is a restraining order slapped on government by the Founders. But that does not mean you should deride power, or scorn those who have power, or give your power away in order to appease those who resent your power and aim to take it from you. As Ronald Reagan said in 1974, "we cannot escape our destiny nor should we try to do so. The leadership of the free world was thrust upon us two centuries ago in that little hall in Philadelphia...We are indeed, and we are today, the last best hope of man on earth."[31]

"The Constitution is a restraining order slapped on government by the Founders."
—Michael Prell

Frederick Douglass knew, back in 1859, that when a self-made man succeeds and gains power, there are those who will scorn him and try to take his power away. Douglass knew that success often must come "not only without the voluntary assistance or friendly cooperation of society, but often in open and derisive defiance of all the efforts

[31] Governor Ronald Reagan, January 25, 1974

of society and the tendency of circumstances to repress, retard and keep them down."[32] He knew what Ayn Rand knew when she wrote of a reflexive "response of hatred, not toward human vices, but toward human virtue...hatred of the good for being the good."[33] And he knew that naysayers and Underdogmatists—when they scorn success and those who succeed—only sharpen the determination of those who succeed, and that such "detraction paves the way for the very perfections which it doubts and denies."[34]

There is a way to balance power, without scorn, without envy, and without Underdogma. Again; look to America's Founders, who crafted the most brilliant series of checks and balances on power in world history.

> "Give all power to the many, they will oppress the few. Give all power to the few, they will oppress the many. Both, therefore, ought to have the power, that each may defend itself against the other."
> —Alexander Hamilton, Constitutional Convention, 1787

As distinguished professor of economics Walter E. Williams told me, "the founders of our nation recognized that government is the source of evil, and the reason why government is the source of evil is because the essence of government is coercion." That is why "in a free society, the essential role of government is to stop [others, includ-

---

[32] *The Mind of Frederick Douglass*, Waldo E. Martin Jr., University of North Carolina Press, 1984

[33] "The Age of Envy," *Return of the Primitive*, Ayn Rand, 1999

[34] *The Mind of Frederick Douglass*, Waldo E. Martin Jr., University of North Carolina Press, 1984

ing government] from taking your money [and power]. Liberty explains why Americans are so much at the top, and it's the attacks on liberty that begin to explain the big problems that Americans have."[35]

America was built on an idea, and the idea is this: for the first time in history, a nation declared in its founding document that man's rights were unalienable, that his rights came from the Creator, not from government. The Declaration of Independence stated "that to secure these rights, Governments are instituted among Men, deriving their just powers from the consent of the governed." As Newt Gingrich wrote, "this is the proposition upon which America was based, and when Thomas Jefferson wrote these lines, he turned on its head the idea that power only came from God through the monarch and then to the people."[36] The Declaration made government the servant of the people, and it gave government the solemn duty to secure the rights that were given to man by the Creator. This made America the first nation in world history to put personal rights above state rights. To borrow a phrase from Tony Robbins; America was the first nation to put "personal power" above state power. The Declaration of Independence also held that "all men are created equal." But it did not promise all men that they would live their entire lives equally, or achieve equal outcomes. Alexis de Tocqueville correctly called American equality the "equality of conditions,"[37] writing that, because our

---

[35] Professor Walter E. Williams, George Mason University, Rush Limbaugh guest host—interview for *Underdogma* January 2, 2010

[36] *Rediscovering God in America*, Newt and Callista Gingrich

[37] *Democracy In America*, Alexis de Tocqueville, 1835

abilities are all different, "man cannot prevent their unequal distribution."[38] Among the unalienable rights spelled out in the Declaration are the rights to "Life, Liberty, and the pursuit of Happiness." If one man's pursuit of happiness makes him wealthier than another man, it is the duty of the American government to *secure* that man's wealth, not to disparage him for having earned it, or to confiscate it, or, as Barack Obama said, to "spread the wealth around"[39] to underdogs.

The power of America is in the idea of America. The American spirit. American exceptionalism. Its founding principles. The founding documents. The philosophical foundation upon which your power was earned. *That* is the reason why America has become the most powerful nation in world history in the historical blink of an eye.

> "We are no different DNA-wise than any other human beings on the planet. No central authority appointed us a world superpower. It happened. We created it ourselves. We did it with the distinct features that we in America were born to as a result of our Constitution and our Declaration of Independence. Nobody elevated us. There was no world order which said the United States is elevated as a group above any other nation. And I don't know that anybody in the United States looks at ourselves that way. We don't look at ourselves as better than anybody else. We look at ourselves as an outpost of freedom the rest of the world wants to join, emulate, in many places they want to tear

[38] *Democracy In America*, Alexis de Tocqueville, 1835

[39] "Obama Fires a 'Robin Hood' Warning Shot," Charles Hurt, *New York Post*, October 15, 2008

> us apart, too, but this whole notion here that any world order that elevates one—so bye-bye American exceptionalism and hello world order. Somebody has got to come in and cut somebody down to size. And that somebody is us."
>
> —Rush Limbaugh, *The Rush Limbaugh Show,* June 4, 2009

American exceptionalism requires exceptional Americans. In 1773, in Boston Harbor, a handful of exceptional Americans gave birth to this nation with America's first Tea Party. As I write these words, a new Tea Party movement is rising up to keep the American spirit alive, and I am honored to be a part of the movement as a writer and strategist for the Tea Party Patriots. Unlike the revolutionaries in Boston Harbor, today's Tea Party Patriots are not seeking to replace a system that has failed to secure your liberties. They are seeking to preserve a system that has secured your liberties far better than any other in world history—before it is destroyed by Underdogmatists who oppose the founding principles that made America great. The Tea Party Patriots are rising up to preserve the American spirit, which is the foundation of the United States, the foundation of its greatness, and the foundation of its well-earned power. As Hugh Hewitt told me, "we are a 'leave us alone' people, and when the government refuses to do so, spontaneous populism erupts."[40] This time, spontaneous populism is erupting—not just in one

Join the TEA PARTY THREAD at www.under-dogma.com.

[40] Hugh Hewitt, interview for *Underdogma*, January 3, 2010

harbor—but across the country. Millions of people, from every state in the nation, are coming together to keep the American spirit alive.

"Reagan would have loved the Tea Party people."
—CNBC host Larry Kudlow, interview for
Underdogma, February 11, 2010

There are those who wish for another Ronald Reagan to lead America at this pivotal moment in history. I disagree. Ronald Reagan was a leader who led a movement. The modern-day Tea Party is a movement in search of a leader. The power is now in the hands of the people. Just like the Founders intended.

This is how to defeat Underdogma. By returning to America's founding principles and rekindling the American spirit. ***The American spirit is the antidote to Underdogma.*** I call upon you to embrace that spirit—and to do so unapologetically and soon.

Afterword

> "Not too long ago two friends of mine were talking to a Cuban refugee, a businessman who had escaped from Castro, and in the midst of his story one of my friends turned to the other and said, 'We don't know how lucky we are.' And the Cuban stopped and said, 'How lucky you are? I had someplace to escape to.' In that sentence he told us the entire story. This [America] is the last stand on Earth."
>
> —Ronald Reagan, "A Time For Choosing,"
> October 27, 1964

WHEN RONALD REAGAN SPOKE OF America as "the last stand on Earth," and of the Cuban refugee who felt lucky to have America to "escape to," his words reached out to millions of people around the world. Including me. I was not born in America. For me, America was a place to "escape to." As Ronald Reagan wrote in "The Hope of Mankind," "sometimes I think we need to remind ourselves of what it is we're trying to preserve in this country...Every once in a while all of us native born Americans should make it a point to have a conversation with one who is an American by choice. They can do a lot to firm up *our* resolve to be free for another 200 yrs."[1] As an "American by choice," I feel compelled to do everything I can to stop Underdogmatists from diminishing America's power and the power of the American people. Their goal is to dim this "shining city upon a hill" so that its brilliance no longer outshines any other. My goal, in writing this book, is to stop Underdogmatists—by lifting the veil of Underdogma, showing you the empathetic bridge they have built to our near-universal love for the underdog, and detonating that bridge so they can never again cross it to pick power from our pockets. America is "the last stand on Earth." For now. I hope this book contributes, in some way, to preserving the United States of America as the last place in the world to "escape to."

[1] "The Hope of Mankind," September 21, 1976; *Reagan; In His Own Hand*, Free Press, 2001

TO BE CONTINUED . . .

As long as Underdogma and Underdogmatists continue—we will continue to expose and oppose them.

Visit www.under-dogma.com to see, and contribute to, up-to-the-minute reports on Underdogma in current world affairs, in our neighborhoods, in our personal lives—and in today's fast-breaking stories.

About the Author

MICHAEL PRELL is a writer and strategist for the Tea Party Patriots. He is a Pollie Award–winning advertiser who has served Israel's Prime Minister Benjamin Netanyahu, Canada's Prime Minister Stephen Harper, and hundreds of conservative leaders on four continents. Michael has also worked with the Dalai Lama, Dr. Phil, the global Chinese dissident community, "America's Rabbi" Shmuley Boteach, and he was a crisis manager during the Northeastern Blackout of 2003. He has written for The American Thinker and The Epoch Times, and his writings have been featured by Rush Limbaugh and Glenn Beck.